INSIDE TRACK

INSIDE TRACK

A Successful Job Search Method

by

William Lareau

NEW CENTURY PUBLISHERS, INC.

Copyright © 1985, by William Lareau

All rights reserved. No part of this book may be used or reproduced in any manner whatsoever without prior written permission from the publisher except in the case of brief quotations embodied in critical reviews and articles. All inquiries should be addressed to New Century Publishers, Inc., 220 Old New Brunswick Road, Piscataway, N.J. 08854.

ISBN 0-8329-0408-2

Library of Congress Cataloging-in-Publication Data

Lareau, William
  Inside track.

  1. Job hunting. I. Title.
HF5382.7.L36 1985   650.1'4   85-25823
ISBN 0-8329-0408-2

DEDICATION

To Darlene, for her love and support in helping me find the work I do best.

And to suffering job seekers everywhere, in whose company I discovered the need for this book.

Contents

Introduction

1. Let's Get to the Bottom Line 3
2. The Real World of the Job Search 7
3. Planning and Strategy Selection 23
4. The Resume: Your Magic Bullet 41
5. Stategy Number 1: Responses to Classified
   Job Advertisements 85
6. Strategy Number 2: Mailings to Headhunters 103
7. Strategy Number 3: Direct Solicitations to Executives
   and Organizations 114
8. Miscellaneous Strategies of Passing Interest 131
9. Somebody's Got to Do It: Administration
   and Recordkeeping 141
10. Hand-to-Hand (and Phone-to-Phone) Combat:
    The Interview 151
11. Using Your Personal Computer As a Job Search Aid 190

Appendix. Facing the Dragon: How to Handle Getting Fired ... 202

Index 215

INTRODUCTION

This book was written to help you find a job as fast as possible, whatever your situation. Being out of work is one of life's most rotten circumstances. Like everyone else, I've been there. I don't want to go through it again, and I don't want you to have to endure it any longer than necessary. Unfortunately, it's difficult to get honest advice about job searching. Far too many of the people writing books and columns on the subject are personnel executives, headhunters, or career counselors. Taking their advice at face value is like asking politicians about integrity; they have too much of a vested interest in their reputations to be perfectly candid. Thus, most job search books either have painted a lily-white, fairy-tale view of the job search world or they have encouraged out-of-work job seekers to embark on journeys of self-discovery before they get serious about finding a job. If you're out of work and need to find a job, you don't have time for such nonsense.

I wrote *Inside Track* to deal with this problem. I don't go out of my way to agree with the powers that be in the job search world; *Inside Track* isn't intended for them. *Inside Track* is intended to help you get a job in spite of them. If a commonly suggested technique is worthless, I don't beat around the bush; I tell you it's worthless and why. Where there are ways for you to take advantage of some of the system's inefficiencies, I show you how to do it.

I have no doubt you'll find that *Inside Track* is the most detailed and comprehensive job search book you've ever read. Good luck (even with *Inside Track's* help, you'll need it).

INSIDE TRACK

INSIDE
TRACK

Chapter 1

Let's Get to the Bottom Line

The bottom line is that you want some practical, no-nonsense information about finding a job. If you're in the middle of a job search or you're about to start one, you need concrete, step-by-step help, and you need it now. If you've recently finished a job search, you're probably wondering if there's any way on earth to make the next one less horrible. If any case, you want to know what works and what doesn't, and you want it in a format that's easy to use. You want results, and you're looking for a book that will help you get them without a lot of wasted time and effort. You're sick of job search books that promise help but contain nothing but vague guidelines, cute gimmicks, and pats on the back to the authors' colleagues who are personnel executives and headhunters. You've had it with ridiculous tactics dreamed up by college placement counselors who have never had a job in the real world of business. Well, I've got good news for you. The bottom line is that *Inside Track* is the last job search book you'll ever have to buy.

Inside Track presents no cute theories, no off-the-wall gimmicks, and no useless general advice about job searching. You want practical, step-by-step, how-to-do-it-in-the-real-world help, and that's what this book presents. *Inside Track* will show you how to find a job in as short a time as possible with a minimum of suffering. Every aspect of your job search campaign will be explained, with detailed instructions and examples which you can quickly modify for your own use. *Inside Track* presents a realistic and accurate description of the job search world's processes and inhabitants. *Inside Track* takes the position that the typical job search is about as enjoyable as snorkeling for a dead cat in a settlement pond on a hot day. There's no way any normal person could possibly find any pleasure in such an endeavor. *Inside Track* won't insult your intelligence by trying to sell you a bill of goods about how exciting and rewarding a job search can be. At its best, job searching is a demeaning, humiliating odyssey into the world of the confused, the limited, and the incompetent. When you're faced with your next job search ordeal, the strategies and techniques presented by *Inside Track* will help you to complete your snorkeling and groping in the job search pond more quickly and effectively.

Inside Track will assist you in developing realistic insights and instincts by showing you how every aspect of the job search world operates. In Chapter 2, you'll find out how different types of job openings are created. You'll be shown how the recruiting process works, all the way from the job description to the job offer. The typical personalities and hidden motivations of all the players will be detailed and explained. Once you're familiar with the employment processes and operational dynamics of typical organizations, you'll have valuable insights into what works, what doesn't, and why. You'll understand why a lot of commonly touted job search strategies and gimmicks, which appear reasonable to the naive, are actually useless wastes of time and money.

The precise, step-by-step instructions presented here will enable you to take full advantage of your new insights. For example, you'll be shown exactly how your resume must look. You won't be shown fifty examples and then forced to wonder which one you should use. That's not help; that's a reading exercise and a waste of your time. *Inside Track* will show you the exact layout format to use for your resume. You'll be provided with guidelines for selecting stationery, colors, type style, and secretarial support for its production. After reading Chapter 4, you'll be able to quickly put together a winning resume which will be in the top 1 to 3 percent of those submitted for the jobs you want. *Inside Track* will show you how most effectively to describe your job experiences, highlight your education, and construct an outstanding summary of qualifications which will grab the readers' attention and encourage them to read more about you. You'll be shown lengthy lists of the most effective resume words, and you'll get detailed instructions on how best to use them in your resume. You'll also find material that you can incorporate into your resume with minor changes. Your *Inside Track* resume will be the best one you'll ever see.

Job search success depends on much more than resumes and correspondence. Resumes and letters are critical, but they're only one part of the job search challenge. *Inside Track* will show you how to organize and execute every aspect of a comprehensive job search. Chapter 3 discusses the selection of job search strategies and the disadvantages, strengths, and costs of each in terms of time, effort, and money. You'll learn how to determine which techniques are most appropriate to your particular search situation. Considerations of time pressures (such as when you're out of work and need a job *fast*), security (you can't take even a small chance that your present employer will get even a hint that you're looking), and convenience (can you handle ten headhunters calling you every day?) will be explored for each of the four major job search strategy areas presented. For eleven different job search situations, you'll learn how to allocate your time and resources among the four major search strategies.

Inside Track presents detailed, step-by-step instructions for all of the most effective job search strategies. Once you decide which strategies are right for you, this book makes it easy by supplying you with readily adaptable samples and forms for all correspondence; all you've got to do is fill in your information and get it typed up. For example, you may elect to make direct contact with executives one part of your search effort. If you decide that it's appropriate for you (this type of networking doesn't work as well as the experts say), Chapter 7 will show you how to do it right. You'll not only learn techniques for five direct solicitation strategies, but you'll also find out how to construct superior correspondence, research your targets, and select executives. You'll even learn how to construct and use a remarkably effective telechart for telephone solicitations.

Responding to classified advertisements is an important strategy for most job seekers. Chapter 5 presents detailed instructions that will enable you to maximize your odds of being selected from the hundreds of responses most ads generate. You'll discover what personnel officers want to see when they open your envelope, what they don't like, and how to use the readily adaptable examples of cover letters that are presented. You'll learn how to answer ads with techniques ranging from the "bare-bones" approach to the "face down through the cactus with supplementary qualifications section" treatment.

Chapter 8 discusses a variety of additional job search techniques which aren't generally effective but may be occasionally useful. You'll learn why job search gimmicks such as "this one's on me" and "super tough talk" look great but seldom work. After reading Chapter 8, you'll be less inclined to waste your time on the flashy but useless techniques many so-called experts recommend.

An important part of many job searches involves sending resumes to headhunters. Most people don't do it correctly. If you decide this strategy is appropriate to your search, Chapter 6 will show you some simple and extremely effective techniques to make it work. You'll discover how to design your materials so they'll get into the hands of the right headhunter and hold his or her attention for the critical ten to fifteen seconds that will determine whether they'll take a chance on calling you. In addition, Chapter 6 will provide you with a source for inexpensively obtaining extensive up-to-date lists of established headhunters who have the good jobs.

When potential employers or headhunters call, you'll have about five minutes to convince them that you're the one to bring in or recommend for the face-to-face interview. Chapter 10 outlines techniques for increasing your odds of winning the phone interview and making the final cut into the group that will get interviewed in person. You'll learn what to say and what not to say, how to rehearse your technique, and how to project power and authority over the phone. After winning the phone interview, the real challenge comes with the face-to-face interview. Chapter 10 provides detailed instructions for handling every phase of the interview process. In addition, it provides extensive lists of the most common interview questions and guidelines on how they must be answered. After reading and applying the principles of Chapter 10, your interviewing skills will dramatically improve.

Inside Track deals with all of the other critical areas of job searching such as clothing selection, references, thank-you letters (Chapter 10), and recordkeeping (Chapter 9). *Inside Track* even provides tips on how best to apply the power of a personal computer to your job search efforts. Chapter 11 outlines strategies for using a personal computer to generate resumes, correspondence, and recordkeeping data.

Unfortunately, many job searches are necessitated by an involuntary termination—getting fired. The odds are that this will happen to you someday, deserved or not. Proper handling of the termination will enable you to get the subsequent job search under way as soon as possible. For the inevitable day when you'll be turfed, this book's Appendix presents step-by-step guidelines to help you handle the horror. You'll be told what to do when it happens, how to attempt to delay it if you think it's coming, how to handle it when it occurs, and how to get the best deal out of it.

After you've read *Inside Track*, I am confident you will view the job search world and the ordeal of looking for a job from a more realistic and insightful perspective. More to the point, you will be able to mount a comprehensive and effective job search campaign which will get better results than you ever thought possible. Good luck!

Chapter 2

The Real World of the Job Search

This chapter will show you what you're up against in the job market. The truth is quite a bit different from what the business world tells us in their standard self-congratulatory magazines and mutual admiration society news releases. Only when you've got a firm understanding about the job search and recruiting process, only when you've got the *Inside Track* about what's really going on, can you effectively plan and conduct a job search that will get you maximum results with minimum effort and suffering. This chapter will describe how job slots are created, how they are filled, how personnel types and headhunters operate, what they're looking for, how they look for it, why they look for it, what happens to your resume when it arrives at someone's office, how resumes are screened, how applicants are evaluated, who makes the decisions, and how job offers are put together. You'll know what's really going on behind the blank stares and rude receptionists of most personnel departments. You'll then understand the rationale behind the *Inside Track* strategies of job searching which are presented in later chapters.

Basic Truths About the Job Search and Business World

Let's get started right at the beginning with some basic truths that few people ever think about. If you don't face them and design your job search to deal with them, you're going to suffer through a longer and more trying job search than those conducted by individuals who understand what's going on.

Basic Truth 1. The job search world is not different from any other aspect of life. Many of the people and organizations involved are insecure, anxious, and intellectually limited.

The significance of this basic truth (BT) is that many of the actions and decisions made by people involved in the job search process are not logical, not tied to an external, objective standard of comparison, and not necessarily related to anything you do. You must design your search strategies and materials to take advantage of the intensely subjective and personal basis upon which most selection decisions are made. The *Inside Track* approach does this.

Basic Truth 2. The business world in general and its personnel selection systems in particular are a disorganized and chaotic jumble of gerrymandered systems which are constantly being compromised, modified, ruined, and/or replaced by legions of marginally competent people.

Many people compromise their job search chances because they haven't faced this BT. The business world appears to be very organized, very systematic, and very logical. It isn't. Don't equate carpeting, glossy annual reports, and nicely dressed executives with smoothly running systems. After the fact, most executives can build logically appearing explanations of their past actions. Before the fact, they're just as unsure and ignorant about what'll happen as you are when you take a chance on a new dishwasher. In the job search arena, if you deceive yourself into believing there's a well-planned and all-knowing system behind the facade, you'll waste a lot of time playing to an audience that's not there. Even worse, you'll overlook opportunities to take advantage of the confusion.

Basic Truth 3. Your technical qualifications are less important than the intangibles.

When compared to factors such as your personal appearance, your bearing and demeanor (do you look and act as they expected?), your personality, and the ever-famous "cut of your jib," your technical qualifications are of secondary importance in qualifying you as a top candidate for a job. You've got to concentrate on giving them what they think they want, not what they actually should want if they knew what they were doing. Everyone will talk about objective technical qualifications when discussing candidates, but the final decision won't be made on that basis. The emphasis on nontechnical information occurs because people continually process all sorts of subjective information about candidates from resumes, telephone conversations, and in-person interviews. Most of the analysis actually takes part as a result of nonverbal cues, and a large part of it occurs subconsciously. We all do this all the time whenever we're interacting with people. We do it more intensely when we first meet or hear about someone because we have so little existing data about them on which to base our reactions. Given this quite natural and normal process, it's easy to understand why technical job skills play such a small part in the evaluation. For one thing, most interviewers (and 99 percent of personnel people) don't know all that much about the technical aspects of a particular job. But they all think they know people. Therefore, they base their selection decisions upon personal impressions and subjective biases. The importance of these intangibles will become more obvious as we examine various aspects of the typical recruiting process throughout the remainder of this book.

For every job there are hundreds of applicants who possess all of the required degrees and experience. The person selected will be the one whose intangibles are the best. In fact, for every position there are usually dozens, if not hundreds, of candidates whose technical qualifications far exceed those of the selected individual. Most of these technically superior individuals won't even get called for an interview because of subconscious or subjective factors. These intangibles run the gamut from using a stationery color or type face the interviewer doesn't like to having gone to a school the screener doesn't like, and so on. Subjective criteria such as the above often operate to kill an applicant's chances even as the resume is being screened. Many more function during telephone and in-person interviews. Countless thousands of interviews have been lost because the candidate was too timid (the interviewer preferred more assertiveness), the candidate was not timid enough (the interviewer wanted a meek candidate), the candidate had a mustache (the interviewer didn't like them), the candidate did not have a mustache (the interviewer did like them), and so on. As a result of these types of subjective intangibles and many others even more strange, the person who possesses the best technical qualifications for the job seldom gets it. The *Inside Track* method deals with this circumstance by showing you how to incorporate an optimally effective set of intangibles into all facets of your search.

Basic Truth 4. An optimally successful job search is conducted by consistently performing the highest probability actions until you get the result you want.

The intangibles discussed above change from person to person and from situation to situation, so there's no way to anticipate and plan for every possible job search situation. The *Inside Track* job search method is based upon the premise that you can't accurately predict what will happen each and every time you interview or send a resume. The intangibles in any one situation are too complex for you to be able to control or manipulate them all, even if you had the time and resources to try. Faced with this situation and the need to find a job, the *Inside*

Track job seeker must develop a long-term, probabilistic view of the job search process. Your goal is to determine the most effective strategies for your search needs and then carry them out without worrying about minor successes, temporary setbacks, or distractions. In any one situation, the intangibles will most likely influence the decision. The *Inside Track* method is designed to optimize your odds over the vast array of typical job search situations and challenges by helping you to organize and executive a well-planned search which presents both your technical qualifications and your intangibles in the maximally effective manner.

The Creation of Job Openings

Your approach to job seeking and your implementation of search strategies must be based on a firm understanding of how job openings are created and filled by employers. There are basically two ways for a job slot to become available:
1. The former occupant of the position is terminated (died, fired, quit, or retired), and a replacement warm body must be recruited.
2. A new position is created because of expansion, reorganization, or empire building on the part of an aggressive manager.

While the final stage of the recruiting effort is about the same for both of the above situations, a lot of the behind-the-scenes activities differ in ways that affect many search strategies.

In most organizations, it's no problem for a manager to start the recruiting process in order to fill a vacated job slot. If the organization is doing OK, it's usually just a formality of submitting a personnel requisition (called a "rec," pronounced "wreck") which is approved by one or more higher-level executives. The requisition then goes to personnel, and the search for a body is on.

It's much more difficult for a manager to obtain permission to create and fill a new position than it is to hire a replacement warm body for an existing position. The creation of a new slot means that a new job description has to be written, funds have to be allocated that aren't presently in the budget (unless the manager was clever enough to squirrel away the funds in advance), and many people have to give the new slot their blessing. All of these things take time. When an organization is doing well and expansion is occurring, individual managers still face a difficult challenge when they attempt to increase staff in their departments. Every other manager in the organization is simultaneously engaged in the same desperate struggle to get a lion's share of the new slots that are available. Everyone knows that the gravy train will soon end as all the new people, equipment, and buildings spur more bureaucracy, reduce efficiency, and ultimately eat up the profits and force an end to the good times until the next business cycle. As a result, an empire-building manager must work feverishly against tremendous competition to get extra slots while the money faucet is running. It's even more difficult to add a slot when times are tough. When a downturn hits, most organizations have a knee-jerk response that deals with the problem by freezing work forces and forbidding the addition of new employees.

It's for the above reasons that the often suggested ploy of sending a cover letter, sometimes called a broadcast letter, and resume directly to executives is a low-probability strategy. No matter how good you look, it's horrendously difficult for anyone in an organization to create a slot for someone who's not already in the plan. Maybe the president of a big organization or division can do it, but middle managers can't. As the following discussion will demonstrate, the odds are not much better if you're hoping to chance upon an empty replacement slot that they need to fill and that calls for someone with your qualifications. If they have such an opening, they'll advertise for it, and you'll have to fight it out with the hundreds who answer the ad. If it's being filled from within, you don't have a chance of edging out the in-house candidate. Thus, the odds of getting anything from a broadcast letter to organizations are very small. Chapter 7 presents techniques that will optimize your chances if you decide to try this approach. Carefully read Chapter 3 on strategy selection before you decide.

The Typical Recruiting Process

This section will outline a typical recruiting effort from start to finish, step by step. It will give you an idea of how things work behind the scenes. The example will incorporate all of the usual screw-ups, inefficiencies, and foot dragging normally associated with the recruiting process. If you're not familiar with personnel departments or large bureaucracies, some of the foul-ups may seem too extreme and bizarre to be credible. Believe me, the example is a charitable characterization of what goes on in many organizations. Although some organizations run their recruiting operations in a more efficient manner than the one shown in the example, most don't, and even the best ones have a lot of bad days. You'll run into your share, and it helps to know what to expect.

For purposes of easy narration, let's assume that the organization doing the recruiting is JB Industries (JBI), the recruiting manager is Mr. Notin, the headhunter is Mr. Gotabody of Tightpack Associates, and the job opening has been created because Fred Sawthelite, a marketing analyst, is resigning. Fred reported to Mr. Gladhand, the V.P. of marketing who must initiate the replacement process.

Day 1. Fred hands in his two-week notice on a Friday at 2:00 P.M.

Fred gets lucky and isn't hustled out the door with no severance pay. Nothing else happens that day because personnel offices never do anything on Friday afternoons.

Day 4. On Monday, Mr. Gladhand calls personnel and tries to find out how to submit a rec for a replacement (his secretary is on vacation, and he doesn't know what to do). By 4:00 P.M., he gets the form and instructions and submits it to typing.

Day 5. First thing in the morning, Mr. Gladhand takes the requisition to his boss, Ms. Jacobs, the executive V.P., to get her signature, the first of two he must obtain. He's told by Ms. Jacobs's secretary that she's out of town and won't be in until Thursday. Mr. Gladhand leaves the rec with the secretary.

Day 7. At 2:00 P.M., Mr. Gladhand gets a call from Ms. Jacobs's secretary to pick up the signed rec. He picks it up and takes it upstairs to mahogany row to get "Jim Bob" Jones, president of JBI, to sign the rec. Ol' Jim Bob signs it (after reminiscing about the good old days for thirty minutes), and Mr. Gladhand races down to personnel to get them to place an ad in the Sunday paper. He is told by Mr. Notin that the paper's cutoff for Sunday classifieds is Thursday noon, so it'll just have to wait for next week.

Day 14. The ad, written by Mr. Notin, is placed by JBI's ad agency, Bilzalot and Associates, to run in the Sunday paper on day 17.

Day 17. The ad appears in the town's major Sunday paper.

Day 18. The responses to the ad begin to come in from desperate job seekers who got the early edition and put their resumes in the mail before Sunday noon. The responses arrive with stacks of mail including hundreds of responses to other jobs, unsolicited resumes, brochures from consultants, internal mail, and general correspondence. The young, uneducated, and bored receptionist sorts the mail while answering phones, typing letters, fetching coffee, handing out applications, giving typing tests, and shepherding candidates to appointments with recruiters.

Day 25. Mr. Notin, who has decided to "handle this one myself," begins to sort through the hundred and fifty responses to the ad that have accumulated over the past seven days. He selects ten candidates for phone interviews.

Days 26–29. Mr. Notin calls the ten candidates for a preliminary phone interview. He manages to make contact with seven, five of whom he schedules for an interview during the next week.

Day 29. Mr. Gladhand calls Mr. Notin to find out where all the applicants are. He's upset that it's been over four weeks since Fred resigned and he hasn't seen one candidate. Mr. Notin gives him the standard personnel line that "these things take time."

Days 32–36. Mr. Notin interviews three of the five people he had invited. One person canceled, and Mr. Notin forgot one appointment, went to lunch, and missed it. That candidate is rescheduled for the next week. One person makes the cut and is scheduled to meet with Mr. Gladhand the following week. An additional ninety resumes arrive, and Mr. Notin selects another six for phone interviews.

Days 39–43. Mr. Notin conducts the phone interviews with all six candidates and invites three for interviews the week after next. (He'll be out of town at a personnel convention the week of Days 46–50.) He interviews the one he missed the week before and rejects the candidate. Another thirty-four resumes arrive, and five are interviewed by phone and set up for personal interviews for the week of Days 53–57.

Day 41. Mr. Gladhand interviews the candidate forwarded by Mr. Notin and is appalled at the person's lack of qualifications for the position. He calls Notin and tells him he expects better results, "especially since it's been almost six weeks since Fred quit!" He's told by Notin, "These things take time." He agrees, under Mr. Gladhand's urging, to run another ad in next Sunday's paper.

Day 45. The original ad runs again.

Days 46–50. Mr. Notin is at a personnel conference, his fourth of the year. Another fifty-seven resumes arrive for the position.

Days 53–57. Mr. Notin interviews seven of the eight candidates he had screened by phone the week before his trip. Worried about the building irritation of Mr. Gladhand over not getting anyone for the job, Mr. Notin lowers his standards and passes four of the seven on to interviews with Mr. Gladhand. For the seventy-nine resumes that have accumulated, he lowers his standards and orders the receptionist to schedule personal interviews with fifteen candidates he selects from the pile.

Day 62. Mr. Gladhand interviews two of the four candidates and decides that one of them is great. He tells Mr. Notin to put an offer together. Mr. Notin meets with the compensation manager, and they "look at the curves" (the regression scatter plots of grade levels and pay rates). They decide that the offer must be $24,000 per year. Mr. Gladhand is incredulous; the candidate is already making $23K and is looking for $27–28K. Mr. Notin sticks to his guns.

Day 63. Mr. Gladhand goes to Ms. Jacobs and enlists her aid in the struggle to get a decent offer together. She agrees and calls the director of personnel, Ms. Fremble. Ms. Fremble says she'll look into it.

Day 64. Ms. Fremble meets with Mr. Notin and the compensation manager, both of whom argue for "keeping these offers in line with our overall pay grades." Ms. Fremble agrees and calls Ms. Jacobs to inform her of the decision. Ms. Jacobs tells Mr. Gladhand that maybe it would help if she interviewed the candidate. He agrees and calls Mr. Notin to ask him to arrange the interview, but Mr. Notin has left early. (It's Friday, and he's in personnel.)

Days 60–64. During this week, Mr. Notin interviews twelve candidates and schedules six of them for interviews with Mr. Gladhand.

14   INSIDE TRACK

Another forty-three resumes arrive, and Mr. Notin selects seven for interviews the following week. On Day 63, Ol' Jim Bob bumps into Mr. Gladhand in the executive men's room and asks him how the search is going. Mr. Gladhand says that he's only had one decent candidate in almost nine weeks and they can't even put together a decent offer. J.B. says he'll "look into it."

Day 67. Mr. Gladhand contacts his prime candidate and sets up an interview with Ms. Jacobs on Day 70, the first day she has open.

Days 68–69. Mr. Gladhand interviews four candidates and finds none of them acceptable (although he's getting desperate, not having had an analyst to sort his marketing magazines for almost ten weeks). Mr. Notin continues to sort resumes and screen candidates.

Day 70. Ms. Jacobs is impressed with the candidate she interviews and wants to raise the offer to the candidate's demands of a minimum of $27K per year. She tells the candidate they'll get back to him in a day or so (and she actually believes it).

Day 71. Ms. Jacobs tells Mr. Gladhand to set up a meeting on Day 74 (Monday) between the two of them and Ms. Fremble, Mr. Notin, and the compensation manager. Unfortunately, Ms. Fremble has a convention to go to on Days 74–76, and the compensation manager has a local personnel association meeting on Day 77. As a result, the meeting is set for Friday, Day 78.

Day 78. At the meeting, it's agreed to "bend the rules a little" and offer the candidate $26.5K. (Incidentally, the total tab for all of the personnel association luncheons, conventions, and meetings for JBI over the past year was $55.7K.) Mr. Gladhand can't contact the candidate that afternoon or all weekend. During the previous week, he interviewed five candidates and none was acceptable.

Day 81. Mr. Gladhand contacts the candidate and informs him of the offer. The candidate says that he must decline since he hadn't heard anything in over a week and had accepted another offer for $27K. Mr. Gladhand is now really upset. He storms into Ms. Jacobs's office and tells her they've got to do something. She agrees and goes upstairs to see Ol' Jim Bob. He stops practicing his putting long enough to tell her to have Ms. Fremble "put a headhunter on this one—we'll just have to eat the fee."

Day 83. Ms. Jacobs finally contacts Ms. Fremble (who had been out at a regional personnel association meeting) and informs her of J.B.'s orders. Ms. Fremble puts a call in to the headhunting firm of Tightpack and Associates, whom JBI has on retainer for executive level searches.

Day 84. Mr. Gotabody of Tightpack Associates returns Ms. Fremble's call and agrees to initiate the search. She agrees to send the job description and related materials about the job to him.

Day 85. Neither Ms. Fremble, Mr. Notin, nor Mr. Gotabody does anything. (It's Friday, and they're all in personnel.)

Days 88–92. Mr. Gotabody calls a few of the people he's placed in

THE REAL WORLD OF THE JOB SEARCH   15

marketing jobs and asks them if they know anybody he might use. If it were a higher-level job, such a request would be tantamount to asking, "Do you want the job?" but it's not in this case because Tightpack doesn't usually deal in jobs that pay less than $40K per year. At the same time, Mr. Gotabody writes up an ad for the job and has it placed in the *Wall Street Journal* to run on Day 96. This ad will get a much better response than Mr. Notin's efforts for two reasons. First, Mr. Gotabody's ad is much more on target (i.e., Mr. Gotabody knows what he's doing), and, second, the *Wall Street Journal's* ads are scanned by more professional-level job seekers than those of any other single paper. He also more carefully scans the reams of unsolicited resumes that cross his desk every day.

Days 95–99. The ad runs on Day 96. Because all of the job ads in each of the four regional editions of the *Wall Street Journal* also run the following week in the *National Business Employment Weekly*, the ad will bring in a heavy stream of responses for weeks to come. On Day 97, Mr. Gotabody spots an unsolicited resume that crosses his desk. It's perfect for the job! He calls the person and conducts a fifteen-minute phone interview. The candidate is articulate and appears to be a great prospect. He arranges to have the candidate fly in for an interview on Day 105, the first day each of them has free. Mr. Gotabody is particularly pleased because the candidate's trip expense will eat up a large part of JBI's retainer and therefore enable Tightpack Associates to bill JBI for more, especially if they find someone for the job. Responses to the ad begin to come in, and Mr. Gotabody scans them carefully.

Days 102–106. The responses are flooding in now at the rate of twenty to thirty per day. On Day 105, Mr. Gotabody interviews the candidate and is very pleased. He tells the candidate that he'll set up an interview with the client. A series of interviews is set up with Mr. Notin, Ms. Fremble, Mr. Gladhand, and Ms. Jacobs on Day 123, the first day when all of them are available.

Days 107–122. Mr. Gotabody screens three hundred fifty resumes, conducts twenty-five phone interviews, and interviews another three people in person. The retainer is nicely eaten up by expenses, and JBI is billed for an additional $15K of time charges. He finds two candidates to send to JBI if candidate number one doesn't make it.

Day 123. The candidate arrives at JBI and is separately interviewed by Mr. Notin, Mr. Gladhand, and Ms. Jacobs (Ms. Fremble had an emergency personnel convention to attend), taken up to meet Ol' Jim Bob, lunched at an expensive restaurant, and given a tour of the physical plant. At the end of the day, the candidate is told, "We'll get back to you in a day or so," and then dropped in a cab.

Day 124. All of the JBIers agree that the candidate is great. Mr. Notin calls Mr. Gotabody, and they discuss what the offer should be. Mr. Gotabody has talked with the candidate already and knows that everything went great. When he talks with Mr. Notin, he realizes that he's got a winner and a fat commission on the hook. He wants the percentage fee to be as big as possible, so he recommends that they make an offer in the $32–33K range. He knows that his recommendation as a consultant will carry considerable weight and will serve to make the candidate seem more appealing (higher cost equals higher perceived value equals bigger commission).

Days 125–127. An offer is put together. The compensation manager and Mr. Notin don't like it, but they know they'd better be quiet this time around. On Day 127, everyone agrees to an offer of $34K in order to "bring the candidate on board with a good feeling."

Day 130. The candidate is called by Mr. Notin, and an offer is made. The candidate asks for a day or two to think about it.

Day 132. The candidate calls Mr. Notin and accepts the offer. Arrangements are made to have the candidate's household moved. The candidate agrees to start work on Day 165.

The job search took more than twenty-two weeks, almost six months! In the interests of conserving space, Tightpack was permitted to fill the job very quickly. Usually, headhunters will take almost as long to fill a position as the company would. In some cases, of course, the headhunters will be called in right at the start, and the length of the process will be limited to only their foul-ups. The above example is an actual job search history (with names changed, of course) related to me by the candidate who was a fellow employee of mine. Between extra expenses, Tightpack's fee, relocation expenses, and the salary increase from the $26.5K they originally sought to pay, JBI had to spend $38.5K more to fill the position than if they had offered $28K to the original candidate whom Mr. Gladhand liked and who was seeking $27K. More amazing is the fact that the candidate who finally got the job had responded to the original ad placed by Mr. Notin. (He had been receiving several major out-of-town papers during his job search.) Mr. Notin had rejected the resume because he didn't like the format when he scanned it for three seconds.

As an individual job seeker, you can get to any stage of a search process such as the above and then get rejected. That's why you must maintain as much activity as you can, especially if you're out of work. You can't afford to be betting on only one or two prospects and then have them fall through. It takes too long to develop each one from the start to a decision point. You've got to have as many in the pipeline at all stages of development as possible.

A Few Words About Personnel Departments

They see themselves as an end product.

Personnel work is a service, overhead function. In their nonproduct-oriented environment, personnel types are generally not as involved with profit and performance issues as the rest of the organization. Instead, they become guardians of the system and keepers of policies and procedures. They learn to use the system to control things. After a while, they become the system and generate more of it. Since they aren't producing anything, they walk a fine line between manipulating the system to exercise their power and taking great pains not to aggravate anyone who has influence. Making the situation worse is the fact that a lot of inadequate people are drawn to personnel work because of the power they perceive it gives them over others. They erroneously see their positions as hire–fire figureheads. (Personnel actually makes few hire–fire decisions.) You can spot these types in an instant during an interview. They're the ones who use up all of your interview talking about their work load, their status, their new title, how tough they've got it, their busy schedule, and so on. Most of them made a feeble attempt to work in operational environments and were thrown out, were pressured to leave, or got scared of the work and escaped to personnel.

If you're going to be successful in dealing with personnel types, you have to appreciate the implications of the above situation. Personnel types take *no* chances; they will do nothing that puts them at risk with the rest of the organization. They will not take a chance on recommending a candidate who has an unusual but interesting background. Instead, they'll stick with what's safe and mundane—there are fewer risks. They never rock the boat, and they never stand up for anything except the policies and procedures.

They don't know what's going on in the organization.

Even if a resume screener or interviewer wanted to take a chance and be bold, they usually don't know enough about the organization's jobs or products to be able to deviate from the parameters and qualifications as they understand them from the job description, the position requisition, or comments made by the hiring manager. As a result, the personnel people generally have only a superficial, jargon-level understanding of what's going on. The people in personnel know they're out of touch, but they'd never admit it. This anxiety about being discovered makes them even more reluctant to take chances or expose their inadequacies.

Candidates are selected out, not in.

Recruiters cope with this sorry situation in the only way they can: they make their unique contributions by screening out candidates with any irregularities or problems. Not only does this permit them to demonstrate that they're hard at work, but it also virtually eliminates the possibility that anyone will criticize them for sending up a candidate with a different or unusual set of qualifications. Rather than focusing on finding the candidates who can do the best job for the organization, they focus on screening out candidates who might make the personnel department have to explain its actions. A not unrelated point is to understand that most personnel departments don't really actively search for candidates in the sense that they go out and creatively beat the bushes. Personnel departments more or less set out the bait, either through an ad or through a headhunter, and then screen whatever wanders by. They view their function as one of keeping out the undesirables rather than aggressively attempting to attract the best candidates they can get. It's not difficult to see that a lot of great candidates never get interviewed.

Executive Recruiters (Headhunters)

Many job seekers believe that the origins of executive recruiters—headhunters—can be traced back to the days of slave merchants and white slavers. They claim that, in terms of ethics and morality, the profession has been in constant decline ever since those early days (which they claim headhunters refer to as the Golden Era). This negative view of headhunters is based partly on a misunderstanding of the role that headhunters play. It's also based on experiences in dealing with a lot of incompetent headhunters. A little knowledge up front will help you avoid many of these negative experiences. This knowledge will also help you to work most effectively with the capable headhunters who contact you.

Executive recruiting firms work on a fee-for-service or retainer basis for organizations that require or prefer assistance in locating job candidates. Although some work independently, most executive recruiters work as consultants for small search firms.

There are two basic types of search firms. Contingency recruiting firms get paid by the client organization (the company with the job opening) only if they locate someone for the job who gets hired. Retainer or noncontingency recruiters get paid a retainer for fees and expenses which is then supplemented if the fee or expenses for finding a particular candidate exceeds the retainer. There are few differences between the two types of firms that will affect your search strategies. It's probably generally true that retainer firms have somewhat stronger ties to the client companies than do contingency recruiters. Retainer firms usually work more intensely for a smaller number of companies. As a result, retainer recruiters on the average know the jobs a little better than contingency recruiters. In practice, however, there's such a wide variety of search firms and individual recruiters that any differences between the types in general are washed out by individual differences. If a search firm offers to fly you back to their office for an interview just to "have a chat," you can bet it's a retainer search firm that is trying to demonstrate how hard it's working by showing the client all sorts of expenses and thereby justifying the same or a larger retainer next year.

Individual recruiters are paid mainly by commission. A lot of firms don't pay them any draw or advance. All the recruiter gets is an office, a desk, a phone, and secretarial support. If the recruiter doesn't place anyone, his or her family doesn't eat. This is an important point to consider when using recruiters. They don't have the time or the inclination to worry about your interests. They're in the meat business, and you're only a roast beef. If the client is in the mood for lamb, the headhunter won't stop to check your marbling. They're in business to find bodies for their clients. If they do it well enough and often enough, they'll have a loyal source of job orders. If not, they're out of luck and maybe out of business. Unless you are a highly placed personnel executive, your favor or good will means less than nothing to them.

The fees involved can be quite impressive. Although some firms are discounting, this is not yet widespread. The typical fee for filling a $50K-per-year job is 30 to 60 percent of the annual salary. The headhunter and the search firm split the fee (which is always paid by the employer), with the headhunter getting proportionately less if he or she received a draw, health benefits, and so on. In any case, both the agency and the firm do very well on any one successful search. Many headhunters make $50–200K a year. Of course, many more are forced out of the business because they don't have the skills, contacts, or luck to make any placements.

Since headhunters don't work for you, don't believe anything they say. Don't trust them to do anything they say they will. Don't expect them to follow up. Don't expect them to demonstrate the slightest courtesy, although the ones who are doing well are generally quite nice. If they say they will get back to you by Friday, expect the call next month—maybe! Remember, to them you are just a piece of meat, and tomorrow may be veggie melt day. The key here is not to waste a lot of emotional effort on what they say they will do. Treat every interaction as a totally independent event which has no connection with the past or future. If they say they will call back, just forget it. If they call, fine. If not, fine.

Job Assistance/Career Development Outfits

There are several well-known national firms and countless local ones that claim they will help you find a job. They operate under the labels of career development, executive development, career counseling, and executive placement. All they will help you do is lighten your wallet, waste a lot of time, and instill a false sense of hope which will restrict your own efforts for months. These firms typically charge from $1000 to $10,000 or more depending on how much you make or want to make and how much they think they can soak you for. The experience of a friend of mine, now a company president, is representative of the dozens of people I've talked to who have used these firms. My friend tried it because he had the bucks, was curious about how they worked, and wasn't looking very seriously for another position. Also, to his slight discredit, he actually thought they might be able to save him some effort. The salesperson, calling himself a career development consultant, told my friend that the cost would be $4000 firm. My friend played hard to get over a period of three weeks and eventually got the price whittled down to $2500.

Here's what he got for his $2500:

1. A one-hour session with a shrink, worth maybe $75 on the open market in a big city. The stated purpose of the interview was to explore what his real strengths and interests were. (If you haven't got that straightened out before the search starts, don't fool with it at that point, especially if you're out of work. Get a job, and then deal with it.) The actual purpose of such interviews is to impress the unsophisticated with the precision of the entire search strategy. ("See, we even use psychologists!") Take it from me. I'm a licensed psychologist, and there's nothing I can find out or do as a shrink in one hour that's going to help you find a job any quicker or write a resume that is any more effective. It doesn't matter what your interests and goals are if you need a job *fast*.
2. Fifty copies of a custom-designed and typed resume, worth maybe $150 from a first-class outfit. (You can do better by using Chapter 4 of this book.)
3. Several mailings to executive recruiters of the resume and a cover letter for a total of about two hundred fifty letters.
4. A mailing of about two hundred fifty letters to what were billed as "highly qualified leads." These leads consisted mainly of people who had been prior clients and were supposedly inclined to assist new clients by networking.
5. Assurance that he could use their resources anytime in the future.

Not much of a bargain for $2500. And he got it cheap! What's worse, these firms usually insist that you make no major search efforts on your own while they're "busy" on your case. A lot of time gets wasted. My friend got no leads over a six-month period. Don't waste your time and money on these unscrupulous operators. You can do much better yourself.

Employment Agencies

Avoid employment agencies at all times. They'll waste your time and lead you only to lower-level jobs. In general, they deal with hourly, secretarial, and some other entry-level office jobs. They solicit or receive job orders from wide arrays of clients in different industries. (Some are specialized, but most can't afford that luxury.) They usually don't know anything about the jobs or the industry. They probably don't even know the people at the various companies other than to talk with them occasionally by phone. If you put in an application with an agency, they'll attempt to match you up with a job order and then send you over for an interview. They don't care if you're not especially right for the job because they're just playing the odds. Unlike a headhunter, who will be careful to send over only good candidates in order to build his or her reputation and avoid getting the client angry, employment agencies know that the same job order is probably out with three to ten other agencies. They throw every available candidate at the job in the hopes that the employer will select one of theirs. The employers don't much care about this type of shoddy screening because they just want warm bodies, and skills aren't that important; they never use employment agencies for higher-level jobs. Unless you're just starting out and are desperate beyond reason, you don't need the grief.

The fee is another problem. More than half the time, agencies expect you to pay. It can be as much as 15 percent of your gross earnings. Don't deal with agencies if you can avoid it. Use headhunters instead. If you do have to work with an agency, refuse to consider anything but fee-paid positions in which the employer pays the fee to the employment agency. Even then there may be catches. Be aware that if you quit within a year you may be expected to reimburse the employer.

It's Not As Bad As It Sounds

If some or all of this chapter's information was new to you, you may be a little shocked or depressed about the quality of people and systems that you'll have to work with during your job search. Don't overreact. The same messed-up systems and people are involved in every aspect of human life. Things still get done in spite of this. Those folks out there in the job search world (and the business world in general) may be confused and intellectually limited, but they're fair about it. They're confused and intellectually limited with everyone; you're not going to be any more at risk than all of the other job seekers. In fact, now that you have a clearer notion of what's really going on, you're in a position to increase the odds in your favor by taking advantage of the confusion and flaws in the system and its people. Thousands upon thousands of job seekers have found good jobs without any understanding of how the job search world operates. If you implement the *Inside Track* job search method described in the following chapters, you'll have outstanding materials, and you'll know how to use them. You'll be doing as much with a bad situation as possible.

Chapter 3

Planning and Strategy Selection

Many activities profit from spontaneous and unplanned execution. Roughhousing with children, certain artistic endeavors, and sex are a few of the many activities whose enjoyment is heightened when the spirit of the moment is permitted to take charge. Spontaneity adds to the emotional thrill and intensifies feelings of personal involvement. That's the advantage of letting our childlike impulses take over for a few minutes every now and then. A job search is not one of those now and thens. About the last things you'll need more of during a job search are emotional thrills and intense personal involvement. Your emotional stability is going to be dragged around by the choke chain of life in a very "thrilling" and intensely personal manner during the job search; you don't need the extra suffering you'll get by kicking off a job search without careful planning.

Some thoughtful up-front planning will benefit you in another equally critical way. Desperate people sometimes do strange and irrational things. Looking for a job can get desperate pretty fast, especially if you're suddenly and unexpectedly unemployed or if you're slowly being driven crazy in a bad job. Careful and disciplined up-front planning will set a course that will help you ride out the tough spots. Once you've got a plan, you won't be as inclined to waste time and effort by postponing critical steps or trying quick fixes. A plan will bolster you emotionally during periods of little action when you feel depressed and guilty because you think it's your fault that the phone's not ringing. If you've got a job search plan, and if you stick to it, you'll know you're doing all you can; you'll feel better, and you'll get better results. You've got to take the mature, objective, and probabilistic long view of the search. Careful planning provides you with that perspective and helps you to maintain it.

STEP 1: Don't Tell Anyone at Work That You're Looking

The first step in planning your job search is *not* a detailed analysis of what you want, how you can get it, and so on. The detailed analysis is the second step. The first step, if you're employed, is to keep your mouth shut at work about your job search plans. Typically, when you get to the point where you feel you must look for another job, you're a little bitter and disappointed that things aren't working out the way you had hoped when you first started the job. You'll be harboring a lot of resentment by the time you've decided to throw in the towel. In that state of mind, the most natural thing to do is to strike back. Subtly at first, and then more blatantly as nobody responds and begs you to stay, you make it clear that you're unhappy, are considering looking for a job, and "don't need to take this stuff anymore." Your secret fantasy is that the news will eventually get to someone important who will implore you to stay. If this has happened more than once in the last ten years in the entire world, I'd be extremely surprised. Everybody has his or her own problems, and nobody really cares what you do (unless you do it to them). If the word gets around that you're looking, you may suddenly find yourself out of your old job before you find the new one. That will do some things to your odds of quickly finding a job that nobody needs. Being out of work when you're looking is a major handicap you should avoid at all costs.

STEP 2: Analyze Where You Are and Where You Want to Go

The biggest single strategic problem with most job searches is that job seekers do not carefully analyze what they really want, how they plan to get it, and what resources they've got or need to get. Whether or not you have a detailed ten-year career plan or you were summarily fired this morning without warning (there probably were warnings but you didn't see them), you shouldn't jump head first into the search. Give yourself a few days to carefully plan your search priorities and determine your job search goals. Answer the following questions:

If you're still employed

1. Is it really that bad where you are?
2. Have you carefully analyzed your discontent to track down its real source, to make sure it's the job and not some personal or social problem that's soured you?
3. Do you realistically think it will be any better at another job? (If your answer to this question is always yes, you need to read *Conduct Expected: The Unwritten Rules for a Successful Business Career*, New Century Publishers, 1985, by this author. You're probably expecting too much and are therefore always going to be disappointed.)
4. How much time can you devote to the job search?

5. How will you handle getting away for interviews?
6. How likely is it that your present employer will find out that you're looking?

If you're out of work

1. How much time can you hang on (to your house, marriage, health, etc.) without a job? How desperate are you?
2. Can you get some temporary work that will provide you with some income to hold things together? (I'm talking about not only high-level consulting but hourly work as a laborer, security guard, or such, that will enable you to pay the rent. This is not a time to let pride stand in your way. Assume that the worst will happen, and work to prevent it.)
3. What are you going to do about the fact of your termination? (Job seekers who are unemployed, for whatever reason, are considered tainted by employers.)

For everyone

1. Do you just want (or need) to get any job you can?
2. Do you want more money without concern for the type of job?
3. Do you need a positive career step at this point? Can you afford to hold out rather than take anything that comes along?
4. Do you want to get out of town or overseas?
5. Can you relocate? What are your limitations and preferences? (You've got to talk with your family before you start responding to ads and contacting headhunters. There's no sense wasting time on leads for jobs to which you couldn't relocate.)
6. Do you really have the experience you need to make it to the next step (both to get the work done and to look like a reasonable candidate to the employer)?
7. What about the industry? Does it matter?
8. Do you have any contacts who might help?
9. What kinds of references will you get from past employers and associates?
10. What are your ethical concerns about lying if your situation is desperate?

All of these questions must be given some thought before you implement a campaign to find your next job. Even if you've just been thrown out the door, take a few days to think about what you really want, what you've got to have, and what assets you possess that will help you get it. Be realistic and practical. If you don't spend a few days assessing your situation, you'll waste a lot of your initial efforts by drafting poor resumes, answering the wrong ads, delaying the start-up of long-term strategies, and so forth. Don't worry if you can't come up with definite answers to all or even half of the above questions; most people never do. That's not the point. The purpose in thinking about these questions is to enable you to put together the best job search possible in your present situation.

Your search strategies, materials, and goals must support each other in a consistent and logical fashion. With a plan, you'll save time, minimize wasted effort and emotional distress, and increase your odds of success. As you read through the rest of this book and begin to get your search plans firmed up, flip through this chapter occasionally and consider the various questions, trade-offs, and implications of the goals you've set for yourself. This periodic "global review" will assist you in keeping your plan, materials (resumes and correspondence), and interview presentations consistent and mutually supportive.

Don't procrastinate on getting started with the actual search effort itself, particularly if you're unemployed. Being out of work is bad news, and it won't go away without herculean effort. Don't do what a lot of unemployed, so-called high rollers do. They take off for a few weeks of vacation and waste time because they think they're sure to find something in a few weeks when they finally start looking. Several months later, they find they're almost broke and haven't gotten to the first phase of the job search. Get to work on your plan right away, keep it practical, and then get busy doing things rather than more planning.

Forget the existentialism

Keep your plan focused on tactics and materials, not philosophy. Many job search books advocate a lot of soul searching about who you are, where you want to be in life, what you do best, what you like, what will "actualize" you as a human being, and other existential concerns. One of the worst times in life to do your soul searching is when you're out of work; you're too driven by emotions, self-doubt, and pressure to take stock of yourself objectively. More critically, if you're like the typical person who's out of work, you don't have time for the luxury of sitting back and getting your head together; you need a job as fast as you can get one. *Inside Track* deals with applied job searching, not pie-in-the-sky self-analysis. I'm concerned with getting you back to work if you're out of work or into a better job if you're stuck in a bad one. If you feel you're lost and adrift and don't know what to do about your life, you probably should explore the meaning of life and your place in it. But if you're currently out of work and not independently wealthy, trust me—now's not the time to do any self-analysis. Get a job, and then worry about the meaning of life after work. You'll find self-analysis easier with a full stomach and a roof over your head.

STEP 3: *Strategy Evaluation*

Chapters 5, 6, and 7 each present detailed instructions for implementing a particular job search strategy. Chapter 8 presents a number of additional strategies which can be useful in specific situations but are generally less effective than those of Chapters 5, 6, and 7. There are many different variations within each type of strategy. You've got to keep the big picture of your search in mind as you select individual strategies. Each strategy has strong points and drawbacks. More critically, each strategy is differentially appropriate to your search on each of several criteria. For example, if you're comfortably working in a job that is acceptable, you probably aren't in a hurry to locate your next position; you can afford to take your time to look for just the right next step. In that case, one strategy that might be effective is called "Let's be friends." This technique, one of many described in Chapter 7, involves low-key, long-term networking with executives. If you've got eighteen to twenty-four months in which to explore the possibilities, it's a good technique. On the other hand, if you're desperate and running out of time and money, such networking wouldn't be effective because of the low probability of short-term results.

The same type of evaluation can be made of each strategy on additional factors such as the amount of your time required to get things started, the cost per item launched (e.g., how much it costs to send each letter), the average time before responses begin arriving, and so forth. Figures 3.1 through 3.4 each rate one of the general job search strategies presented in Chapters 5 through 8, respectively, on ten separate evaluation criteria. The ratings are composites of each strategy's performance in searches in all industries and for all position types.

The ratings shown in the figures are based on the following assumptions:
1. The strategy is conducted in a technically precise fashion. That is, all letters are well written in accordance with *Inside Track* guidelines, phone calls are handled with competence, and the resume used is a well-prepared *Inside Track* version.
2. The candidate's real or imagined background is relevant to the job, and the candidate can substantiate written and verbal claims to the interviewers' satisfaction.
3. The candidate lives in a metropolitan area which presents at least some variety of job possibilities or has access to appropriate job search materials or leads for other geographical areas to which relocation is a possibility.

4. For several of the evaluation criteria, Figures 3.1 through 3.4 present categories of *you do* and *you pay*. The *you do* column presents ratings that pertain if you do the typing, mailing, and so on. The *you pay* column presents corresponding data for a candidate who pays a word-processing service to produce all letters. If *you pay*, it's assumed that you'll be using a secretarial service that utilizes word-processing equipment that can easily edit and mailmerge your letters. (See Chapter 11 for information on mailmerging and word processing.) The *you do* ratings assume that you can do as good a job as a service.
5. If *you do*, it's assumed that you can type a little, at least twenty words per minute, and that you can produce letters that don't look like they've been through the wash. If you really aren't a passable typist and can't prevent shoddy, multicorrected or poorly edited letters from going out, don't try. Pay someone else to do it right.
6. For the sake of simplicity, all of the cost data assume that your time is free. Of course, it's not, especially if you've got a limited amount of it. Keep that in mind as you evaluate the trade-offs of paying for secretarial support versus doing it yourself. If you're out of work and can't find or don't need part-time or temporary work, you might as well do things yourself, but only if you do it right. It makes no sense to crank out letters that give a bad impression. Even if you're running out of money and have the time to do them yourself, don't try if you can't do a first-rate job.
7. It's assumed that you're looking for a job for which there's a reasonable demand. The rarer the openings, the longer it's going to take and the fewer chances you'll get. If you're in a high-demand field, you'll get more responses in a shorter time. The ratings are generalizations for the average situation and are intended to serve as comparative guidelines among all the strategies, not as absolute indicators.
8. The final assumption is that the user of the strategy will possess sufficient intelligence to apply the strategy properly. For example, Figure 3.1 estimates as very low the probability that your present employer will find out about your job search as a result of your responses to classified ads. Let's suppose a job seeker works as a production manager for the only red widget firm in Glenside, California. If the seeker is stupid enough to answer a blind ad soliciting candidates for V.P. of manufacturing for a "red widget industry leader" and the box address is Glenside, guess who's going to be fired very shortly? If you follow the suggestions and observe the cautions in the chapters that describe each strategy, you won't create problems or compromise your results.

Where certain other variables could significantly affect time, costs,

PLANNING AND STRATEGY SELECTION 29

probabilities, and so on, they are mentioned in the discussions that accompany the figures.

As you read the following chapters, you'll observe that each of the strategies can be pursued with various levels of effort. For example, a mailing to headhunters (Chapter 6) could consist of a specifically written letter resume (Chapter 4) sent to only ten narrowly targeted headhunters who work in a specific industry. The same general strategy of mailings to headhunters would also encompass a mailing to every identifiable headhunting outfit in the country. The odds of success, the number of responses, and the quality of the responses are only a few of the evaluation criteria that would be markedly different for these two variations of the mailings to headhunters strategy. Think of the variations you might apply as you read about each strategy. Figures 3.1 through 3.4 present average ratings across these types of variabilities so that you may get a general sense of each strategy's applicability. Don't make any firm strategy selections until you've read the subsequent chapters that describe them in detail.

The definitions of the ten evaluation criteria rated in Figures 3.1 through 3.4 are as follows:

1. *Cost to launch each item.* The cost to "do" each item. In answering ads, for example (Figure 3.1), the cost is for postage and stationery if *you do*. If *you pay*, the cost also includes word-processing support done by a secretarial service. Refer to Chapter 11 for additional information on using word-processing services or your own computer system. For strategies that require phone calls and research to launch each item, the costs will appear low as your time is considered free in the figures.

2. *Your time required to launch each item.* The average number of minutes it takes to launch each item, whether it's making a networking phone call to an executive or typing a letter or both.

3. *Does it target the job you're seeking?* The strategy's ability to put you in touch with jobs that are reasonably close to what you want and which you would accept if everything worked out.

4. *Time lag from launch to responses.* The average time it takes to receive 25 percent of the total positive feedback (phone interviews for good leads) you'll get from people who were contacted by means of the strategy.

5. *Callbacks per hundred items.* The number of times per hundred launches that you'll get a phone interview or an outright (no screening) invitation to a face-to-face interview.

6. *Average quality of each callback.* The likelihood that you'll get good leads. Not all feedback from your ad responses, mailings to headhunters, and direct solicitations will be of high quality. Often, after you've responded to an ad that seemed perfect for you, you'll get a phone call and discover that the job is totally

different from the one described in the ad. Or you'll get a phone call from a novice headhunter who totally misreads your interests and qualifications and wants to put you in the running for a job you'd never get or wouldn't take if it was offered.

7. *Your time to handle each callback.* The average time required to respond to each callback. With every strategy you're hoping for at least a phone interview. Talking on the phone takes time. If you're conducting an *Inside Track* job search, you'll also have to follow up each phone call with a thank-you letter. This also takes time (and money; see next criterion). This rating item gives you an idea of what to expect in terms of each strategy's demands on your time.
8. *Cost to handle each callback.* The average cost incurred to respond to each callback. As explained in item 1, this category presents costs for both the *you do* and the *you pay* situations. Included are both phone and correspondence expenses. The phone expenses are estimated on the basis of the probable mix of local and long-distance calls.
9. *Personal interviews per hundred launches.* The average number of invitations to personal interviews you can expect from every hundred items launched. Not included in the estimate are invitations you would decline because the phone interview uncovers things you don't like.
10. *Probability of employer finding out.* The likelihood that your employer will discover your job seeking activities through an unscrupulous third party. It doesn't happen often, but it's not unheard of.

Strategy 1: Responding to Classified Ads

The ratings of this strategy are presented in Figure 3.1. This is the most commonly used job search approach. Almost everyone uses it (although not very well). As appraised here, it consists of a cover letter and a resume sent in response to a classified advertisement in a newspaper, professional or industry journal, or magazine. Chapter 5 presents the how-to of this strategy. It is particularly critical because many organizations use it exclusively for external recruiting. As Figure 3.1 shows, this strategy gets uniformly high ratings. It's the best single strategy if you are going to use only one. The costs and time involved are no greater than with any other strategy and much less than with most of the others. At the same time, the hit rate (callbacks per hundred items) is high and the quality of callbacks is very good. If you more narrowly define your search parameters and go after only a very specific type of job for which you're qualified and have credentials, you could easily get the hit rate up to thirty per hundred launches. In

Evaluation Criteria	You Do	You Pay
1. Cost to launch per item	$0.40	$1.25
2. Your time required to launch each item	30 min	10 min
3. Does it target the job you're seeking?	Good	
4. Average time from launch to responses	2 weeks	
5. Callbacks per hundred items	10	
6. Average quality of each callback	Very good	
7. Your time to handle each callback	30 min	20 min
8. Cost to handle each callback	$2.40	$3.25
9. Personal interviews per hundred launches	5	
10. Probability of employer finding out	Very low	

Figure 3.1 Evaluation of Strategy 1: Responding to Classified Ads

that case, the personal interviews would increase to about twenty per hundred.

This pattern holds true for all search strategies. If you focus your strategy more narrowly, your return per item goes up very fast. The problem is that the narrowing of the focus shrinks your target population and gives you less to shoot at. That's one reason why it pays to be as noncommittal as possible about your requirements for salary and working conditions in resumes and cover letters. You don't want to shrink your target population (by being summarily rejected by the screener) before you get a chance at least to talk with them on the phone.

The costs to handle each callback may seem high. Don't forget phone charges. Many times you'll be required to return a call to a headhunter or potential employer. Very often, they don't offer to allow you to call collect (and it's not a good idea to ask about this during the first call; it takes the conversation to a "do something for me" stance much too soon). Many will offer and even encourage you to call collect. If they insist, do it. If you're trying to impress them that you're a high roller or doing pretty well financially, don't call collect.

Strategy 2: Mailings to headhunters

The step-by-step procedures for this strategy are presented in Chapter 6. Figure 3.2 displays its overall average ratings. This strategy consists of sending a cover letter and resume to a number of headhunters or

Evaluation Criteria	You Do	You Pay
1. Cost to launch per item	$0.40	$1.25
2. Your time required to launch each item	20 min	2 min
3. Does it target the job you're seeking?	Fair	
4. Average time from launch to responses	4 weeks	
5. Callbacks per hundred items	5	
6. Average quality of each callback	Good	
7. Your time to handle each callback	30 min	20 min
8. Cost to handle each callback	$2.40	$3.25
9. Personal interviews per hundred launches	1	
10. Probability of employer finding out	Low	

Figure 3.2 Evaluation of Strategy 2: Mailings to Headhunters

headhunting firms. This strategy's strength is that it can generate a lot of action. It can also put you in touch with many high-level jobs. An added plus is that many organizations place considerable trust in the headhunters they use. A referral by a trusted headhunter immediately puts you in the final pool of candidates. If you properly balance your materials to be specific about what you can do (everything) but not too specific about what you'll take in terms of position, location, and salary (within the limits of your search), it will be easier for the headhunter to believe and make the client believe that you're just what they've been looking for, whatever that might be. Note that if you make a thousand launches (that's not an incredible number of launches for this strategy), you'll get fifty callbacks. This brings us to the strategy's main drawback: it takes a lot of time. It's not that you've got to spend a lot of time on each callback; it's just that you'll have a lot of them to handle. Since each will require about thirty minutes of your time for the phone conversation and sending a follow-up note, you'll have to devote twenty-five hours of total time to handling the phone calls and getting the thank-you letters out. If you're currently employed, you might not have that much time available. This problem can be dealt with by narrowing the focus of the mailing so that the number of callbacks will be reduced and their quality will be higher.

If you're out of work, this strategy is excellent when used with a broadly focused cover letter. You'll get many more callbacks than the average shown, and you'll have the time to handle them. Of course, you'll have to deal with a lot of marginal headhunters who don't know what they're doing, but enough will call with decent leads to make it worthwhile.

Strategy 3: Direct solicitation to executives and organizations

This broad strategy encompasses as one of its variants the faddishly popular but not particularly effective networking. Chapter 7 discusses a wide range of direct solicitation strategies, including telephone networking and how to do it correctly. Direct solicitation involves direct contact by mail and/or phone with specific individuals who might have or know about a job possibility. Figure 3.3 presents an assessment of this strategy's criteria.

You'll notice that the number of callbacks per hundred launches appears pretty good. Don't be misled. Many of these will be "guilt" calls or interviews which the interviewer conducts as a courtesy to (or in fear of) the person who referred you. That's why the number of interviews is so low; guilt interviews don't count. Even if you do this strategy the right way, which is to send a mailer to selected executives and follow up with phone calls, you're not going to get much, simply because so many of your letters will go into the trash.

As Figure 3.3 clearly demonstrates, this strategy is a poor choice if you're in a hurry to find a job. It's also a poor choice if you don't have copious amounts of free time to use for the launches. The times are

Evaluation Criteria	You Do	You Pay
1. Cost to launch per item	$0.40	$1.25
2. Your time required to launch each item	120 min	60 min
3. Does it target the job you're seeking?	Poor	
4. Average time from launch to responses	10 weeks	
5. Callbacks per hundred items	8	
6. Average quality of each callback	Fair	
7. Your time to handle each callback	30 min	20 min
8. Cost to handle each callback	$2.70	$3.55
9. Personal interviews per hundred launches	0.5	
10. Probability of employer finding out	Moderate	

Figure 3.3 Evaluation of Strategy 3: Direct Solicitation to Executives and Organizations

very high because of the effects of the large numbers of phone calls it takes to locate and contact each launch for telephone networking. It's then necessary to follow the chain of referrals with more phone calls until a decision maker or choice contact is made. All variants of this strategy require additional research time (not included in the estimates) to research targets for the mailings.

The heart of the strategy is to get close to decision makers who'll have the power to hire you or enough influence, knowledge, or contacts to refer you to someone else who'll hire you. As Chapter 2 demonstrated, there are few people even in the largest organizations who possess that type of power.

As a result of these limitations, this strategy isn't recommended unless your main interest is in building some career development contacts for future use and you've got a lot of time available with which to do it. Chapter 7 will show you how to use this strategy effectively to build these long-term relationships.

A final caution on this strategy: high-level executives maintain a much closer network within and across industries than you might think. If you start sending out a lot of letters and making a lot of phone calls to executives, particularly within a small community or industry, there's a not insignificant chance that your present employer might find out. The odds of this happening are low, but it occurs more often when using this strategy than with any other. Select your targets with this in mind.

Strategy 4: Miscellaneous

Figure 3.4 assesses the overall ratings of this strategy, which isn't so much one strategy as a collection of odds and ends, most of which have an element of the outrageous or the theatrical about them. They're often very appealing, especially to a desperate and emotional job seeker. Once again, remember that a lot of strategies that appear intuitively appealing are, in reality, worthless. Chapter 2 has provided you with the reasons why most of them don't work. When you read about them in Chapter 8, you'll recognize their weak spots. They're presented in detail so that you'll know what to avoid and what not to do. They're also presented for a more practical reason: you may not listen, you may get excited by the emotional appeal of some of the outrageous approaches, and you'll try them. Since you're reading this book, the least I can do is show you how to minimize your wasted time and possibly get a long-shot result.

Figure 3.4 demonstrates that the time and cost requirements for miscellaneous strategies overall are about the same as they were in Figure 3.1 for answering ads, except for callback costs. That's where the similarity ends. The miscellaneous strategies have long lead times

PLANNING AND STRATEGY SELECTION

Evaluation Criteria	You Do	You Pay
1. Cost to launch per item	$0.40	$1.25
2. Your time required to launch each item	30 min	10 min
3. Does it target the job you're seeking?	Very poor	
4. Average time from launch to responses	6 weeks	
5. Callbacks per hundred items	3	
6. Average quality of each callback	Fair	
7. Your time to handle each callback	30 min	20 min
8. Cost to handle each callback	$1.40	$2.25
9. Personal interviews per hundred launches	0.15	
10. Probability of employer finding out	Low	

Figure 3.4 Evaluation of Strategy 4: Miscellaneous

for responses, the responses you'll get will be only fair, and most of them will be off target for the jobs you want. Don't waste your time with the strategies shown in Chapter 8 unless you've completely exhausted all possible applications of strategies 1 through 3. (I've only seen such exhaustive searches a few times.) Then, if you want to have a little fun and are willing to waste your time, go ahead and try a few.

Allocation of Resources to Search Strategies

It's probably clear to you by now that you'll have to employ a number of strategies in most job search situations; just using one probably won't touch all the bases you've got to cover. On the other hand, even if you're out of work and desperate, you don't have the time or money to do everything possible. The question is, just where should your effort go? How much time and money should be devoted to one strategy before, instead of, or while you implement another one? Figure 3.5 provides some general guidelines for allocating time and resources among strategies in a variety of common job search situations. The job search strategy numbers in Figure 3.5 correspond to the same strategy numbers used in Figures 3.1 through 3.4.

Figure 3.5 presents recommended percentage allocations of time among the four main strategies. Allocation of money would follow the same recommended percentages although you'll find that your time will usually be the critical limiting factor, particularly if you're still employed and trying to do most of the actual work yourself. Of

36   INSIDE TRACK

	Job Search Strategy			
Job Search Situations	1 Ads	2 Head- hunters	3 Solici- tations	4 Misc.
Employed and:				
1. Just window shopping	35	40	25	0
2. Desperate to get out	50	50	0	0
3. In a dead end but not desperate	35	40	20	5
4. Want to focus on long-term career growth	10	15	70	5
5. Looking to make a move in twelve to eighteen months	15	40	40	5
Unemployed and:				
6. Desperate	65	35	0	0
7. Not desperate; can afford to wait six months	45	40	10	5
8. Just relocated to new area; need job soon	60	30	10	0
9. Just out of school	40	20	30	10
10. Returning to job market after absence	70	10	20	0
11. Seeking part-time or temporary work	40	0	40	·20

Figure 3.5 Recommended Allocations of Resources Among Strategies for a Variety of Job Search Situations

course, if you decide to send word-processed letters to two thousand headhunters, you're most likely going to run into some financial barriers before your time runs out.

Figure 3.5 presents separate sections for the job search situations of the employed and the unemployed. The critical difference between these two groups is the time pressure that the unemployed typically face. Even if you think your financial situation will permit you to ride out the unemployment period, you may find, as have many job seekers, that it takes a lot longer than you feared. The recommendations of Figure 3.5 take this factor into consideration. For the unemployed, priority is given to those strategies that yield the greatest short- to medium-term results. Thus, if you're out of work and desperate (situation number 6 in Figure 3.5), you should direct 65 percent of your resources to responses to classified ads (strategy 1), 35 percent to mailings to headhunters (strategy 2), and no time to strategies 3 and 4. If, on the other hand, you aren't particularly interested in changing jobs but would just like to make sure you're not missing anything outstanding in the world of job openings, situation 1 outlines the recommended allocation of resources. You'd allocate 35 percent of your resources to strategy 1, 40 percent to strategy 2, and 25 percent to strategy 3.

Be flexible in applying the recommendations of Figure 3.5 to your situation. You may find that you'll be pressed to the limits of your available time in answering all of the appropriate classified ads and don't have time even to think about headhunters. This is the situation in which many data processing and engineering professionals occasionally find themselves. (We all should have such problems when we're looking for a job!) If there were so many great ads that you were running out of time just to answer them, you'd have to either: (1) Get more selective about the ads and respond to fewer of them so that you'd have time for other strategies, or (2) forget the headhunters and all other strategies and hope that the ads alone would lead you to the best job.

I recommend that you pursue a balanced mix of strategies whenever possible. If there are so many ads in your field that you can't respond to all of them, there are probably lots of goods leads with headhunters as well.

Of course, most of the time the problem is not too many ads but too few. You may find, operating in any of the situations shown in Figure 3.5, that you can respond to all appropriate ads with a small amount of your total available time. In that case, simply direct your available surplus resources to the strategy with the next largest resource allocation. Don't be content simply to do the minimum. You can never do too much as long as you do it properly.

When first laying out your plans (after you've read this whole book), take a look at Figure 3.5 and determine the strategy that seems best for your situation. Then refer back to Figures 3.1 through 3.4 and consider the time and cost requirements you'll have to meet in order to implement the strategies you've selected. Don't forget to tailor the time and cost estimates to your typing speed, the cost of word-processing support in your locality, and whatever other elements you'll be using for your search.

The process of developing a search plan is not a step-by-step procedure. It's a holistic, gradually evolving, subjective exercise. The purpose of this chapter is to get you properly focused on the issues that have to be dealt with. Don't be alarmed if you're still not absolutely sure about the exact mix of strategies that is right for you when you've completed this book. At that point, if you've digested the material presented, thought about it in terms of your requirements, and begun to get your search going, you'll be in great shape.

How Long Will the Search Last?

A critical concern in any job search is how long it will last. The answer is particularly important if you're out of work and desperately trying to hang on to the house, car, and so on, until you find a job. It seems almost as bad (but isn't) if you're employed but hate your job and want to get out. Figure 3.6 provides estimates in weeks of job search length in a variety of situations, from the start of the search until an offer is accepted. It presents separate estimates for employed and unemployed job seekers in both a good market (there's a reasonable number of jobs out there) and a bad one (appropriate openings are few and far between). Estimates are made according to the starting salary of the new job. (The number of openings decreases as the salary level increases, so it's harder to find an appropriate one.)

The estimates of Figure 3.6 are approximate guidelines only. They're based on the assumption that you're looking for the next step up from what you've got in terms of responsibility, salary, career growth, or technical expertise. If you're willing to settle for essentially the same job as what you had before, subtract 20 percent from the appropriate estimate (fifty weeks would become forty weeks). If you're willing to settle for a position at a level one step lower than your last or present job, subtract 25 percent. (It doesn't help much more to go lower because most employers will view such a move as indicating that you're a loser.) All of the estimates assume that you conduct a comprehensive *Inside Track* job search and that you are, or can appear to be, qualified for the job you're after. If the job market in general, or in your specialty in particular, is very good or very bad, you'll have to subjectively adjust Figure 3.6 to determine the probable length of your search. If you're being especially selective, add 15 percent to the search times. If you're qualified and willing to accept a wide array of position types, subtract 15 percent.

Figure 3.6 is not intended to tell you exactly how long your search will last. Nobody can tell you that. Its main purpose is to demonstrate that your search may take a lot longer than you think. Be prepared for a long struggle, and don't do anything to compromise your chances,

Salary of New Position (K/year)	Poor Market		Good Market	
	Unemployed	Employed	Unemployed	Employed
11 – 20	13	11	9	8
21 – 30	25	23	19	17
31 – 40	40	36	30	27
41 – 50	57	52	42	38
51 – 60	71	64	54	47
61 – 75	93	83	68	61
76 – 100	115	105	85	75
100 +	125	116	92	82

Figure 3.6 Estimates of Job Search Length in Weeks

such as quitting a job before you find another one or delaying the start of your search.

A Final Word: Stick to Your Plans at All Times

After reading Chapter 2, you know in advance that the job search will be marked by incredible failures and setbacks, by false hopes and dashed expectations, and by excruciating near misses. There will be all sorts of great jobs for which you'll never even get to interview, there will be jobs in which you'll give a great interview but never get a call (or get yours returned), and there will be positions for which you'll be interviewed three or four times and then get turned down with no explanation. Know now that all of these things are going to happen; know it and believe it even before you start planning your search.

As the days, weeks, and months pass, as the disappointments mount, you'll be tempted to change your plans, strategies, and goals in midstream. Don't let this happen without careful planning. It's OK (and sometimes essential) to make changes if you objectively decide that the changes are necessary. But don't modify your tactics as a result of emotional pressures. You'll be tempted to make changes when you're scared and depressed. Recognize where the motivation comes from. If things are deteriorating and you absolutely must have any job you can find to save the house, change your plans and objectives and do what you have to do to survive. There's nothing wrong with that. But be honest with yourself. If you absolutely want the objective you first established but you're considering making some changes in your plans purely for emotional reasons, stay on course. Keep your objective in mind when you're preparing resumes, writing cover letters, selecting ads to respond to, and answering questions during interviews. Your plan, and not transient emotional states, must be the driving and guiding force behind all that you do and say during the job search.

Chapter 4

The Resume: Your Magic Bullet

The single most important tool in any job search is the resume. More than 99 percent of all job offers for managerial, technical, and professional positions (excluding moves within an organization) involve a resume at some point. If the resume is bad, the applicant is out of the race or severely handicapped before the starting gun goes off. You can make a lot of job search mistakes that will hurt you, but using a poor resume is the absolute worst. If you blow a few interviews, it's no big deal; there will be many others. A shabby resume, on the other hand, will hurt you with every employer who receives it. You'll miss countless opportunities you'll never know about. Nobody will call you and say, "Ms. P. O. Orresume, I'm Mr. Jones of JB Industries. I just wanted to call and let you know we got your resume. It was so poorly prepared and inappropriate that we'd never consider having you in for an interview. I thought you'd like to know." If your resume has problems, nobody will bother to tell you. They'll call someone else for the interview.

In spite of their critical, fundamental importance to job search success and the large amount of attention focused on them in the job search media, the resumes of the vast majority of job seekers range from horrible to merely adequate in form, content, or the application for which they're used. Averaged over all job types, not more than 10 percent of the white-collar work force can put together a passable resume, much less a great one.

Resume Myths

Why are most resumes so bad? Aside from the effects of gross incompetence and sloppy production values, the main problem is that most job seekers, as well as most so-called resume experts, have fallen prey to a number of dangerous myths about resumes, job seeking, and the business world. Since they are led astray by false and confusing advice, it's to be expected that most job seekers can't put together a decent resume. Let's take a look at these dangerous myths.

Resume Myth 1. Resumes aren't as essential as they used to be.

Every so often the job search world is swept by another fad claiming that resumes are passé and that personal phone calls, networking, qualifications briefs, and letter resumes have replaced them. Forget this nonsense. Resumes haven't been replaced and probably won't ever be replaced. Even if the employment screening process is eventually accomplished between computers (yours and theirs), the purpose of the intercomputer communication will be to provide the employer's computer with a profile of your qualifications: a resume. Resumes are used because they serve a very practical purpose: they provide a concise and easily handled means of summarizing and presenting a candidate's qualifications. Periodic antiresume fads sweep the job search field in much the same way that ridiculous, laughable styles sweep the world of fashions each year. The designers wouldn't make any money if they tried to sell the same old stuff every year. Faced with this obvious danger to their expensive life styles, fashion designers invent something new each year. It's no different in the job search world. The experts have to keep churning out articles on the latest thing in order to keep their names in front of potential clients. One year resumes will be called qualifications briefs. The next year the fad designers will show a line of letter resumes in their fall collections. Don't fall for it.

Resume Myth 2. You're up against thousands of outstanding resumes and applicants.

It's a demographic fact that most job seekers possess only average intelligence, which isn't very much intelligence at all. Thus, it should come as no surprise that most of them can't put together an effective resume. In spite of this situation, the media of the job search world are continually trying to convince job seekers that they're competing against hordes of sharp young tigers who are churning out piles of excellent, customized resumes for every job they go after. They push this myth because they want to sell their latest bit of resume advice. If you were to fall for this propaganda, you'd be continually tinkering with your resume in a frenzied quest to make it absolutely, completely perfect. It's important for you to ignore this myth. You're not up against thousands of great resumes. Most of them are trash. Your goal is to make it into the interview pile along with the few great resumes and the small number of good ones that will always be there. It's a lot easier (and less nerve-wracking) to fight your way into this company than it is to try to create the perfect resume. Such a quest would be futile anyway; the idiosyncrasies of resume screeners make it all a game of odds once you get into the last few percent that will be closely considered as interview material. Each screener has a set of expectations that are unique to that screener alone. There's not much you can do to ensure that your resume will be the absolute best for a particular resume screener (unless you know the individual personally). The very things that make a resume perfect to one person make it flawed to another.

The *Inside Track* approach to resume construction is to produce a resume that will appeal to the greatest number of typical screeners in the greatest number of typical job search situations. That's all the resume you need because that's the best anyone can do. Don't waste your time trying for more.

Resume Myth 3. There are thousands of different types and styles of resumes, and only one of them is right for you.

As with myth 2, this myth is encouraged and propagated by the so-called experts who make a living by feeding on the anxieties of job seekers. If you were to believe that there was only one specific but as yet unknown (to you) style that would work for your resume, you'd be more apt to seek professional help to write it. Planning on this reaction, all sorts of career development consultants and college placement types continually flood the job search media with articles that make it seem as if preparing a good resume is more difficult than writing the great American novel. Multitudes of career development consultants and resume shops have sprung up to help job seekers put together the perfect resume for a fee. These resume gurus claim to be able to do magic and technical things for your resume that you can't do. Personnel types and headhunters support this charade because they see so many bad resumes and because such hype makes their industry seem more technical (and helps them sell their own articles on how to write resumes). The whole sorry process is total nonsense. There are a lot of poor resumes out there, not because it's so difficult to put one together but because there are a lot of incompetent people who can't drive correctly, can't raise their children properly, and can't put in a good day's work. When these people, as well as more competent individuals such as yourself, are misled by reams of contradictory and shoddy advice, it's a wonder there's even one decent resume out there.

Don't fall for it. You can have an excellent resume, and it's not difficult once you know how. Your resume, whatever form it takes, must meet certain criteria and must perform several functions. The *Inside Track* approach incorporates the best of these criteria and operating characteristics so that your resume will appeal to the most screeners in the most effective manner.

Resume Myth 4. The purpose of a resume is to get you a job.

The purpose of a resume is not to get you a job. No organization ever hires on the basis of a resume without examining the goods in person. Therefore, a resume can't "get" you a job (unless you've got unbelievable connections). A resume's only purpose is to get you an interview. You will have to get the job by winning the interview. All the resume can do is get you into the office or onto the phone. Once you've gotten that far, your resume is of little further importance for that particular position. This may seem like a mundane and obvious point, but it's not. It has considerable significance in terms of the content and conceptual design of a resume. If resumes were used as the sole criterion with which to select employees, they would have to contain all sorts of detailed minutiae exhaustively listing the candidate's personal data, work activities, personality characteristics, hobbies, family life, and so on. This type of information would have to be provided in order to show the real you. As things work in the real world, the interview is the means for establishing and demonstrating the real you. A resume's only purpose is to present the safe and expected information that will get you in for an interview. If you use the resume to attempt to perform the interview's function, it will look strange. Worse, you might inadvertently display a bit of personal trivia that sets off one of the interviewer's many unique internal alarms. That's very bad for your chances of getting invited for an interview.

Resume Myth 5. Employers exhaustively analyze each and every resume for technical qualifications, job skills, and specific experience.

Since even a few small typos can kill an otherwise good resume's chances, it might seem logical that each resume is subjected to a scrupulously careful analysis and examination. Nothing could be further from the truth. Aside from those resumes that are horrendously inappropriate, very few are rejected as a result of a careful analysis of technical qualifications, experience, and education. Remember, for every job opening an organization receives at least dozens, often many hundreds, and sometimes thousands of resumes. A good number of those that are rejected will have identical or even better technical qualifications than those that pass muster and make the interview pile. Most resumes are rejected not because they fail to pass a sophisticated analysis of credentials and qualifications but because they do not adequately deal with the reviewer's doubts, fears, and expectations, most of which have nothing to do with the technical qualifications of the applicant or the technical demands of the job.

As you'll recall from Chapter 2, personnel types are insecure and anxious about being second guessed in the decisions they make. When they're considering applicants and resumes, these insecurities are at fever pitch. Headhunters are even worse; they are simultaneously driven by both their clients' and their own anxieties. These people make only the safest, most palatable, and least risky decisions available to them. A resume that contains any indication of the least bit of risk to them (should you join the organization as a result of their actions) will be rejected out of hand. Your resume must be safe, respectable, and reassuring. You must never show in any way that your general character, job history, expected educational background, sexual orientation, military experience (if any), or past work performance are not completely normal and blemish-free. You will be guilty of repeated counts of resume manslaughter if you send yours out into the world with such flaws as the following.

1. *Admitting you were fired.* If the candidate is hired and doesn't work out, someone can say, "Good Lord, Bob, this clown was fired before and you brought him in for an interview with us?" Even if you have been fired and you're not inclined to lie about it when asked, there's no need to tell anyone about it before you get to the interview. If you do tell them, you probably won't get interviewed. Despite personnel executives' protestations to the contrary, it's an almost automatic exclusion if you admit it up front; there will be just too many perfect, blemish-free resumes as alternatives. Once you get to a face-to-face interview, you have a better chance of working around an admitted involuntary termination. The interviewer will have had a chance to get to know you and will have more time invested which he or she will be loathe to waste. Job seekers have discovered many different ways to deal with a termination on their resumes. One interesting technique is to become a consultant for the period of the termination. This is a particularly good strategy because everybody who is not a consultant is jealous of and impressed by people who are (or claim to be). When these job seekers want to conceal a recent or past termination, they simply say that they went into independent consulting for a while to try their luck. When asked why they left consulting, they must have a good reason or they'll seem like losers or quitters. A commonly used reason is, "There were too many eighteen-hour days. I don't mind ten- or twelve-hour days, but eighteen was too much." Also good is, "I wanted to spend my time doing satisfying work, not selling" (unless you're trying to get a sales job). Job seekers who use this approach generally have some cards and stationery printed, and they're in business. If they also have an expensive attaché case, a three-piece suit, and a phone, they are consultants! And, like most real consultants, they don't have any work. Some job seekers using this approach have actually stumbled upon consulting work!

2. *Showing gaps in your job history.* This is an indication that you're hiding something, or that you've been out of work. It's a big red risk flag. Knowing that many employers won't bother to check job dates (and that many of the checks won't ever be answered), unscrupulous job seekers have been known to extend the starting or termination dates of one or more of their past positions to even out their career progression. When I've discovered such ruses, some of the applicants have been ingenious in their explanations. ("That damn secretarial service. I should have known they'd mix up the dates with the ones on my spouse's resume.") What can you say to such creativity? If only more employees would put that kind of effort into their jobs!
3. *Showing too many jobs.* More than one job every two years is too many. The perceived risk is that you'll leave them after a short time. Nobody wants to take a chance on a job-hopper, whatever the cause or the justification for the job changes.
4. *Showing less education than the job requires.* It's a paradox that at the same time that our educational systems are under justifiable attack as second rate, the business community is more in love with degrees then ever before. In past decades, when B.A.'s, M.A.'s, M.B.A.'s, D.B.A.'s, and Ph.D.'s were hard to come by, they weren't a hot item in most employment situations. Now that you can get a B.A. anywhere for just showing up at class, and you can get an M.B.A. or M.A. in one to two years at any old school, every ad specifies a B.A. as mandatory, and most list higher degrees as desirable or preferred, if not mandatory. If they demand or prefer an M.B.A. (which means they'll get dozens and maybe hundreds of resumes with M.B.A.'s) and you don't show one, your resume will die a fast death in the reject pile. If you don't have the required education to look credible in your field, I'd advise you at least to visit a school and sign up for one of the "two-year degree magic" programs. Nobody much cares where the degree comes from or what you actually learned; it's just a piece of paper, but a damned important one!
5. *Showing no experience in the industry.* They won't waste their time interviewing someone without experience in their industry if anyone else is available. For most jobs, you can be sure they'll get at least fifty to two hundred fifty other resumes, most of which will show specific industry experience. Nobody is going to risk criticism to take a chance on a candidate whose resume will not look safe to the rest of the organization.

A resume reviewer's decision to reject is not usually based on a conscious awareness of factors such as the above. Most often their decisions will be subconscious (with many personnel types, *unconscious* might be the more appropriate term) and not evident even to themselves. For this reason, you must avoid anything out of the business world's ordinary, day-to-day routine. For example, this means that pink, green, and blue stationery are dangerous; seldom is business correspondence conducted with these colors. The use of such paper might be perceived by some screeners to connote nonmastery. It is for these same reasons that you must avoid the mention of any nonessential personal data. You may think it's a real achievement to have a black belt in karate, but there are many people who will perceive that type of interest as indicating someone who's a ruthless and tough person. Many insecure screeners would be threatened by such interests. More typically, that type of information would put off the screener because it would forcefully indicate that you have extensive, time-consuming nonwork activities. Almost everybody does, but you'll look less industrious compared to others who don't show such information. You can't risk the effect that even the most harmless bit of personal information might have on the reviewer. Believe it; resumes get rejected more on the basis of screeners' unique and highly personal biases than for failing to pass objective analyses of qualifications.

Resume Myth 6. Gimmicks and flashy approaches work.

This is one of the most dangerous resume myths because it seems so logical. After all, if you were a recruiter facing hundreds of resumes every day, wouldn't you be grateful to find one that was so different and unique that it just jumped out at you? Well, you might notice it, but if you were the recruiter you'd be a little worried about it. You'd be worried that the resume writer was unorthodox and dangerously creative. You'd worry that the person behind the resume might be too aggressive and maybe a little too flashy. For example, fancy multifold resumes with five type styles get a lot of attention, but screeners worry that the designer is a little flaky. They worry that someone might question their judgment if they brought the designer in for an interview. As a result, flashy approaches and gimmicks get noticed, get talked about, maybe get passed around the office for a few laughs, and maybe even get tried by the screener on his or her next resume, but they never get the owner called in for an interview. Forget the humorous approaches, the drawings behind the printing, the tough talk, and the five-part foldout booklets. They'll get noticed, but they won't get you an interview. Chapter 8 explores the mechanics and drawbacks of these techniques in detail.

What Your Resume Must Do

Given that you'll no longer be falling for the common myths about resumes, let's jump on to the *Inside Track* about what resumes are supposed to accomplish. If your resume is going to be effective, it has to do a number of things to and for the people who will read it. These critical functions will determine many of the resume's design and content characteristics. The general framework and format of the *Inside Track* resume has been designed to satisfy these functions. Some of the things that the *Inside Track* resume will do are the following:

1. Meet the standard conventions of the business world in terms of style, content, and materials. The resume must look like a proper piece of business correspondence and must appear professional and conservative in terms of organization, vocabulary, and physical appearance.
2. Demonstrate a positive tone of optimism, achievement, and professional growth. This is accomplished through word selection, phrasing of job responsibilities, and careful attention to proper descriptions of your accomplishments.
3. Avoid tripping any of the typical screener's subconscious alarm buttons. This is achieved primarily through careful selection of content to eliminate superfluous and unfavorable information. If there are serious problems, avoid mentioning them until the interview if you can.
4. Demonstrate that you can meet their ideal expectations for the perfect candidate. This is done by using appropriately aggressive words and, at the same time, demonstrating by job achievements, career progression, and tone that you are absolutely not aggressive at all. They want someone who will talk and look aggressive but will sit around on his or her thumbs with everyone else once he or she is hired. This impression is conveyed by careful use of aggressive words in a very conservatively designed resume.
5. Satisfy their minimum technical qualifications for the position in question. If you're totally unqualified, even the *Inside Track* resume isn't going to get you into many interviews. On the other hand, careful composition of the responsibilities and achievements sections of your resume can stretch the perceived competence of your qualifications quite a lot. Resume screeners are hoping they'll find what they want so they can get some closure on the open job requisition and feel good. Proper design of the resume will build these hopes and make your qualifications appear more complete and appropriate for the position.

The *Inside Track* resume will perform the above functions better than the best custom resume you can buy, since you'll be using an extremely effective format and custom tailoring it to your own situation. If you follow the design guidelines in this chapter and then pay scrupulous attention to the recommended production details (typing, copying, and so on), you'll make it to a lot more interviews.

Building Your Resume the Inside Track Way

Now that you're familiar with some of the general aspects of proper resume focus and design, let's get down to practical matters and show you how to build a great resume. An example of the *Inside Track* resume format is shown in Figure 4.1. The resume is that of a fictional Sally Candoeze, an office administrator. Before we get down to details, let's look at Sally's resume and review some of the general features you'll be incorporating into your resume. (Two additional examples of the *Inside Track* resume format are presented in Figures 4.23 and 4.24 at the end of this chapter. Review them before you design yours.)

Keep it short. First of all, it's a two-page format. This is not a coincidence; it's a planned result. Your resume must *never* be longer than two sides of an 8½ by 11 sheet of paper. It's preferable to use both sides of a single sheet (hence the FOR FURTHER DATA, PLEASE SEE REVERSE SIDE statement on Sally's resume) rather than using only one side of two sheets of paper.

This is a critical design feature for two reasons. First, the desk of the typical personnel type or headhunter is awash with resumes and cover letters. If your resume is on one piece of paper, it's easier for the reviewer to handle, and there's less probability of a page being lost in the giant pile of rejects, job descriptions, and empty fast-food containers. With hundreds of resumes all over the place, nobody is going to worry if they lose a page from one of them; they'll just forget about that resume (win a few, lose a few) and pick someone else for the interview. Aside from your concerns about missing pages, anything you can do to make your resume easier to handle will please the reviewer (if only subconsciously). Further, a two-sided sheet conveys a feeling of very professional preparation; it looks as if it required more planning and effort.

A single-sheet resume (or one side of each of two sheets) is critical for a second important reason. You want to appear organized and businesslike. A long, rambling resume won't give that appearance. Don't talk yourself into thinking you need more than two pages. I've seen countless resumes from people with only two or three jobs that ran to five and six pages. The impression given by such lengthy resumes is that the owner either was impressed with his or her own minor achievements or couldn't get organized enough to get things under control and concisely summarize them in two pages. You don't need to generate that type of disorganized or pompous impression in anyone. Long resumes also demonstrate a lack of respect for the reviewer's time and a lack of business knowledge and courtesy. If you send in a resume longer than two sides, you'd better have enough content to make it worth the trouble to read it. Few people have enough meaningful information to make a long resume appropriate.

555 Luckawana Place (202) 555-5555
Washington, DC 20018

RESUME

of

SALLY CANDOEZE
Administrative Manager

OBJECTIVE

Challenging administrative position which requires extensive experience in office operations as well as comprehensive personnel supervision skills.

SUMMARY OF QUALIFICATIONS

*** <u>Resourceful, Take-Charge Manager</u> An aggressive and polished administrator with comprehensive skills in the administration and day-to-day supervision of technical and support personnel and systems.

*** <u>Planning and Analysis</u> Adept in policy, procedure, and work-flow analyses and reports. Wide-ranging experience in the analysis and collection of data for use in annual reports, marketing plans, and budgets.

*** <u>Communications</u> Excellent verbal and written communications skills. Extensive experience in the design and preparation of reports, briefings, and special studies.

*** <u>Client Relations</u> Successful experience in handling customer relations, including billing and service adjustments, sales, and customer support.

*** <u>Office Systems</u> Thoroughly experienced in the coordination and administration of automated office systems, including payroll, new accounts, and receivables.

PERSONAL DATA

DOB 5/21/55; married; excellent health.

EDUCATION

B.S., Accounting, BRONSKI STATE COLLEGE, Potowski, NJ, 1977.

<u>FOR FURTHER DATA, PLEASE SEE REVERSE SIDE</u>

Figure 4.1 Basic *Inside Track* Resume Format (Page 1)

SALLY CANDOEZE   Page 2
                            EXPERIENCE

<u>March 1981–present</u>   **GIBSON AND GIBSON ARCHITECTS**
                                              Washington, DC
ASSISTANT VICE PRESIDENT, ADMINISTRATION

<u>Responsibilities</u>: Coordinate and supervise approximately 65 support and clerical personnel. Administer secretarial, duplication, communications, drafting, and mailroom functions. Interview applicants, make hiring recommendations, coordinate training, develop schedules and staffing requirements. Develop office procedures and administer policies. Review operations and improve systems. Prepare budget data and special reports for executives as required. <u>Achievements</u>: Developed new annual budget preparation system. Reduced secretarial staffing 10% by more effective scheduling and use of part-time personnel. Managed installation of new phone, computer, and drafting systems. Prepared comprehensive report for president which analyzed office automation alternatives.

<u>December 1978–February 1981</u>   **DRECK INDUSTRIES, INC.**
                                                    Potowski, NJ

OFFICE MANAGER

<u>Responsibilities</u>: Supervised the office operations and systems of a large consumer products company. Administered 23 clerical staff responsible for order processing, client service, accounting, and sales support. Prepared preliminary budget and annual plan information for executive review. <u>Achievements:</u> Coordinated special task group to implement new marketing campaign. Developed improvements to new order processing system which reduced new order processing time by 8%. Prepared request for bids and evaluated submissions for new communications system.

<u>September 1977–October 1978</u>   **JACKSON PIG BELLY PROCESSORS, LTD.**
                                                    Potowski, NJ

SUPERVISOR OF WORD PROCESSING

<u>Responsibilities:</u> Supervised the word-processing department of a large food-processing company. Directed and planned the activities of a word-processing department of 6 persons. Interviewed applicants, trained new personnel, prepared equipment requests, and coordinated the delivery of word-processing support. <u>Achievements:</u> Reduced turnaround time on all requests by 17%. Supervised the installation of a new system and the training of all personnel. Prepared a number of special reports for executives.

                REFERENCES AND FURTHER DATA UPON REQUEST

Figure 4.1 *(Cont'd)* Basic *Inside Track* Resume Format (Page 2)

Sally's *Inside Track* resume is comprised of a number of discrete sections. Let's briefly review the general format and content of each section before we get down to the basics of designing the corresponding sections of your *Inside Track* resume.

The first page contains the following sections and content:

1. *Header.* Your name, address, phone, and perhaps your typical job title ("Administrative Manager" in Sally's resume). This is the section above the double solid line.
2. *Goal or objective.* If appropriate, a short statement of what you're after.
3. *Summary of qualifications.* Your assets and strong points. This section is constructed after the second page (experience) is put together. The summary of qualifications (SOQ) gives you an opportunity to wax poetic about your assets and outstanding achievements right up front in the resume and without the burden of fitting them into a job history. Coupled with the descriptions of your achievements on the second page, the SOQ allows you to present the same information in two different places. Your experiences and skills will appear much more impressive, and you'll be perceived as a very organized job seeker for having the sense to put together an SOQ.
4. *Personal data.* A small amount of safe and expected personal information.
5. *Education.* Schools, degrees, certificates, extra courses taken, and so on.
6. *Miscellaneous outstanding achievements.* An additional section can be added if you've got something really special that is relevant to the job you're applying for. (Sally didn't have anything for this section.)

Page 2 presents your work experience in detail. Each job you've had (or are going to mention) is described in a detailed job experience section (JES). Each JES consists of three parts:

1. *Heading.* Dates of employment, job title, name and address of the organization.
2. *Responsibilities.* What you were typically expected or tasked to do in the position.
3. *Achievements.* Specific and/or extraordinary accomplishments that support your candidacy.

For 99.99 percent of all job seekers, the above *Inside Track* resume format is all you'll ever need. Don't make frivolous deviations from this format without very good reasons.

Step 1: Constructing your experience section

The first step in building your *Inside Track* resume is to put together the second page, which details your work experience. You'll construct a

THE RESUME: YOUR MAGIC BULLET 53

Month 19XX–Present   **CURRENT EMPLOYER NAME**
                                       City, ST

YOUR JOB TITLE

Responsibilities: Administer the (your area) operation and coordinate day-to-day activities. Supervise staff of (number). Analyze and develop (problems you work on). Process (whatever the main paper flow is) and suggest improvements in policy and procedures. Achievements: Decreased (something bad you reduced) by (some percentage; usually 6–20% is believable and hard to refute even if someone tried to). Developed entire new (you must have written or suggested something that was done). Increased (profits, volume, productivity) by (some percentage) through (developing, revising, implementing, installing, etc.) the (whatever it was).

A. JES for current position

Month 19XX–Month 19XX   **PREVIOUS EMPLOYER NAME**
                                       City, ST

PREVIOUS JOB TITLE (IF IT'S A LONG ONE AS THIS IS, MAKE IT SINGLE SPACED AND TWO LINES)

Responsibilities: Monitored and supervised (function). Coordinated (department name) activities and prepared special reports for (some high-level department or person). Documented changes in operating guidelines and trained managers in new procedures. Documented (some ongoing function's activities) and processed (the paper). Achievements: Completely revised (function) operation and procedures which resulted in a (some percent) (decrease or increase) in (something).

B. JES for previous positions

Figure 4.2 Sample Job Experience Sections (JES)

---

separate JES for each of your last three positions if you've had that many jobs. If you've had more, the earlier jobs will be mentioned in a final combination JES. Each JES should be formatted in the manner of the two samples shown in Figure 4.2. This enables you to present a lot of data in a very polished and organized fashion.

1. *Job dates.* Months are written out in first-letter capitals (FLC), not abbreviated. The year is expressed numerically and not separated from the month by a comma. (Too much punctuation contributes to a choppy appearance.) Don't put in exact dates such as January 15, 1992; such detail appears compulsive and is of little value to anyone. Underline the entire date entry. If you're not presently working and will let the fact speak for itself (it never says anything good), substitute the appropriate month and year for the word *present*.
2. *Organization name.* Written on the same line and to the right of the date entries in boldface full capitals (BFC) as shown or full capitals (FC) as a second choice. Have it right justified (the right-hand

side of each line of print ends at the right margin). Put the organization's city and state on the line below, right justified, with the name of the city in FLC. Use the two-letter post office code for the state, in FC with no periods (e.g., ME for Maine). Don't present the exact street addresses of employers. It looks too busy, takes too much room, and demonstrates detail that's not appropriate in an accomplished businessperson's resume. More importantly, you don't want them contacting current or former employers without your permission. (Most won't, but there's no sense in making it easy for the real idiots out there.) For the same reasons, never put in an employer's phone number.

3. *Job title.* Place the job title in BFC (or FC as an alternative) on the second line below the date and even with the left margin. Use the most impressive title you can get away with. For example, if you are or were an office supervisor, you could claim the title of office administrator. Remember, your resume will be going head to head with a lot of inflated titles, so use the best one you can come up with that you can defend if someone asks about a discrepancy. ("Oh, well, the official title in personnel was supervisor, but everyone called it administrator.") Even if you don't inflate any of the duties, pumped-up titles will make the entire resume read a little more impressively. If the title is a long one, end the first line at least seven spaces before you'd run under the city and state data. This approach is displayed in part B of Figure 4.1.

4. *Main body of the JES.* This is made up of two sections:
   1. Responsibilities
   2. Achievements

The use of this format for the main body of each JES is essential for two reasons: (1) it will give your resume a more organized appearance than the typical resume, and (2) it permits you to say good things twice. The responsibilities sections permit you to list your specific duties in as much detail as appropriate. The achievements sections permit you to call out additional or the same activities, which will then appear even more impressive simply because they're listed as achievements. For example, in the responsibilities section of the JES for Sally's Gibson and Gibson job, she claims that one of her responsibilities is to "Prepare budget data and special reports for executives as required." Even if she only did it once, it's a responsibility. Then, in the achievements section, she states, "Prepared comprehensive report for president which analyzed office automation alternatives." This double mention of the same activity makes it seem like she was doing more work. It also makes the report sound like something special enough to be called an achievement. The use of separate responsibilities and achievements sections also makes the resume easier for the reader to interpret. If you make it easier on them, they'll not only read more of your resume, but they'll also read more into it.

The wording and tone of the experience section is critically important. You want to leave the reader with the feeling that you're a person of action, organization, and directness. Of course, actually acting this way in most organizations would be a serious mistake. (Those of you who doubt it should read my recent book, *Conduct Expected: The Unwritten Rules for a Successful Business Career,* while you've still got a career left.) The trick is to design your resume to read as if you're someone who knows that the game is to appear accomplished and aggressive but will just play along when you get the job. You do this by choosing the aggressive words that the business community endorses and then incorporating them into an organized and properly somber resume design. Readers will feel reassured even if they don't know why.

The selection and proper use of appropriate *action words* is critical in order to give your experience section the right impact on a reviewer. Never use the word *I* in any part of the resume. They know it's you and your resume. If you use *I*, you'll have to use it a lot, and it will make everything seem incredibly self-centered. It also takes up valuable space. Even though a resume is the essence of self-aggrandizement, you've got to make yours look and read like a piece of business correspondence which you've selflessly written for the reviewer's benefit. The entire experience section, in both the responsibilities and achievements areas, must be constructed from phrases that start with action words. Never use complete sentences such as "I was responsible for administration and operation of the communications department of the computer center." Instead, use "Administration and operation of the communications department of the computer center." The effect is more businesslike, direct, and urgent, which suggests you're a no-nonsense person who doesn't beat around the bush. If you're currently employed, use the present tense of all action words (as in "Coordinate and administer") in the responsibilities section of your present job. For all achievements sections and for the responsibilities sections of prior jobs (or all jobs if you're out of work), use the past tense (as in "Coordinated and administered").

Figure 4.3 presents a comprehensive list of action words which can be used to describe what you've done. The action words are more than just effective verbiage that you'll use in your resume. They can help you to compile the material from which you'll build the responsibilities and achievements sections of your resume. Use them to analyze each job you've had. Work on one job at a time. Go down the list word by word, and try to think of anything you did in the job that fits with the word. For many, you won't come up with anything, but you'll quickly find that all sorts of little projects and accomplishments will come to

accelerated	cooperated	gathered	optimized	reviewed
accomplished	coordinated	generated	ordered	revised
achieved	corrected	governed	organized	revitalized
activated	corresponded	grouped	originated	routed
actuated	counseled	guided	overhauled	safeguarded
adapted	created	harmonized	oversaw	saved
addressed	criticized	headed	participated	scheduled
administered	decreased	identified	performed	secured
advised	delegated	illuminated	pinpointed	selected
alerted	delivered	illustrated	planned	served
analyzed	detected	implemented	positioned	serviced
anticipated	determined	improved	prepared	set up
appraised	developed	increased	prescribed	shaped
approved	devised	indexed	presented	shut down
arbitrated	diagnosed	influenced	procured	simplified
arranged	diagrammed	informed	produced	slashed
assembled	directed	initiated	promoted	sold
assisted	disapproved	innovated	provided	solved
attracted	disciplined	installed	presided	sorted
audited	discovered	instituted	processed	sparked
authored	dispensed	instructed	programmed	speeded up
built	disproved	interpreted	promoted	staffed
calculated	disseminated	interviewed	proposed	started
cataloged	distributed	introduced	protected	stimulated
charted	documented	invented	provided	straightened
checked	doubled	investigated	realized	streamlined
closed up	edited	issued	received	strengthened
collected	effected	launched	recommended	structured
compiled	eliminated	lectured	reconciled	studied
completed	enhanced	led	recorded	suggested
composed	enlarged	logged	recruited	terminated
compounded	established	made	rectified	tested
conceived	evaluated	maintained	reduced	tied together
concluded	examined	managed	refined	took charge
conducted	exceeded	maximized	removed	took over
conferred	executed	minimized	rendered	trained
confined	expanded	moderated	reorganized	transacted
conserved	expedited	modernized	replaced	translated
consolidated	facilitated	modified	reported	triggered
constructed	fashioned	motivated	represented	upgraded
consulted	forecasted	navigated	researched	used
contracted	formulated	negotiated	reshaped	verified
contributed	founded	obtained	restored	wrote
controlled	funneled	operated	revamped	

Figure 4.3 Recommended Action Words

THE RESUME: YOUR MAGIC BULLET 57

mind as you think about each word. Write down the action word and then the achievement. For example, let's say as you read the word *analyzed* you recall that you often were required to do some calculations on sales figures for one of your past bosses. You would then write, "Analyzed sales data for management." Do this type of association exercise for each action word. Then, to make sure you haven't forgotten anything, take another piece of paper and write down everything you can recall about your typical schedule of events and activities at that job. Consider group activities as well as projects on which you worked alone. Think of typical business trips. Think about special projects you prepared or annual planning. If an additional item comes up, look through the action word list and find the word that best describes the activity. Once you've completed a separate analysis of this type for each job that's going on the resume, divide each job's list into responsibilities and achievements. The responsibilities are the usual and typical activities you performed on a regular basis. If you're writing your resume up a little (the euphemistic beefing up or lying everyone does on a resume), you might want to put some of the more glamorous and higher-level achievements in the responsibilities section. For example, let's say you only rarely got into the executive boardroom, and about all you did on those rare occasions was to run the lights and the slide projector for your boss. If you were being painfully honest, you would either leave the item out or put it in the responsibilities section as "Assisted superior in presentations to management." That doesn't sound too impressive. If you wanted to write the item up a little, you might put it in the achievements section as "Coordinated several briefings to top executives." This would make your coordination appear to be more significant in that it appears to be something special. If you wanted to make it look as if such activities were a regular event and no big deal in your schedule, you'd put it in the responsibilities section. This would make you sound even more high-level because it would appear as if you were spending a lot of time with top-level management. Of course, keep in mind that you may eventually have to explain elements of your resume in person; don't get reckless unless you can handle the heat.

In the achievements section, be sure to use lots of numbers. It's essential to get in at least one or two *increased, decreased, saved*, or similar action words in the achievements section of each JES, followed by percentage or dollar amounts. Phrases such as "Reduced turnaround time in processing orders by 8%," "Increased volume by 14% with 4% decrease in staff," and the like are very impressive to employers. Use at least one or two of them in each job's achievements section. The typical businessperson is blissfully wedded to simplistic numbers as the ultimate measure of effectiveness. Give them what they expect. Don't be too concerned with having to back them up; it would be too difficult for anyone (including the interviewer or your previous employer) to know enough about your day-to-day operations to refute or validate your claims.

For each JES, you want to end up with no fewer than four responsibilities clauses and four achievement clauses. It's advisable to combine phrases if there are more than eight in either section. Too many short phrases will look disorganized (unless you've got a lot of meaningful and discrete duties to mention). Thus, on Sally's resume, "Interview applicants, make hiring recommendations, coordinate training, develop schedules and staffing requirements" appears grouped rather than as separate phrases (as in "Interviewed applicants; made hiring recommendations on applicants," etc.). Be careful not to include things that are mundane or expected. I once received a resume where the candidate for a management job actually put down "Open mail" as one of his activities. The candidate was probably trying to appear meticulously detailed in his resume. Instead, he appeared meticulously naive and inappropriate. Going to meetings (at your own or your boss's level), giving presentations, writing memos, and similar routine duties should be mentioned only if they represent something special for someone at your level. For example, if you were fresh out of college and had done the above as a summer intern, it would be appropriate to mention such activities because most of your peers and competitors for the job probably wouldn't have such experience. If you're a seasoned business veteran, all of the above would be assumed and would kill your resume if you used them.

The actual length of each JES will be determined largely by how many jobs you've had and the scope of your duties in each. The overall consideration is that you've got to limit all the JESs to one side of a page. More recent jobs should get the bulk of the attention unless you've had career problems or changes and your best or most representative work is in a past job. Let the size and detail of each JES be determined by the importance of the job to the resume's specific purpose. Jobs further back than six years, unless they're in the first three or meet the above conditions, shouldn't be described in separate JESs. Combine them by using a single JES such as the one shown in Figure 4.4.

There's no need to provide detail on these past positions unless

---

Prior to September 1975

PROJECT DIRECTOR, Gamma Industries (September 1973–October 1975),
SENIOR ANALYST, Sledge Corporation (July 1967–August 1973),
PROGRAMMER, Hypertechnology, Ltd. (February 1965–June 1967).

Figure 4.4 Sample Job Experience Section for Noncritical Jobs

you're just reentering the job market after a hiatus, maybe returning to work after the children are grown. In that case, describe the jobs that will support your candidacy with the most detailed JES, even if they're in the past. Never, under any circumstances, provide any information about why you left a position. You can deal with that type of information in the interview when you've got an opportunity to elaborate and defend yourself in person.

Jargon is very important in resumes. Before you finalize any of your resume content, carefully examine a large number of ads for jobs like the one you want. The ads are written by the folks who will screen your resume. The jargon words they use in the ad are the ones they'll be looking for as they sift through the mountain of resumes. If you have exactly the qualifications they want but you use common, non-jargon, or out-of-date words to describe your qualifications, your resume isn't going to appear as on target as the resume of a lesser-qualified person who uses the jargon of the ad. It's a good idea to cut out every ad you see for jobs in your field and keep them in a file folder. As you design your resume or periodically rewrite it, scan the ads and determine if there isn't another jargon word or two that you can substitute for regular speech. If you're going to use the recordkeeping system recommended in Chapter 9, you'll be automatically developing your own jargon reference bank of ads which you can use in the future. If you're not about to get started on a search at this point, plan ahead and start to build up a file folder of ads now. When the time comes, you'll have a very helpful reference for jargon words. Don't get carried away with being too technical in either jargon or content, but remember, whatever your area, the people who write the ads are the ones doing the screening.

Step 2: Putting the second page together

Once you've got a JES completed for each position, you're ready to put the second page into its final form. Start with the second page header as shown in Figure 4.5. At least three lines from the top of the page, place your name (exactly as it will appear on page 1 of your resume) flush with the left margin in FC. Write "Page 2" in FLC and numerals on the same line, right justified. Skip a line, and center in BFC (or FC as a second choice), the word EXPERIENCE. If you're in a professional field (legal, medical, academic), use the expression PROFESSIONAL EXPERIENCE.

YOUR NAME	Page 2
EXPERIENCE	

Figure 4.5 Page 2 Header

Start the first JES at least double spaced below EXPERIENCE. Triple space if you've got the room. Each JES should be formatted as shown in Figure 4.2. At the bottom of the page, after the last JES, double space down (triple space if you've got room), and center and underline the phrase "REFERENCES AND FURTHER DATA UPON REQUEST" in FC.

Step 3: Constructing the summary of qualifications section

Once you've put together a JES for each of the jobs you're going to use on the resume, you're ready to put together the summary of qualifications section (SOQ) which will go on the first page. The SOQ is the first substantive section of the resume that the reviewer will read after your name. If the SOQ isn't good enough, it will also be the last thing he or she will read. You've got to build an extremely effective SOQ so the reviewer will be curious about where and how you managed to develop such a superior set of credentials. This will encourage the reviewer to read the back of your resume. If you can get the reviewer to do that, your resume will be getting more attention than the majority of resumes which are tossed into the reject pile because the screener didn't find anything interesting in the five to ten seconds he or she glanced at it.

More than just a curiosity arouser, the SOQ will also serve to orient the reviewer's expectations in your favor. It works in this way. If the opening is for a personnel administrator and you claim in one of your statements in the SOQ, "Comprehensive experience in all facets of personnel administration and operations," the reviewer is going to be hoping that the search is over and he or she will get a kudo for finding someone to interview. The reader will be expecting and hoping to find support for your contention on the second page of your resume. The screener will be more inclined to do two very important things: (1) read more of your resume before making a yes or no decision while searching for the critical information they want, and (2) err in your favor while evaluating the extent of your experience's relevance to his or her company's needs.

These natural tendencies will increase the odds that more of your resume will get read. If the reviewer does read more of your resume, he or she will have more to lose by deciding you're not the one he or she is after. This will work in your favor because nobody likes to admit a mistake, even a small one. (In this case, the error would be having been suckered into reading too much of an inappropriate resume.) People (especially in personnel and headhunting) will deny that this mechanism operates. Fear not; it operates on all of us all the time. It's merely the resume-reading version of the self-fulfilling prophecies we all use to interpret or manipulate reality in our favor.

Figure 4.6 displays an SOQ section for a typical middle manager in

THE RESUSE: YOUR MAGIC BULLET 61

SUMMARY OF QUALIFICATIONS

*** <u>Dynamic Take-Charge Manager</u> A well-organized and prudent professional with a positive attitude and exceptional energy.

*** <u>Planning and Finance</u> Adept in the preparation and administration of operating plans and budgets. Successful experience in computer-assisted spread-sheet analysis.

*** <u>Communications</u> Outstanding verbal and written communications skills. At ease before groups and familiar with formal written communications techniques.

*** <u>Interpersonal Skills</u> Work well with personnel at all levels. Exceptional ability to facilitate group efforts.

*** <u>Personnel Supervision</u> Extensive and successful experience in the motivation, training, and direction of subordinates.

*** <u>Comprehensive Technical Knowledge</u> In-depth knowledge of diffused array radar transmission technology. Solid foundation in guided array antennas and energy source design.

Figure 4.6 Representative Summary of Qualifications Section (SOQ) for an Engineering Middle Manager

an engineering firm. In any field, an effective SOQ will contain technical qualifications statements that detail the applicant's particular areas of technical expertise. (The Figure 4.6 example has only one; each of the two additional sample resumes at the end of this chapter has several.) The technical qualification is the bottom one in Figure 4.6. A banker would substitute appropriate technical qualifications that would deal with his or her finance and banking expertise. Aside from the technical qualifications that are unique to the industry or specialty, the other qualifications shown in the SOQ of Figure 4.6 represent skills and assets categories that are more or less standard to white-collar middle managers across most industries and jobs. Employers expect these types and categories of qualifications in the ideal candidate, even if they don't ask for them. The outstanding resume shows them all. Representative statements for the generally expected qualifications categories for middle-management job candidates are shown in Figure 4.7.

For most middle-management resumes, you could simply use the SOQ statements shown in Figure 4.7 just as they're written, and your SOQ would make your resume look better than 95 percent of all resumes. (This is partly because of the amazing fact that about 75 percent of all resumes don't use any type of SOQ.)

The first SOQ statement in Figures 4.6 and 4.7 is a personal character statement. It's important to include such a statement that highlights the wonderful and unique personal qualities you bring to the job. These statements are nothing but self-congratulatory hype, but if you

62   INSIDE TRACK

*** <u>Personal Character Statement</u> A flattering description of your sterling qualities.
*** <u>Planning and Finance</u> Adept in the preparation and administration of operating plans and budgets.
*** <u>Communications</u> Outstanding verbal and written communications skills. At ease before groups and familiar with formal written communications techniques.
*** <u>Interpersonal Skills</u> Adept in fostering easy and cooperative relationships with all levels of personnel. At ease in dealing with executives. Skilled in the coordination of group efforts.
*** <u>Personnel Supervision</u> Extensive and successful experience in the motivation, training, and direction of subordinates. Experienced in employment interviewing, conducting performance appraisals, and handling disciplinary problems.

Figure 4.7 Generally Expected Qualifications Catagories and Representative SOQ Statements for Middle-Management Jobs

don't do it nobody else will. You must be extremely careful to design your personal character statement so it's appropriate to the specific industry or organization at which the resume is targeted. For example, if you were after a sales management position, you might want to use a personal character statement like the one in Figure 4.8.

The personal character statement of Figure 4.8 would give a reviewer the feeling that the resume belongs to a real tiger of a sales manager. The words *aggressive, take-charge, dynamic, success-oriented, persuasive, confident, high-energy,* and *excel* sound like the qualities almost everyone associates with a hard-driving sales manager.

You have to tailor your personal character statement to the personality of the industry or occupation you've targeted. If, rather than going for a sales management job, you were after a chief accountant's position, the personal character statement shown in Figure 4.9 would be more appropriate. Admit it, it sounds just like everyone's ideal accountant. The words *methodical, well-organized, detail-minded, professional standards,* and *deadlines* all reinforce the general perception of an ideal accountant. Just as important, once such a qualifications statement is made, everything that's read in the rest of the resume will be viewed through the filter provided by the personal character statement.

If, in one of his JES achievement sections, the sales manager claims

*** <u>Aggressive, Take-Charge Manager</u> A dynamic, success-oriented manager who demands and gets the most from subordinates. A persuasive, confident, high-energy individual with a need to excel.

Figure 4.8 Personal Character Statement Appropriate for a Sales Manager

*** <u>Methodical, Well-Organized Manager</u> A detail-minded and participative manager who can maintain the highest professional standards and meet deadlines.

Figure 4.9 Personal Character Statement Appropriate for a Chief Accountant

to have "increased volume 22% by keeping sales personnel out on the road longer," a reader, having seen the SOQ personal character statement in Figure 4.8, is going to think, "That's exactly what I expected such a hard driver to do!" Not only will the reader be impressed by the achievement, but he or she also will better remember the claim because it will support the expectations the SOQ statement set up. Everybody likes and needs consistency, and they look for it all day long, even when they screen resumes. Help them to find it in your resume by making sure that your personal character statement echoes the tone and style of your achievements, as well as the personality of the industry in which you're seeking a job.

Before you put together your personal character statement, think carefully about the ideal candidate for the job and industry at which you're targeting your resume. Words like "*profit-conscious*" sound great to organizations that see themselves as aggressive, but they're the kiss of death when applying to outfits like public utilities and nonprofit concerns. If you're after a type of job that's common in many different industries, such as a personnel or finance position, you might need to have several resume versions, each with a different industry-specific personal character statement. If it's not feasible for you to use more than one resume version, keep your personal character statement universally positive, general, and so innocuous that it cannot possibly offend anyone. Figure 4.10 presents a widely applicable personal character statement suitable for general use. The reviewer will read it and believe it. The natural assumption is that you wouldn't say it if it wasn't true; they want to believe you'll solve their problem. Do it and prosper.

Some descriptive and generally positive words for use in your personal character statement (as well as throughout your resume and other job-related correspondence) are presented in Figure 4.11. Before you construct your personal character statement, give some careful thought to the characteristics of the folks in your industry who are respected and the manner in which they're described. Use those types of words when you describe yourself.

*** <u>Hard-Working and Professional Manager</u> A dynamic and considerate manager who takes pride in outstanding performance and performs well under pressure.

Figure 4.10 Personal Character Statement for General Use

accurate	dependable	good-natured	positive
active	detailed	high-energy	practical
adaptable	detail-minded	honest	precise
adept	determined	imaginative	productive
aggressive	dignified	independent	professional
alert	diplomatic	industrious	proficient
ambitious	discerning	inspiring	purposeful
analytical	disciplined	intuitive	qualified
articulate	discreet	keen	realistic
artistic	economical	kind	reliable
assertive	effective	knowledgeable	resourceful
astute	efficient	logical	self-controlled
attentive	eloquent	loyal	self-reliant
capable	energetic	mature	sincere
cheerful	enterprising	methodical	sociable
competitive	enthusiastic	modest	stable
composed	exacting	objective	stamina
confident	executive	observant	systematic
congenial	extroverted	optimistic	tactful
conscientious	fair	orderly	thoughtful
considerate	follow through	organized	tolerant
consistent	forceful	patient	truthful
contributor	forward-thinking	perceptive	understanding
cooperative	frank	persevering	versatile
courteous	friendly	personable	vigorous
creative	generous	poised	well-educated
democratic	genuine		

Figure 4.11 Words for Use in Developing Personal Character Statements

Of course, rather than just making slight modifications of the examples I've provided (which will work fine), you'll probably want to tailor the wording of your SOQ and JES sections to suit your own style and preferences. If you do, don't fall into the trap of always using the same word, such as *comprehensive*, to characterize your experiences (as in Comprehensive experience in labor relations"). Mix up your choice of words so that the resume maintains interest. Figure 4.12 presents a list of words that provide variety as modifiers of the word *experience*. Use different experience modifiers in each SOQ statement so there's no repetition or monotony.

Don't overuse the word *experience* itself. You can substitute any one of a number of phrases that mean more or less the same thing and in some cases may be more descriptive. Vary the content of your resume's SOQ statements by using some of the expressions shown in Figure 4.13 as substitutes.

administrative	intensive	significant
applied	major	sound
comprehensive	management	structured
executive	outstanding	substantial
extensive	performance-oriented	successful
first-hand	positive	technical
ground-floor	practical	thorough
hands-on	profitable	versatile
in-depth	proven	well-rounded

Figure 4.12 Modifiers for the Word *Experience*

Step 4: Construction of page 1

Once you've completed the design and construction of your SOQ, you're ready to put together the remainder of page 1.

Header. The header goes at the top of page 1 and tells the reader what the document is and who it comes from. The format of the header is shown in Figure 4.14. Note that your name and RESUME are the only items that are in FC. This will serve to call attention to them and reinforce the fact that you are forceful, direct, and not afraid to be aggressive (in appearance). The phone number should be right justified. Center each line. Some people contend the phrase *resume of* is redundant and unnecessary. They reason that since everyone will know it's a resume, the phrase is just pedantic nonsense. These folks don't understand the overall effect a resume strives for. The phrase isn't put in to let them know it's a resume; even the most limited personnel type will recognize what it is without help.

The *resume of* is used to demonstrate in a very subtle way that you recognize and respect the conventions of the business world just as you do when you use the salutation "Dear Mr. Smith" in a business letter. Everyone knows the *Dear* is unnecessary and very often exactly the opposite of the writer's true sentiments. We all use it, however, because it's expected business etiquette and part of the charade we all play. As a job applicant, you must take every opportunity to show that you're a

ability to (in)	foundation in	productive in
adept in	have mastered	proficient in
capacity for	know-how in	skilled in
effective in	knowledge of	strength in
efficient in	knowledgeable in	success in
equipped to	mastery of	well-versed in

Figure 4.13 Alternatives for the Word *Experience*

1234 Street Address (000) 000–0000
City, State 00000

RESUME

of

YOUR NAME
Optional Title in First-Letter Capitals

Figure 4.14 Header for Page 1

conventional, traditional, charade-by-the-rules person. Using the phrase *resume of* is one of the many ways you can reinforce this image.

The optional title is written in FLC if you decide to use it. If you're going to try to get by with only one resume version, you'll probably want to omit the title as it might not be appropriate for all of the jobs to which you'll apply. For example, if you're an engineer and you're using a single resume to apply for both engineering management positions and technical, hands-on jobs, it would be inappropriate to have the title "Engineering Manager" beneath your name; your candidacy for the technical jobs would be compromised. Reviewers might assume you had misread the ad as being for a management position. Even worse for your chances, they might assume you want a management position but are desperate and are considering hands-on positions as a last resort. You could suffer the converse effect if you applied for a high-level technical position; they might assume you're a management type who doesn't really have what it takes to do a hands-on job. In this type of situation, if you want the little extra image and effect on readers that a general title can give, go with a nebulous title such as "Engineering Professional." While it says nothing specific, it will orient readers, if only a little, into believing you have career direction. It's not as good as a specific title, but it can't hurt. Finish up the header by running two solid lines all the way from the left to the right margins. This separates the preliminary information from the job-related data and helps maintain an organized appearance.

Objective. The objective is placed two lines beneath the header. (Triple space if there's enough room to triple space between all of the first-page sections.) Flush with the left margin, place the word OBJECTIVE in BFC. Double space down, indent six spaces, and place the body of the objective (right justified).

The objective is a powerful way to influence the expectations of the reviewer. The use of an objective demonstrates to the reviewer that the resume belongs to someone who is looking for exactly the job they are offering and who is specifically interested only in their type of organization. This will impress them that you are a discerning and unique individual who is more worthy of an interview than the masses of applicants whose resumes appear disorganized and unfocused on any particular position. A positive-sounding, rather general type of objective can do this because most people associate their jobs and industries with a number of common and flattering adjectives such as *aggressive* or *dynamic*. If you use such words to describe what you're after, they'll be inclined to believe that you've targeted their industry or company. Figure 4.15 displays a rather general objective which would be appropriate for most administrative finance positions in the majority of for-profit organizations. This objective would make you look great to the typical company. Every for-profit organization thinks it's dynamic and believes that it places a premium on results (even if the only results they want are no waves). Everyone also thinks (or at least pretends he or she thinks) his or her job and the working environment are challenging and dynamic, even if the staff can hardly stay awake at their desks.

The more detailed and specific your objective is, the more positive will be the impression you'll make. You'll seem like a heads-up, focused individual. The converse side of this influence is that an objective that is too specific will turn off many of the reviewers for one reason or another or simply will not be appropriate to all organizations. The optimal solution is to have several resume versions, each of which has an objective (and optional title) that is unique to each of the different jobs, industries, or environments you've targeted. If you're trying to get by with one resume (which is a *big* mistake), leave the objective out.

Summary of qualifications. The development of your SOQ statements was described earlier. The entire SOQ section is placed directly under the objective, or the header if you aren't using an objective. Double space down from the objective or header and place SUMMARY OF QUALIFICATIONS in BFC flush with the left margin. Each qualifications statement should be indented six spaces. Highlight each statement by placing three asterisks flush with the left margin. Single space and right justify each statement with double spacing between statements. Figure 4.6 (as well as Sally's resume in Figure 4.1 and those shown in Figures 4.23 and 4.24) demonstrates this format.

Personal data. The personal data section is placed beneath the SOQ

OBJECTIVE

Challenging financial administration position in a profit-conscious organization that places a premium on results.

Figure 4.15 Objective Appropriate for Most For-Profit Positions

section. Double space down from the last SOQ statement and place PERSONAL DATA in BFC flush with the left margin. Double space down and indent the data itself six spaces. If it runs to two lines, single space and right justify. Employers want and expect to see a number of things they'll use to discriminate automatically against certain groups according to their personal and organizational prejudices. Unfortunately, there's nothing you can do to counter this situation or defend yourself.

For example, many employers don't like to hire women for certain jobs. If they see that a candidate for one of their "male" jobs is a woman, her resume gets trashed. If they want only young people and they see that a candidate is too old for their tastes, another resume goes down in flames. You can't defend yourself by leaving the information out. They'll probably be able to infer the information from another part of the resume. (It's not hard to see that someone named Sally is a female or that someone who graduated from college in 1955 is about fifty-one years of age in 1986.) If they don't get it from the resume, they'll discover it when you come in for the interview. In either case, you'll be out of it. You might as well let them practice their illogical and stupid strategies on your resume. If they're going to trash you on one of their prejudicial items, at least you won't have to waste your time interviewing in person with a bunch of losers.

Don't try to make things vague by leaving out data if you think you have a problem area, such as age or sex. Your entire resume will look watered down. Older workers sometimes leave out all dates in an attempt to elude the age issue. The result is that everyone automatically assumes they're trying to hide age data, even if they aren't. Sometimes you'll see a very vague resume and assume it's an older person trying to cover up the age issue. It's a real surprise to discover occasionally (when the owner calls in to find out why an interview invitation hasn't been forthcoming) that it's a young person with horrible resume-writing skills. Employers sometimes see extreme cases of this from candidates who have been out of work for some time. These people will sometimes leave out all dates and jobs and·attempt to gloss it over with a functional resume that outlines skills and experiences without showing jobs. Forget it. Screeners want to see jobs and dates more than anything else. Rather than wasting time on a vague resume, they'll find another candidate among the hundreds of other resumes they've received. Since you've got to put in some personal data, stick to the minimum, safe data shown in Figure 4.16. If you're single or divorced, leave out the marital status. Personnel types say that being divorced or single doesn't influence them, but they lie a lot. Children are good either way for men. If a man has children, the reader will perceive that he's more stable and traditional (part of the community and all that). If a man has "no children," the impression will be "Here's a tiger who's really devoted to his career and who won't be leaving early for little league games and complaining about a lot of travel."

PERSONAL

DOB: XX/XX/XX, marital status, number of children, excellent health.

Figure 4.16 Format and Content of Personal Data Section

Remember, they're trying to satisfy their expectations as they read, so they're always hoping for the best. For women, it's not a good idea to state the number of children unless there are none; then it's a plus. Everybody is concerned that sick children mean Mommy is going to miss some work. No children implies career woman.

Unless you're about to die from a terminal disease, state your health as excellent. Stating that your health is excellent adds positive energy to your resume. If you've got some obvious problems that will be apparent in an interview, state "excellent health" anyway (it's all in how you feel, right?) or don't mention health at all. Anything less than excellent will seriously decrease your resume's chances because nobody admits health problems on resumes. Don't list hobbies, sports, domestic tidbits ("I have a beautiful wife and three wonderful children"). Any little thing may turn off a reviewer for no apparent or logical reason. There's no sense in taking risks to show them more than they expect.

Education. Double space down from the last line of the personal data section and place the word EDUCATION in BFC flush with the left margin. Double space down and indent each entry six spaces. Two sample education sections are shown in Figure 4.17.

Each item in the education section is entered in the following order and manner:

1. *Degree.* Capital initials and periods as in B.A. or M.B.A.
2. *Area of concentration.* FLC as in Psychology or Marketing.

EDUCATION

      M.A., Industrial Engineering, FLOTSAM UNIVERSITY, Backhoe, TX, 1974.

      B.S., Electrical Engineering, STATE TECH, College City, OR, 1969.

Sample A

EDUCATION AND CERTIFICATIONS

      CERTIFICATE, Advanced Physical Therapy, UNIVERSITY OF RALPH, Los Angeles, CA, 1983.

      CERTIFICATE, Holistic Massage, VELEMERE MASSAGE SCHOOL, Van Nuys, CA, 1981.

      B. A., Physical Education, STATE UNIVERSITY, Cabbage, MN, 1975.

Sample B

Figure 4.17 Two Representative Education Sections

3. *Name of school.* FC as in UNIVERSITY OF OREGON.
4. *City and location of the school.* City in FLC with state in FC using the two-letter postal service abbreviation as in OR for Oregon.
5. *Year of award.* In numerals as in 1965 or 1978.

As shown in Figure 4.17, the first line of each education item is indented six spaces from the left margin. Each item is single spaced within itself. Any second lines of a single item are indented another three spaces. Double space between items.

Note that in sample A, the items are not separated by double spacing. Use this method if you're getting tight on space.

Sample B represents the ideal in terms of spacing, particularly if you wish to call extra attention to relevant education. You may not have the room for this spacing if your SOQ is lengthy. If you have additional items such as certificates or licenses, change the title of the section from EDUCATION to EDUCATION AND CERTIFICATIONS or PROFESSIONAL PREPARATION. Put your highest or most relevant degrees or certifications at the top of the section so they'll be the first ones read.

Optional special achievements section. A final optional section can be included if you've got something special and appropriate. Professional licenses and especially relevant certifications might go in this section. For example, if you were using the data shown in sample B of Figure 4.17 to design a resume for use in applying for physical therapy positions, it would be appropriate and smart to call out the certificates in a separate additional section. This approach is shown in Figure 4.18.

The special section shown in Figure 4.18 is formatted in exactly the same manner as the education section. Since the two physical therapy certifications would be critical in assessing candidates' qualifications for the job, the special section would be very effective. Even though dozens of resumes might have similar certificates, the resume that calls out the data in a special section will appear more organized and will be easier for the reviewer to process.

If an item is not directly related to the job in question, don't put it in a special section. For example, if you're applying for a job as a cost accountant, it's irrelevant to mention that you've got a private pilot's

---

EDUCATION
   B.A., Physical Education, STATE UNIVERSITY, Cabbage, MN, 1975.

PHYSICAL THERAPY CERTIFICATIONS
   CERTIFICATE, Advanced Physical Therapy, UNIVERSITY OF RALPH, Los Angeles, CA, 1983.
   CERTIFICATE, Holistic Massage, VELEMERE MASSAGE SCHOOL, Van Nuys, CA, 1981.

Figure 4.18 Sample of an Optional Special Achievements Section

license. On the other hand, if you were applying for a job as an aeronautical engineer, the pilot's license should be presented in a special section. Even though it might not be directly related to the job itself, such a disclosure would heighten the technical image of your resume. If you don't know for sure or have doubts that something is an asset, leave it out of the resume entirely. You can always mention it during the interview if you get that far.

Page footer. The final item on page 1 should be a centered footer, in FC and underlined, that states, "PLEASE SEE REVERSE SIDE FOR FURTHER DATA." If you aren't going to double side your resume as I recommend, substitute FOLLOWING PAGE for REVERSE SIDE.

Step 4: Fine tuning of page 1

Once you get the first page laid out, play with the spacing between sections in order to get an even look. If you double space between the SOQ and personal sections, use double spacing between all sections. If you've got room, triple space between all sections. Whatever you do, keep it consistent. If you're running short on space, shrink up the SOQ section by combining a few of the statements. Try to maintain at least one-inch margins all around, although slightly smaller margins are acceptable as long as the overall effect is organized, attractive, and businesslike.

Step 5: Editing

Once you get to this point, you'll be halfway to a great resume. You'll think it reads great, and you'll probably be pretty impressed with yourself. In that self-satisfied condition, you can't possibly maintain the calm, critical air of detachment that proper resume design demands. Have a few intelligent people take a very critical look at it. Ask them to note anything that seems confusing, unclear, redundant, or too specialized. Don't show it around at work; that's a dangerous place for anyone to know you're looking. At the very least, have a few friends or your spouse read it for typos, tone, and design. Don't settle on a final proofing the day you finish writing it. Let it sit overnight and then read it again; you'll be a little more detached, critical, and objective. Read it one word at a time, backwards, for typos. There's nothing more infuriating than getting a hundred copies back from the printer and finding a typo. Worse yet is finding one on a resume you've been using for two months. Be careful up front.

Once you think you've finally got it where you want it, carefully print or type it so that you can take it to a professional for final typing. Do *not* type the final copy yourself unless you have the equipment to do a first-class job, which includes being able to produce right justification. It's usually not worth the aggravation, time, and small amount of money you'll save trying to do it yourself.

Step 6: Production

Who should do it. Flawless production is an absolute essential. When you send your resume out to compete with hundreds of others, you'd better make sure that yours is perfect in terms of spelling, punctuation, paper selection, type face, and reproduction quality. Every detail counts, and one small typo will drastically reduce your chances. As mentioned above, do *not* attempt to type your resume at home unless you have a state-of-the-art electronic typewriter or a word-processing package and computer with a letter-quality printer. (If you have the latter, see Chapter 11.) Anything less will not do the job you absolutely must have.

What to look for. Look for a secretarial service or a resume preparation outfit in your area that has a word processor. Call them up and ask if they have a word-processing system that will permit them to store your resume and any letters for easy and fast modification in the future. Ask them if they can right justify and boldface. Ask them if it's all right for you to bring your own paper. If not, don't waste more time with them unless your options are limited. Ask them what they'll charge for copies if you bring your own paper and they copy onto it. Ask them what their rates are and whether they charge by the hour, by the page, or both. Ask if they charge by the page for rough drafts and final copies. A lot of companies quote a low hourly charge to type resumes or correspondence into the system but then charge you per page for output as well. Two or three cuts at a two-page resume can end up costing a lot more than you thought. Don't get impatient and settle for the first place you find. A little extra shopping at this point can save a lot of grief down the road.

You are the boss. Once you've located what appears to be a decent outfit, take your draft resume in. Do *not* allow them to make helpful suggestions about changes in format. If you've read this book, are following the instructions, and have at least average intelligence, you know more about effective resume design than anyone who works for a resume preparation outfit or a secretarial service. It's a basic truth that everyone who works in these organizations thinks they know all about resumes. What they know a lot about is bad resumes because they see so many of them; to them marginal is good. Ignore their advice; it's dangerous. You're using their services to produce your resume, not to design it.

Paper selection. A lot is written about the selection of paper and ink for resumes. Forget what you have read before and pay careful attention. Your resume must show that you are a professional, substantial, know-the-rules, play-the-game type in your profession. At the same time, your resume must stand out as more impressive than the others in the pile. You must balance these two considerations in selecting paper. You want to attract attention, but not all attention is positive. Use an off-white, ivory, beige, or extremely light brown paper. A subdued texture is an important added plus (as in "laid" papers). Do not use any other colors or shiny finishes. Tones of ivory and light beige look more impressive because of their association with the badges of authority, success, and power that those at the top collect and display. Do successful executives have pastel blue desks and green attaché cases? Of course not; they almost always use leather, fine woods, and subdued tones for their furniture and accessories. You must use the power of this association for your resume. Select a paper that mimics these preferences.

Do not buy paper from the place that will do the production of your resume unless they have exactly what you want. They usually have limited selections of not very good paper, and you'll get reamed (pun intended) on the price. If they have a fan spray of six colors of the same paper stapled to a bulletin board, you're not going to find what you must have. Go to a paper distributor and purchase several reams (or more, depending on the scope of your search effort) of a good paper and matching envelopes. In larger cities, there are self-service paper warehouses where you can get outstanding quality and selection at very reasonable prices. Buy enough so all of your job search correspondence (resumes, cover letters, thank-you notes) can be produced on matching paper and envelopes.

Selection of ink color. Never use any ink color but black. That's the expected color for all business correspondence. Anything else looks too nonestablishment, avant garde, or flaky.

Selection of type style. The type style you select must reflect the conservative, professional, and successful you. Avoid type styles that simulate a computer printout appearance. Such a style doesn't connote the conservative image you're trying to project. Absolutely avoid script and italic type styles; they look too informal and relaxed, as if you're not really serious about what will happen to your resume. Don't use gothic or statistical type styles. The best appearance is conveyed by type styles similar to those of the IBM "Courier" line of type styles. If you're going to be typing cover letters for your resume yourself, be sure to match the type style of the resume with the one you'll be using for the cover letters. Less than a perfect match is a problem; get as close as you can.

Selection of type pitch. If you can use a 10-pitch (10 characters per inch) type style, you'll be enhancing the appearance of your resume and making it easier on the reviewer, thus increasing your odds that he or she will read more of it before giving up or making a decision. If you're really pressed for space and can't possibly edit more material out of the resume, then you may have to go with a 12-pitch (12 characters per inch) type style. If so, make sure you leave adequate margins and spaces between sections; 12-pitch printing can look pretty cramped if it's too closed up. You don't want to risk discouraging the reviewer if you can possibly avoid it. Do not use proportional spacing for any job search materials. (Proportional spacing allots less space for an *i* than for an *a*.) Proportional spacing has an overproduced look to it, as if a machine rather than a person typed it. Normal business letters are typed, and that's the impression you want to give, whether you typed the cover letters or a computer did it. (Appearance, not fact, is the important issue here.)

Making copies. When your resume is finally in the word processor and you've made all the corrections you want, it's time to get the master original produced. Ask for two original copies on plain white, nontextured paper. You're going to use one of these originals as the master copy for photocopying or offset printing. The other original is your insurance copy if the copy or secretarial service shreds your original. You could always get the secretarial service to pull another copy out of their word processor, but you might not have time or they may accidentally erase your original. Don't let them print out the original on your selected paper, because any color and texture will interfere with later copying or printing. Plain white paper will permit the best-quality copies.

There's always a lot of discussion in the job search literature about whether you should have your resume duplicated by offset printing or photo duplication (copying machines). There's no doubt that offset printing gives a sharper, more professional appearance. If you're going with only one or two resume versions and you don't anticipate many changes on your resume over the course of the search, offset printing would be a reasonable choice. It's a little more expensive than using a copying machine and it takes a little longer, but the quality is a little better. If you decide to have your resume offset printed, go to a good printer and ask to see some samples of completed work. Bring your paper with you and insist that it be used. Call first; a lot of printers will balk at using your paper because they want to sell theirs and get the markup. They'll tell you that if they use your paper they can't be responsible for problems or quality. If you can get them to sell you the same paper (they can order anything if they want to take the trouble) for about what it would cost you at a paper supply outlet, let them do it. Otherwise, go somewhere else.

I don't argue for exclusively using offset printing, because first-class copying machines can do a job that is almost as good. Several years ago, this was not the case. If you go to a secretarial or photocopying service that has first-rate equipment, you really don't need to go to the extra trouble and expense of offset printing.

THE RESUME: YOUR MAGIC BULLET   75

If you decide to go with photocopying, have them run a test copy using your paper. Have them double side it if that's the way you're going to go. If the copy looks good, have them run off only as many as you'll use in the next few weeks. You don't want to be stuck with a lot of wasted copies if you decide to make some changes. (Don't resist the urge to make such changes; once you start to think a little more about resume design and get some interview feedback, you'll continue to have valuable insights into more effective wording.) If there are any black spots or lines on the copy, forget them and go elsewhere. You shouldn't be able to see anything on the paper but the print. The slightest spot or distortion is totally unacceptable. After copying, put your original in a separate file folder for protection and store it where it won't get wrinkled or dirty. (There's nothing more irritating than running out of resumes and then discovering your original has a big coffee ring in the middle of it.)

Is one resume enough? Unless you're absolutely new to the job market, one resume can't possibly be effective with all of the various types of environments and organization types to which you'll be applying. If you're in middle management, you'll need one resume to point up your technical do-the-work skills and another to emphasize your people-management skills. Don't try to make one resume do both jobs.

It's not hard to develop additional resumes once you've got the first one completed. Simply cut and paste a copy of the first one with your modifications written in. I recommend that you create one version of each of your resumes with an objective and another version exactly the same but without it. You use the version without the objective for those jobs or industries where your objective might be a little off target.

What if you're just out of school? No problem—at least resume-wise; welcome to the rat race! Your SOQ section will consist of statements of your various abilities as reflected by schooling. For example, you can still have an SOQ statement about budgets and planning as long as you've studied it in school. Such a statement might read like the one in Figure 4.19.

Use the same approach for all of your skills areas. Since you might be a little short of experience, put in another personal qualifications statement or two.

Handle page 2 in much the same way. Treat your time in school as a job. Use an activities section rather than a responsibilities section for listing your areas of concentration and important courses. Put anything

---

*** <u>Budgeting and Planning</u>   Comprehensive and extensive preparation in budget and business plan development and analysis.

Figure 4.19 Summary of Qualifications Statement Based on Educational Experience

noteworthy such as good grades, the fact that you worked while in school, or any honors or scholarships in the achievements section. List each school you attended (or are attending) or major course of study as a separate "job" with its own JES. If you've been employed on a part-time basis while in school or have had summer jobs or internships, put them down in separate JES sections, just as if they were separate full-time jobs. In those cases where a job overlaps with school, simply attach the phrase "concurrent with above" beneath the job dates as shown in Figure 4.20.

A complete *Inside Track* just-out-of-college resume is shown in Figure 4.21. Note that Otto's SOQ uses two personal characteristics statements and two technical qualifications statements based on schoolwork. If you're just out of school, load in everything you can about computers; even if they don't use them where you'll be working, they'll be impressed even if all you can do is turn one on. The second page of the just-out-of-school resume looks remarkably impressive (in terms of number of entries) simply because each part-time job looks bigger than it really is. Don't leave out any jobs because they were lowly (such as the laborer job) unless you're running out of room; any work and the consequent entries will serve to make you look more industrious and eager. Everybody expects college students to have worked like pack mules; nobody holds it against them. The organized look of the *Inside Track* resume is particularly effective for the just-out-of-school situation because so few rookies have the perspective to develop such an organized and serious approach to their resumes.

The Letter Resume

Letter resumes occasionally get a flurry of attention in the job search media. While they're not universally appropriate, they can be very effective when you're trying to project a tone of informality. The hope is that the letter resume will lead the reader into believing that you put together the entire resume just for him or her. Personal letters feel more intimate than resumes because resumes practically scream, "What job have you got for me?" You want and need that scream when your resume is fighting it out for attention on the desk of a recruiter or headhunter; the whisper of a letter resume will be lost in the roar of

---

September 1981–June 1982　　　　　　　　**AJAX DISTRIBUTORS, INC.**
(concurrent with above)　　　　　　　　　　　　　　College City, CA

ASSISTANT ACCOUNTANT

Figure 4.20 Sample of JES Header for a Concurrently Held Position

THE RESUME: YOUR MAGIC BULLET 77

114 Maple Street   (705) 111-1111
Bencer, MA 00934

RESUME

of

OTTO OPTIMIST

SUMMARY OF QUALIFICATIONS

*** <u>Resourceful and Hard-Working</u> A dynamic and well-organized Business Administration graduate who is looking for a no-holds-barred, demanding position.

*** <u>Entrepreneurial Approach</u> Continuously employed at least 20 hours per week (usually 30 – 40 hours) while in school. Currently working at two part-time jobs while searching for appropriate full-time position.

*** <u>Comprehensive Finance Training</u> In-depth knowledge of principles of cost accounting, financial analysis, and tax planning as a result of program concentration in these areas.

*** <u>State-of-the-art Computer Skills</u> Comprehensive skills and abilities in personal computer applications for finance. Familiar with XXX mainframes and standard financial programming languages.

PERSONAL

DOB 4/1/64; single; excellent health; willing to relocate.

EDUCATION

B.A., Business Administration (concentration in Finance) BENCER UNIVERSITY, Bencer, MA, 1985.

GRADUATE-LEVEL COURSES, Finance, BENCER UNIVERSITY, Bencer, MA, 1984-1985.

FOR FURTHER DATA, PLEASE SEE REVERSE SIDE

Figure 4.21 Just-Out-of-College *Inside Track* Resume (Page 1)

hundreds of bellowing resumes from the competition. You may not want the scream when you're attempting to approach an executive with a direct solicitation.

It may appear at first glance that a letter resume is nothing but a slightly longer version of a cover letter (such as those shown later in Figures 5.3 and 5.4). The difference is more significant than just length. A cover letter attempts to grab the attention of a busy person and entice him or her to read the accompanying resume with more interest than that given to hundreds of competing resumes. A letter resume, on the other hand, takes a more leisurely, companionable, and

OTTO OPTIMIST   Page 2
                              EXPERIENCE
September 1981–June 1985   **BENCER UNIVERSITY**
                                                              Bencer, MA

BUSINESS ADMINISTRATION STUDENT

<u>Activities</u>: Between September 1981–June 1985, majored in Finance and Accounting. <u>Achievements</u>: Made Dean's list 11 out of 12 quarters. Awarded the Foggybottom Scholarship for academic excellence in Finance in 1983. Attained G.P.A. of 3.4 out of 4.0 in all subjects and 3.8 out of 4.0 in major.

September 1983–June 1984   **AJAX DISTRIBUTORS, INC.**
(concurrent with above)   North Dookfoeld, MA

ASSISTANT ACCOUNTANT
(30 hours/week)

<u>Responsibilities</u>: Maintained daily cash records and sales reports for a plumbing distributor with 35 service and sales agents. <u>Achievements</u>: Developed new posting forms and programmed XXX PC to log and track all sales call costs and expense reports.

September 1984–present   **BRONSKI BROTHERS, PLUMBERS**
(partially concurrent with above)   Bencer, MA

ASSISTANT BOOKKEEPER
(25–30 hours/week)

<u>Responsibilities</u>: Maintain receivables, payables, and cash ledgers for plumbing service company of 120 employees. Assist as required with payroll. <u>Achievements</u>: Assisted in the installation of a PC-driven payroll and tax package. Payroll preparation time has been cut 57%.

June–August, 1982–1984   **DITCH DIGGERS, INC.**
(concurrent with above)   Bencer, MA

LABORER

<u>Activities</u>: Utility person on construction crew.

<u>REFERENCES AND FURTHER DATA UPON REQUEST</u>

Figure 4.2 *cont'd* Just-Out-of-College *Inside Track* Resume, Page 2

---

less promotional tact; it's more of a frank discussion of mutual needs than a, "Hey, do I have what you need!" The down side of a letter resume's intimacy is that it is more trouble to read. The reader must look for certain data (e.g., the education section isn't nicely labeled) and then work a little to decide if the candidate is appealing. If it takes more time and work, the recipient may decide to forget it and go to lunch or take a call. I don't recommend their use for anything but direct solicitations to very high-level executives who have been carefully researched and validated as likely to need your skills. Chapter 7 discusses these direct solicitation techniques in detail. Read it before you attempt to use a letter resume in place of the more hard-hitting cover letter and resume combination.

Figure 4.22 presents the body of a letter resume version of the *Inside Track* resume shown in Figure 4.23. Note that the letter resume of

---

Dear Ms. White:

I have read in several sources that White Memorial Hospital is about to undertake a period of aggressive expansion into new health-care market areas. That is a strategy I heartily endorse. It is stimulating to see that White Memorial, long a traditional leader in health care, has the foresight to make such a bold and necessary move at such a critical time.

Of course, there is more to success than careful planning and bold action. Skilled marketing and operations talent will be essential. There is always a shortage of highly skilled and experienced professionals in these areas.

In health care, the shortage is even more acute, because of the limited numbers of executives who have succeeded in competitive health-care endeavors and, at the same time, understand the special structure and needs of not-for-profit hospitals. I am such an executive, and I would like to talk with you about your executive staffing requirements in the new market areas you have targeted.

I have successfully managed a $2+ million per year branch of a private health-care agency at gross margin of 42%. I tripled the volume of business in three years. Prior to that, I had established, operated, and then sold at a large profit my own health-care services business.

My entrepreneurial skills are augmented by extensive experience in not-for-profit hospitals. I have been a vice president and DON for a 250-bed acute-care facility and a DON for a large university medical center. In both positions I cut costs and personnel while maintaining quality and service and implementing new programs.

Of course, I possess the academic preparation and interpersonal skills you require of a key executive. In addition to an M.B.A. and a B.S.N., I hold a number of certificates from large universities in Public Relations and Corporate Communications. I have successfully organized, staffed, and directed large work groups in many settings; I can bring these skills to your new programs.

I will call you in a week in order to determine whether it would be appropriate for us to get together and discuss your requirements for an executive with my qualifications.

Thank you for your attention. I look forward to speaking with you.

Figure 4.22 Example of Letter Resume

P.O. Box 23506 (502) 555-9999
Smalltown, KY 40222

RESUME

of

MARLENE FLABEAUX
Health-Care Executive

SUMMARY OF QUALIFICATIONS

*** <u>Bottom-Line Orientation</u> Entrepreneurial approach and orientation. Prefer to operate in a lean, profits-first environment. Adept at identifying and developing revenue-producing endeavors. Minimum emphasis on peripheral issues. Have established successful independent firm.

*** <u>Operations and Management</u> Wide-ranging experience involving program administration, budget development and administration, public relations, marketing, and operations (staffing, scheduling, and personnel administration). Hands-on experience in the administration and delivery of services in home health, Medicare, and acute and extended-care environments.

*** <u>Interpersonal and Organizational Skills</u> Consistent record of success in motivating and developing subordinates. Extremely effective in establishing working relationships with all personnel levels. Comfortable and effective in working with executives.

*** <u>Health-Care Marketing</u> Comprehensive experience in the marketing of health-care products and services to private medical practitioners, acute and extended-care facilities, and the public. Experienced in marketing needs analyses, development of marketing materials, direct mail, advertising, long-range planning, and budget development.

PERSONAL

    DOB 1/1/49; married; no children; excellent health.

EDUCATION AND PROFESSIONAL CERTIFICATIONS

    M.B.A., THE FROOFROO ACADEMY, Washington, DC, 1981.
    CERTIFICATE: Public Health, MANTAN STATE COLLEGE, Burn, FL, 1984.
    B.S.N., UNIVERSITY OF RAMON, Albuquerque, NM, 1972.

<u>FOR FURTHER DATA, PLEASE SEE REVERSE SIDE</u>

Figure 4.23 *Inside Track* Resume of a Health-Care Executive (Page 1)

MARLENE FLABEAUX   Page 2

EXPERIENCE

September 1982–April 1985   **LORRENN HEALTH CARE, INC.**
                                                Sherman Oaks, CA

BRANCH MANAGER

Responsibilities: Responsible for general administration and day-to-day operations of a $2+ million/year branch of a nationwide temporary nursing service. Developed and directed marketing, advertising, and public relations efforts. Selected and trained nursing supervisors. Directed and trained office personnel in day-to-day office operations. Achievements: Completely reorganized outdated office systems. Implemented direct mail and qualified cold call marketing campaign to physicians. Implemented local media advertising campaign to end users. Increased weekly billings from 800 hours in 1982 to an average of 2100 hours in 1985.

August 1981–September 1982   **TLC NURSING SERVICE**
                                                       Glendale, CA

OWNER

Responsibilities: Established private-duty nursing service for patients in home and hospital environments. Recruited personnel, implemented marketing campaigns, and established and managed all systems. Achievements: Increased business from zero in August 1981 to 700 hours per week by September 1982.

November 1977–August 1981   **FLOUNDER COMMUNITY HOSPITAL**
                                                      Flounder, ME

VICE-PRESIDENT OF PATIENT SERVICES

Responsibilities: Administration and day-to-day management of all nursing services and four ancillary departments (total personnel 385 FTE) of a 250-bed acute-care facility. Achievements: Reduced nursing staff 7% from previous levels and cut nonpersonnel budget of all five departments by 8%.

May 1972–October 1977   **UNIVERSITY OF SUNBELT**
                                                        Miami, FL

DIRECTOR OF NURSING SERVICES, OPEN HEART UNIT

Responsibilities: Administer highly specialized unit. Achievements: Designed and implemented budgets, policies, procedures, training, and day-to-day operations of the unit.

REFERENCES AND FURTHER DATA UPON REQUEST

Figure 4.23 *(cont'd) Inside Track* Resume of a Health-Care Executive (Page 2)

800 Barrington Road (818) 555–9999
Glenside, CA 94702

RESUME

of

BARRY BRONSKI, Ph.D.

OBJECTIVE

Challenging position that demands outstanding administration skills and superior program design and presentation capabilities.

SUMMARY OF QUALIFICATIONS

*** <u>Training Administration</u> Successful experience in the administration and direction of training programs and staff in commercial, industrial, and military environments. Skilled in the development of budgets, plans, and program promotions.

*** <u>Technical Training</u> Comprehensive experience in all facets of program development including media and effectiveness evaluations. Extensive experience in the application of Instructional System Design principles to technical skills training programs.

*** <u>Management Development Training</u> Expert in the design and presentation of 1–3 day OMD programs for both line and executive personnel. Adept at producing cost-effective audiovisual materials (videotape and film).

*** <u>Communications</u> Outstanding writing skills. Adept in the preparation of proposals, reports, speeches, scripts, newsletters, and briefing materials. Excellent platform and public speaking skills. Extensive seminar leadership, teaching, and group facilitation experience.

PERSONAL

DOB 12/6/47; married; no children; excellent health.

EDUCATION

Ph.D. Organizational Psychology, STATE UNIVERSITY, Pohot, KS, 1978.
M.A. Psychology, BOB'S COLLEGE, Baltimore, MD, 1974.
B.A. Psychology, UNIVERSITY OF ROBERT, Robert, OR, 1969.

FOR FURTHER DATA, PLEASE SEE REVERSE SIDE

Figure 4.24 *Inside Track* Resume of a Training Professional (Page 1)

BARRY BRONSKI, Ph.D.   Page 2

EXPERIENCE

March 1981–Present   **SELF-EMPLOYED**
                                                                                        Glenside, CA

TRAINING AND MANAGEMENT DEVELOPMENT CONSULTANT

<u>Activities</u>: Market and conduct training, research, and programs designed to enhance organizational and management development, productivity, and employee performance. <u>Achievements</u>: As both prime and subcontractor, designed over 120 programs in the areas of team building, techical training, leadership, executive development, and supervisory skills.

June 1978–February 1981   **HPP, INC.**
                                                                            Gunt Crest, MD

DIRECTOR, MANAGEMENT DEVELOPMENT GROUP

<u>Activities</u>: Directed 16-person department that provided corporate resources to five divisions for technical, sales, and management development training. <u>Achievements</u>: Designed and implemented new system for career pathing. Designed, presented, and maintained sales training programs (and accompanying operations/tracking system) for several divisions. Designed and presented many seminars for senior executives in areas of leadership, team building, and communications skills.

October 1976–May 1978   **MYSTIC APPLICATIONS, LTD.**
                                                                           McPork, VA

MANAGER, TRAINING SYSTEMS

<u>Activities</u>: Marketed, directed, and /or conducted training, personnel research, and organizational development programs. Supervised field personnel, designed and conducted briefings, wrote reports and proposals. <u>Achievements</u>: Developed several large-scale, comprehensive technical skills training programs for military simulation training. For FAA, reviewed and revised all training materials for ground equipment and performed manpower planning and succession planning research. Developed several avionics maintenance training programs for US Marines.

EXPERIENCE PRIOR TO 1976

RESEARCH/TEACHING ASSISTANT (statistics and experimental design instructor for graduate-level courses) at State University (1974–1976). INSTRUCTOR, Bob's College (1972–1973).

<u>   REFERENCES AND FURTHER DATA UPON REQUEST   </u>

Figure 4.24 *(cont'd)* Inside Track Resume of a Training Professional (Page 2)

Figure 4.22 doesn't come on all that hard. It's obviously an "I'm looking for a job" letter, but it doesn't scream it out. The fact that it's not a breathless pounding of "I'm great! I'm great!" will impress certain executives; it's the low-key approach they prefer in their senior people. No resume is included. That permits the job seeker to drop the resume off in person during the meeting or to send it if a meeting isn't possible. Read Chapter 7 and the discussion of telecharts for pointers on making the "When do I come in for an interview?" calls. A few tips on writing your letter resume follow:

1. Flatter the readers about their skills, intelligence, and so on, right at the start of the letter. They'll want to see more.
2. Keep the opening discussion related to a concrete plan or action of theirs that relates to your skills. A loose philosophical discussion won't advance your chances.
3. Build a brief case for your value. Relate it to their activities and goals. Tell them you're looking for a more suitable situation. Don't try to hide it once you've softened them up; they know it's coming and expect it. A delay leads them to perceive you as devious or contemptuous of their intelligence.
4. Begin your self-praising with numbers and accomplishments.
5. Stress your breadth of experience.
6. Refer to yourself as an executive if appropriate, or at least as a professional.
7. Briefly sum up the most impressive titles you've held.
8. Briefly sum up your educational background if it's at least acceptable.
9. Tell them you'll be calling in a week.
10. Don't mention any names of organizations you've worked for; it will build their curiosity.
11. Don't mention problems or outline credentials that are less than the standard in your field.

More Examples of the Inside Track Resume

Figures 4.23 and 4.24 present two additional examples of the *Inside Track* resume format. They'll assist you in getting a feel for the effect you're aiming for. The first resume is that of a nursing administration type. The second resume belongs to a training professional. Read through each resume and note the specificity of the SOQ items to various skills and experiences, the wording in general, and the organization of the responsibilities and achievements sections.

Chapter 5

Strategy Number 1: Responses to Classified Job Advertisements

When people speak of looking for a job, this is the strategy most think of first. Many books on job searches dump on the technique of responding to newspaper ads. The so-called expert authors of these books contend that only 10 to 20 percent of all jobs are advertised in the newspapers. They claim that if you only answer ads you'll never get a shot at the other 80 to 90 percent that don't get advertised. There's some truth to this contention but not much. Many jobs aren't advertised; a lot of them are filled by internal candidates, and many lower-level jobs are taken by people who walk in off the street. If you add these two types of recruiting sources together, they comprise a big part of what the headhunters claim are the unadvertised jobs. Responding to ads is almost always the single best or most important strategy to pursue because the ads are right there just begging for responses. Chapter 3 discusses the many reasons why this is a good strategy. Unfortunately, most job seekers can't prepare a decent response to an ad any more than they can put together a decent resume. This chapter will show you how to avoid the common mistakes and make the greatest impact on the reader in your responses to classified ads.

Where to Get the Ads

The best sources of classified ads are newspapers. A very popular source for business and professional jobs is the *National Business Employment Weekly* (NBEW), a sister publication of the *Wall Street Journal* (WSJ). The NBEW contains all of the employment ads that have been placed in the "Job Mart" sections of all four regional editions of the WSJ from the previous week. It's available at larger newsstands or by subscription at about four dollars per week. You can subscribe by calling 212-808-6791 or (800) JOB HUNT. Using the NBEW is more convenient and much less expensive than trying to obtain each day's WSJ. (Tuesday is the big day for WSJ employment ads.) An added benefit of the NBEW is that you'll get the employment ads from every one of the four regional editions. A good proportion of ads placed in the WSJ are run only in one or two regions because many employers want to cut advertising costs. Some employers advertise regionally because they'd rather not pay long-distance relocation costs. On the other hand, many employers know that the NBEW will run every ad carried by all editions, thus enabling them to reach large numbers of job seekers if they place the ad in a single regional edition. Don't worry about the relocation issue and regional ads; if they can't find anyone in their region, they'll pay the relocation. One caution about the NBEW: it runs a lot of filler articles from experts in job searching. Read the articles, but be extremely careful about following the advice they give. Most are written by authors who have their heads in the clouds and are mainly interested in pumping up their own reputations as leading-edge headhunters, career counselors, and personnel executives.

The next best source of ads are the major Sunday papers in large cities. The two best ones are the *New York Times* and the *Los Angeles Times*. They're the best because New York and Los Angeles are the two biggest job markets in the country; they've got the most jobs. A minor added plus is the fact that a lot of out-of-town employers also use them because they know many out-of-town job seekers read them. If you're in a city, be sure to scan carefully that city's Sunday papers. The daily papers are of some value at the lower salary levels, but most of the $20K+ per year jobs will be advertised only in the Sunday papers. Make sure you look in the business section as well as the classified section. Many large Sunday papers, including both the *New York Times* and the *Los Angeles Times*, run a professional employment section in their Sunday business section. If you were to read the classified sections only, you'd miss most of the good jobs.

Two additional publications are outstanding for conveniently locating ads from a variety of major Sunday papers. They are the National Ad Search (NAS) and the National Job Market (NJM). Both contain thousands of classified advertisements taken from hundreds of newspapers across the country. Look for them at major newsstands. The NJM, the largest in number of ads and circulation, provides subscribers (six issues over three months for approximately $30) with free resume kits, federal jobs kits, and listing in their mailer to headhunters. The ordering number is 800-323-7702. The NAS publishes over 2,000 ads weekly and offers subscriptions of various lengths for about $6 an issue. Subscribers are offered a free resume service. You can order by calling 800-992-2832. Keep in mind that many of the employers in the NJM and the NAS are small and either couldn't afford to or wouldn't think of paying relocating costs. They have no way of knowing their ads may be seen by job seekers who are thousands of miles away. If you see a great opportunity, answer the ad regardless of the location (unless the ad states that "candidates must be residents of

RESPONSES TO CLASSIFIED JOB ADVERTISEMENTS 87

_____"), but be aware that your odds of success are lower simply because of the relocation issue.

A few additional sources may be appropriate for your search. If you're looking for overseas or government jobs, there are several tabloid publications that deal exclusively with these areas. Check for them at major newsstands and in ads appearing in the Sunday classified sections of big city newspapers (as well as in the above-mentioned sources).

If you're in a specialized field, you'll find ads in professional magazines and journals. For example, health-care magazines run many ads soliciting candidates for nursing, health-care administration, and related positions. Financial magazines and journals contain many ads for CPAs, accountants, and lawyers. Almost every profession or specialty has its own magazines and journals. Take a look at the ones in your field. The ads in these sources place quite an emphasis on academic credentials and currently popular professional froo-froos and jargon. That's because the people placing the ads are "academics advertising for same." You'll probably also find that they're in no hurry. Journal and magazine ads are generally less likely to pay off than newspaper ads, but they could be hot in your field. Don't overlook them if you've got the time to answer them.

What is a Response to an Ad?

The *Inside Track* response to an employment ad consists of an individually typed cover letter placed on top of a resume, triple folded, placed in a business-size envelope, and mailed to the person or address listed in the ad. This chapter will detail the correct way to prepare and present appropriate and effective cover letters.

Why It's Important to Use a Cover Letter

If you respond to an ad without a cover letter, you might as well not respond at all. There are several reasons why it's essential to use a cover letter:
1. Recruiters expect it. Since they expect it and many people use them, a response without a cover letter will suffer greatly by comparison.
2. It's a convention of the business world. When a piece of business correspondence arrives, it's expected to arrive with a letter, even if the letter is only two lines long. As explained in Chapter 4, you want your resume to be viewed as a proper, polished piece of business correspondence. Without a cover letter, an answer to an

ad demonstrates that the sender doesn't know or care about the conventions of the business world.
3. You've got to increase the probability that your resume will be forwarded to the right person when it arrives. If you simply stuff your resume in an envelope and put it in the mail, it may never get to the person doing the recruiting for the job. The receptionist might forward it to the wrong person or stick it in a "worry about it later" pile. In most personnel departments, nobody worries about anything later.
4. A properly written cover letter increases your chances of getting an interview at least 250 percent over the results you'll get with a poor cover letter and at least 500 percent over the results you'll get from using no letter at all.

Some General Guidelines

Regardless of which ad response strategy you select from the later sections of this chapter, there are a number of guidelines that are fundamental to all properly designed ad response materials:
1. Type all of your cover letters on stationery that matches your resume (8½ by 11 inches).
2. Use either blank stationery of the type described in Chapter 4 or personal stationery with your name and address printed on it. Never use the stationery of an employer unless it's your business and the stationery makes that fact clear.
3. Use a type face as close as possible to the one used on your resume. Less than an exact match is a serious deficit. If you're going to be typing the letters yourself on your own typewriter, take a sample of the type face with you when you get the resume word processed. Insist that they use one as close to it as possible.
4. Each letter must be a typed original. Don't try the obvious and shoddy ploy of typing up the main section of the letter, making photocopies of it, and then individually typing the inside address on each one. It looks terrible, insults the reader's intelligence, and will help your resume into the reject pile. Chapter 11 tells you how to do essentially the same thing with a word processor, but since each letter looks like an original, it's OK.

Levels of Effort

Depending on your resources in time and money, the number of ads you're going to answer, your secretarial skills if you're going to do the typing, and your general inclinations, there are several levels of effort you can expend in responding to ads. As with many other things in life, the more effort you put in the better results you get out. The greater the effort and work put into the cover letter, the greater your odds of making the first cut and getting a call.

Level 1: Bare Bones

Figure 5.1 presents the bare-bones cover letter. This letter says the absolute minimum that's necessary in a proper response to an ad. It's the very least you should do. It doesn't do anything outstanding in terms of special targeting to the job, but it's better than 90 percent of the cover letters that arrive on recruiters' desks.

Joseph Jones
22 Main Street
Glendale, CA 91207
(818) 555-9999

June 23, 1986

Ms. Mary Quitecontrary
Personnel Manager
ACME HUMMINGBIRD MEAT PACKERS, INC.
9999-B Brand Boulevard
Glendale, CA 91207

Dear Ms. Quitecontrary:

I am responding to your June 21, 1986, advertisement in the Los Angeles Times in which you solicited candidates for the position of Supervisor of Packing Operations. My qualifications are an ideal match to those outlined in the advertisement. My resume is enclosed.

My qualifications include an M.S. in avian meat packing from Bird University. I am currently employed by Nadir Sparrow Packers, Inc., of Bellflower, CA, as Supervisor of Feet Processing. I am seeking an increase in challenge and responsibility.

I would be pleased to discuss my potential contributions with you in detail at your convenience. Thank you for your attention.

Respectfully,

Joseph Jones

Enclosure

Figure 5.1 Bare-Bones Cover Letter in Response to an Ad

The bare-bones cover letter of Figure 5.1 contains several elements that are essential in any cover letter:
1. Repeats the applicant's name, address, and phone number on the top of the letter. This demonstrates proper business format, increases the association with your name, and helps prevent the letter from being permanently lost if it's separated from the resume.
2. Uses proper business format. Note that the addressee's name and address are included. Not to do so would make the letter appear to be a personal letter and therefore inappropriate, signaling that the writer was either ignorant or not concerned about the etiquette of the business world.
3. States where and when the ad appeared and the specific job in question. This demonstrates organization and directness on the part of the writer and also serves to assist the initial sorter in getting your resume into the correct pile.
4. States that the applicant is ideally suited for the job, whether it's really true or not. (That's what they're supposed to be determining; you're certainly entitled to your opinion.) This begins to orient the reader to look for the evidence. If you're using an *Inside Track* resume, it won't be hard to find.
5. States that the resume is enclosed. This is a formality expected in proper job search correspondence.
6. Gives a brief statement of qualifications. This serves as a hook to entice the reader to look at the resume. An additional benefit is that the best qualifications are repeated; the more they see them, the more they'll remember them.
7. Contains a sentence stating that the applicant is seeking increased responsibility and challenge. These are positive words that further orient the reader toward viewing the writer as an organized and accomplished businessperson.
8. Asks for a meeting. Such a request is a mere formality because it's expected. It can do a little more. The exact form used in this letter is highly recommended. The words *potential contributions* and *in detail* make it appear as if the writer has some real contributions in mind and isn't afraid to talk about them. This orients the reader toward thinking the writer is very businesslike. This might not be the case if everyone used the exact phrase shown in Figure 5.1, but few job seekers use anything like it at all; take advantage of their appalling ignorance.
9. Thank them for their trouble. It's their job, but if you demonstrate a little formal courtesy they may react with an extra bit of positive feeling which will influence them to stop and glance at the resume even though they're late for a personnel association lunch.
10. Contains a formal closing section. Use "Respectfully," repeat

your name as it's written at the top, and finish with "Enclosure," which refers to your resume. The repeat of your name is redundant and a slight violation of letter form, but it's necessary. You want the reader to see your name as often as possible in order to build an association between your name and your great letter and resume.

It's incredible, but most people don't know how to put together a decent business letter that incorporates the above basic principles. If you use them, you'll be way ahead of the others even before the recruiter starts reading for content.

All you've got to do to use the bare-bone letter of Figure 5.1 is change the date, the ad source, the job title, and your qualifications. If you're unemployed, state "I have successful experience as" instead of "I am currently employed," and then mention the job that best supports your candidacy.

Level 2: Lead 'Em by the Hand

The "lead 'em by the hand" cover letter does all of the things the bare-bones letter does and more. The principal difference is that the lead-'em cover letter points out the specific qualifications that are most relevant to the requirements listed in the ad. In effect, the lead-'em letter expands the second paragraph of the bare-bones letter and customizes its contents to the specific ad. Let's look at an example. Figure 5.2 is a blind ad that appeared in the NBEW.

Read the ad and then look at Figure 5.3, which shows the lead-'em cover letter sent in response.

NUCLEAR FUEL EXECUTIVE

An exciting opportunity exists in this established nuclear utility in the Northeast for an individual with a proven record of accomplishment in the fuel cycle area. The successful applicant will be accepting overall responsibility for direction of the company's nuclear fuel program in a very challenging work environment. To be considered for this position, you should have strong technical competence in all aspects of the fuel cycle, experience in contract negotiations and administration of contracts, a good management background, 10 years experience in the nuclear industry, and a minimum of a Bachelor's degree. If you're up to the challenge, this organization offers an excellent salary and benefits program and relocation assistance where applicable. Please send your resume, in confidence, to Box WJ–XXX, Wall Street Journal.

Figure 5.2 Actual Blind Ad From the NBEW

Samuel Smith
1011 Jefferson Road
Powell, TN 40223
(607) 555–9999

October 20, 1986

Box WJ–XXX
Wall Street Journal
1701 Page Mill Road
Palo Alto, CA 93404

Dear Sir or Madam:

I am responding to your recent advertisement in the Wall Street Journal in which you solicited candidates for the position of Nuclear Fuel Executive. My qualifications are an ideal match to those outlined in the advertisement. My resume is enclosed.

In terms of the specific requirements mentioned in the advertisement, I offer the following:.

*** Extensive background in fueling operations. Three years experience as a fueling technician and two years as manager of a spent fuel processing plant.

*** Experienced in contract negotiations with fuel suppliers, overhaul and construction trades, and foreign governments.

*** Fourteen years experience in the nuclear industry.

*** Seven years experience as a manager including responsibilities in nuclear fueling operations, procurement, and salvage, and three years experience as a supervisor of administration for a large nuclear generation facility.

*** B.S. in Nuclear Engineering with M.S. in Operations Research.

I would be pleased to discuss my potential contributions with you in detail at your convenience. Thank you for your attention.

Respectfully,

Samuel Smith

Enclosure

Figure 5.3 "Lead 'Em by the Hand" Cover Letter

RESPONSES TO CLASSIFIED JOB ADVERTISEMENTS

Note that the lead-'em letter matches each required qualification phrase or sentence in the ad with a corresponding credential or qualification. This sets up an expectation in the screener that the candidate is highly qualified and the resume will be scanned in a very positive light. It also forces the reader to look at the resume to see just how good it is. Since the reader wants to get the search over, he or she will be more inclined to read the resume in detail, hoping to find what's wanted. Few resumes get that type of attention. If yours does, it will have a greater chance of making it to the person who will make the final decision. A few minor style points in the letter are worthy of mention:

1. Note that the letter doesn't give an exact date for the ad. This is because the NBEW, where the ad was spotted by the candidate, doesn't tell you the date on which the ad first appeared. It's not a good idea to mention that you spotted the ad in the NBEW, as that connotes a "desperate job seeker" (which may be true, but there's no sense in decreasing your perceived value as a great candidate). Just mention the WSJ and say the ad was "recent" if you're using the NBEW.
2. Since it's a blind ad, you don't know if it's a man or woman on the other end. If the address doesn't list a person or title, address the letter to "Dear Sir or Madam." That's an expected business courtesy. If the ad gives a name, such as J. Howard, where it's not apparent if it's a man or woman, use "J. Howard" in the address block and on the envelope, and use "Dear Mr./Ms. Howard" in the salutation. If the address lists a title, such as Personnel Administrator, use that title in the address block and on the envelope, and use "Dear Sir or Madam" in the salutation. Again, these are expected formal courtesies. Some experts would have you use "Mr.," "Dear Sir," and "Gentlemen" when there's doubt about the gender of the addressee, but that's too dangerous. There are a great many female managers out there, especially in personnel, who are sensitive to such slights. It's better to play it safe and sound a little more formal, which never hurts in a job search.
3. Note the use of the asterisks to call out each qualification. This is particularly important. As you'll recall, Chapter 4 suggests using asterisks to call out individual summary of qualification (SOQ) items on your *Inside Track* resume. The same type of symbols on the cover letter will provide your entire package of materials with a consistent and carefully planned appearance.

Level 3: Face Down Through the Cactus

The "drag 'em face down through the cactus" cover letter represents the ultimate in cover letter responses. It will be better than 99 percent of all other letters for the job you're after. The only better ones will be those of candidates who use the same principles but are better writers. Don't worry about it; once everyone is invited in for the interview, it's a brand new contest. For most ads that receive two hundred fifty to four hundred resumes, this means you'll have one of the best two or four letters. As long as your qualifications are average, you'll probably get a call. The face-down letter does just what it's name implies: it drags the reader face down through a detailed presentation of every qualification you have that was mentioned or implied in the ad. This approach works because the reader, after sorting through dozens and maybe hundreds of marginally qualified letters and resumes, is highly attuned to the qualifications the ad specified. After finding numerous resumes and letters that don't have any or only a few of the required qualifications, the screener begins to look more intensely for deficits in qualifications, to screen people out rather than in. Your face-down letter's organization and style will not only be a breath of fresh air in the midst of the other applicants' malodorous scrawlings, but it will also be perfectly clear that you've got exactly what they're looking for. In effect, you'll be giving a custom summary of qualifications section written specifically for the ad. Figure 5.4 presents a face-down cover letter that could be sent in response to the ad shown in Figure 5.2.

The power of the face-down letter derives from several points:
1. Everyone likes to see their own writing; it makes them feel respected and important. They'll view your materials more favorably when they've seen that you've quoted their words.
2. It leaves no doubt in their minds that you know exactly what they want. This will reassure them because, as personnel types, they're not all that sure about what the job is really about. Your objective and detailed response will indicate that you're an expert in the area who instantly recognized their needs. This will lead them to believe that you have the qualifications they need.
3. You're talking their language. They'll automatically view you more as "one of us" than "one of them" (other applicants).
4. They'll subjectively enhance their perception of your qualifications. Using their words and then responding to each with a specific qualification leaves no doubt in their minds that you've covered all the bases and have what they need.
5. You'll appear to be a hard-hitting, organized, no-nonsense businessperson just on the basis of your letter's appearance.

If you're going to be using the face-down letter often, construct a file that contains each different quoted qualification item and your corresponding credential or response. It's a good idea to place each unique quote and the qualification on a note card. After you've responded to about twenty ads, you will have seen just about every possible qualification an employer could request in your area of interest. By keeping the qualification card file, you'll have a prepared cre-

Samuel Smith
1011 Jefferson Road
Powell, TN 40223
(607) 555-9999

October 20, 1986

Box WJ–XXX
Wall Street Journal
1701 Page Mill Road
Palo Alto, CA 93404

Dear Sir or Madam:

I am responding to your recent advertisement in the Wall Street Journal in which you solicited candidates for the position of Nuclear Fuel Executive. My qualifications are an ideal match to those outlined in the advertisement. My resume is enclosed.

In terms of the specific requirements mentioned in the advertisement, I offer the following corresponding qualifications:

*** "Strong technical competence in all aspects of the fuel cycle."

Extensive background in fueling operations. Three years experience as a fueling technician, two years as manager of a spent fuel processing plant.

*** "Experience in contract negotiations and administration of contracts."

Experienced in contract negotiations with fuel suppliers, overhaul and construction trades, and foreign governments.

*** "10 years experience in the nuclear industry."

Fourteen years experience in the nuclear industry.

*** "A good management background."

Seven years experience as a manager including responsibilities in nuclear fueling operations, procurement, and salvage, and three years experience as a supervisor of administration for a large nuclear generation facility.

*** "A minimum of a Bachelor's degree."

B.S. in Nuclear Engineering with M.S. in Operations Research.

I would be pleased to discuss my potential contributions with you in detail at your convenience. Thank you for your attention.

Respectfully,

Samuel Smith

Enclosure

Figure 5.4 "Face Down Through the Cactus" Cover Letter

dential for each requested qualification. From then on, it's a simple matter to sort through the file and select the appropriate credentials for any requested qualifications. This technique enables you to concentrate on putting the letters together rather than having to compose a lot of original correspondence for each response. If there are multiple qualifications that are basically the same and for which you'd supply the same credential, put the multiple qualification quotes on top of the appropriate card. This will save you a lot of card shuffling. This technique permits you to use the best wording you've got for each credential on every letter. This won't always be the case if you write each credential off the cuff every time you answer an ad. When you find that you've thought of better wording for a qualification, change your note card on that item. This system will reduce the heavy time demands of the face-down letter approach and will assure you of consistent high quality.

An extra touch

Any of the three letter styles can be augmented with an additional section listing other qualifications you possess but which they didn't ask for in the ad. In this extra section, you tell them that there are a number of qualifications they should expect from the successful candidate. You then point out that, surprise of surprises, you're in possession of those very qualifications. Figure 5.5 gives an example of this supplementary section which can be put into any of the letters right before the final "let's get together and thanks" paragraph. The example shown is one that might be included in the nuclear fuel executive letter of Figure 5.4. If you're going to use the face-down letter, it's not much more work to add the supplementary section. If you're using a

---

In addition to the above minimum requirements which you specify, I possess a number of additional qualifications that I believe you will expect from the outstanding candidates you interview:

*** State-of-the-art knowledge of fueling technology.

Three published papers (in referred journals) dealing with frontier technology in fuel processing.

*** Experienced in dealing with government regulatory agencies.

Serve on private industry advisory council of NRA Fueling Standards Committee.

*** Experienced nuclear power advocate to the community.

Active member of numerous community groups. Frequent speaker on behalf of the industry to local and regional community groups.

Figure 5.5 Example of Supplementary Qualifications Section

RESPONSES TO CLASSIFIED JOB ADVERTISEMENTS 97

bare-bones letter prepared by a word-processing service, you can always include a standard supplementary skills paragraph that does the same thing. Be careful not to include a supplementary section that is too specific or too narrow if you're after a wide range of job types or industries. You may need several basic versions, each of which will have a supplementary section appropriate to a specific type of job opportunity.

The supplementary section gives you an opportunity to mention plusses that might not be exactly related to the job duties but peripherally may cause you to be viewed more positively. This supplementary section is used to put into the cover letter those things that would be totally inappropriate in a resume. As Figure 5.5 demonstrates, the format (spacing, asterisks, etc.) is identical to that of the previous parts of the letter and your resume's summary of qualifications section.

A supplementary section can be very powerful if you've got some solid extra credentials (or lightweight credentials that you can dress up a little). In effect, you're trying to show the recruiter that the minimum qualifications don't ask for enough and that you've got the extra ones they should be demanding. Note that the example doesn't say "I am a great candidate" but rather "I believe you will expect." You avoid bragging and turning off the recruiter, yet at the same time you attempt to up the ante on the other candidates and make yourself appear to be the candidate of choice.

Things to Avoid in Cover Letters Sent in Response to Ads

If you follow the examples and formats shown in Figures 5.1, 5.3, and 5.4, you won't be including any information that will compromise your effectiveness. Things that should not be mentioned or included in cover letters to ads, especially if you decide to get creative (which I don't recommend), are as follows:

1. Any negative information of any kind. Never use the phrase "I don't," as in "have all the qualifications you mention, but," or any other indications that you are at variance with their requirements. If you don't have something they're looking for, don't mention it at all. Concentrate on the ones you do have.
2. Problems. Don't mention illness, reasons why you're looking (other than the expected "seeking more responsibility and challenge"), why you left your last job, the fact that you're unemployed, handicaps, past or current problems of any kind.
3. Salary levels. Never put salary information—past, current, or desired—on the letter itself. You can't afford risking a rejection on the basis of salary data before they've read your entire letter and looked at the resume. Salary data, if provided, goes on the re-

sume, written in by hand in ink. Whether or not and how to quote salary data is dealt with in a later section of this chapter.
4. Cutesy information about your family, hobbies, philosophy of life, or deepest wishes for mankind. The statement that you have "a beautiful wife and three wonderful children" is liable to turn off the recruiter. Don't say anything extra that can't be made to appear directly relevant to the job.
5. References. Never provide the names of references when you're responding to an ad, even if they ask for them. You have no idea what they really want until you talk with them. You can't risk having anyone call a reference and start asking questions until you've had a chance to warn the reference about what the job's like, what you said during the interview (by phone or in person), and which of your outstanding qualifications he or she should emphasize. If you provide references in the letter, you run the risk of the reference getting a call before you do. It's a small risk, but why take chances? A more important concern involves reference courtesy. You're not going to get a lot of help from your references if you make it hard on them. Use them as often as necessary, but keep the inconveniences to a minimum. Wait until you talk with a potential employer on the phone before you provide references. The one exception might be when you're applying for academic or semiacademic positions (such as administration in a university). The tradition in academics is to provide three references with the application. In that field, you don't have much choice but to provide them. When you do provide references, use the format shown in Chapter 10.

Selecting Ads

The selection of ads is a very subjective and personal process. Yet there are a number of considerations everyone should think about as they develop an ad response strategy and when they screen an individual ad.

Blind ads

The topic of whether or not to respond to blind ads receives a lot more attention than it should in the job search literature (the experts again). A blind ad is one in which the identity of the employer is hidden, usually by a box number or by a "confidential reply service" that serves as a mail drop. The traditional wisdom is that many blind ads may not be ads at all but may be market testers in which an organization is attempting to see who's out there and how much the jobs are worth. The contention is sometimes made that some blind ads are put out so

RESPONSES TO CLASSIFIED JOB ADVERTISEMENTS

that large organizations can find out which of their employees are looking for jobs. Forget this type of paranoia; less than half of one percent of blind ads are of these types, if that many. It's just too expensive. A small box ad in the WSJ costs almost $1000; few people are going to spend that much to test the market or see who's looking.

The only time you have to worry about responding to a blind ad is when the job is in the same city as your present employer and it sounds like it's in the same industry or business. If you work for an electronics company in Butte, Montana, and you respond to a blind ad from "an aggressive electronics company" and the city address is Butte, you're begging for it and you'll get it if you respond to the ad. If the ad looks like it might be from your organization, don't respond to it.

There's a plus side to the fear that blind ads generate. As a result of so many people having been brainwashed about their danger, blind ads get only 50 to 60 percent as many responses as open ads. When you answer a blind ad, you've already cut your competition in half compared to open ads.

Salary levels

There are two questions here. The first is, how much should the implied or stated salary levels for the advertised job influence you when you're determining whether or not to respond to an ad? If you've got most of the qualifications for the job and the salary differential between what they're willing to pay and what you're earning is within 20 percent, the answer is, not at all. If the salary differential is greater, such as if the job pays $60K per year and you're going to state that you were or are earning $40K, nobody is going to believe that you're qualified for the job, even if you are. You can avoid mentioning salary in the correspondence, but they'll ask sooner or later. If you're desperate and don't have enough ads to answer, don't screen out any but the most extreme on the basis of salary. If you've got a lot of potential ads from which to select, don't waste your time on the jobs that pay a whole lot more or for which you're not exactly qualified. Too many people with a more appropriate compensation background and all of the qualifications will be responding.

The second, more fundamental question is, should you provide desired, current, or historical salary data when requested in the ad? If the ad requests salary information and you don't provide it, you're reducing your chances of making the first cut. On the other hand, if you do provide it and it turns out that you're earning either too much or too little for their tastes, you won't make the cut either. Whenever they ask for salary information, they're going to get a lot of resumes with it. If they get a lot of good resumes that provide it, yours without such data will have less chance of making it to the interview pile.

Nobody wants to take the effort to call you and then find out that you make too little or too much, especially when they've got good candidates about whom they have no doubts. If you believe the competition will be tough and numerous, provide salary information if they ask for it (unless you're in a position to tolerate lower odds and a longer search). If you think there's not all that much competition (meaning fewer than a hundred resumes), you can safely leave out the salary data. They'll call you if they don't find enough good candidates.

If the ad very strongly demands salary information, as in "No responses without salary data will be considered," there's no sense in responding if you don't provide it. Someone in the organization has a thing about salary information, and all responses without it will be trashed. If the ad doesn't absolutely demand salary data (as when it states, "Respond with resume" or "Send resume and salary history to"), follow the guidelines stated above.

When providing salary data, use a black pen to write in each job's last or highest salary next to the job title on your resume. Don't have the salaries printed on the resume. Write salaries in the form, "$23K per annum," not "$23,000 per year." If there were or are bonuses or other income, write it beneath the salary, as in "$2–4K per annum bonus." Don't go into detailed explanations; just give them a general idea about your compensation.

How close are your qualifications?

Most of the time, you're not going to have the exact set of qualifications the ad requests. You'll be overqualified in some areas and underqualified in others. If you've got a plethora of ads from which to select, it's obvious that you should respond first to the ones for which you're most qualified. If you don't have enough ads that are closely matched to your qualifications, you can expand your limits and take some chances on less than perfect matches. (Be sure that you've taken care of other strategies before you become too flexible in terms of responding to ads for which your qualifications aren't at least average.)

You can easily sidestep most minor qualification problems simply by not mentioning them specifically. For example, if an ad says eight years of experience and you have six, you can probably make the first cut if you simply state "many years of experience" in your lead-'em or face-down cover letter. On the other hand, if the ad says something like, "No candidate without a minimum of ten years experience will be considered," you can be sure that someone in the organization wants ten years of experience and isn't going to take anything less. That type of strong language will result in them getting few resumes with less than ten years of experience. Yours with eight or six years would look really bad. In that situation, you can be sure that any low-level screener is not going to risk career problems by letting a resume slip through without ten years of experience. If the ad states "M.B.A. from top school required" and you "only" have a Ph.D. and an M.A., don't bother; if the screener doesn't see "M.B.A." on the resume, you won't make the cut.

The stronger the language in the ad about any of the qualifications, the less likely will be the possibility that any variances will be accepted. And since the competition will be tough, why bother? People who answer strongly worded ads without the appearance of proper qualifications are getting emotionally involved and wasting their energy and money.

Geographical considerations

It's important to take careful note of the geographical location of the organization placing the ad. If you don't want to move there, don't waste your time responding to the ad unless you're interested in practicing your interview technique or learning some more about the industry. If you're out of work, there's almost no reason not to go to such interviews for the practice if your technique isn't perfect.

If they're paying for it, why not? If the ad says something to the effect of, "Seeking New York City based candidate," they're probably reluctant or unable to pay for relocation and therefore are looking for someone who already lives in the area. If you don't live in the area, don't waste your time with a response unless the qualifications they seek are exactly what you have. In that case, it might be worth a long shot to respond, in the hope that if they don't find anyone local they'll call you. If you're already busy with a lot of other ads, don't bother; the odds against you are large.

It's All a Game of Odds

Even with outstanding *Inside Track* resumes and cover letters, you're going to get a lot of rejections. Don't take it personally. You can never know what's going on behind the scenes to cause your materials to miss the cut (and if you were to find out, you probably wouldn't believe it). As I write this sentence, I'm employed by an organization that took five months to call me after getting my resume—and I was the only one they called! If I had looked through my log book, I would have written them off after three or four months. Now that I know what was going on behind the scenes, it seems reasonable enough. It probably seems outrageous to the other three hundred people who responded to the ad and only got a form-letter rejection.

Don't try to infer or deduce what's going on when you respond to an ad; just launch them and forget them. Do everything you can to produce the best-quality resumes and correspondence possible. Then respond to as many appropriate ads as you can. That's all you can do. If you use the formats provided in this chapter, you'll get results.

Chapter 6

Strategy Number 2: Mailings to Headhunters

This is your second best overall search strategy in most situations. It's one that you can't afford to ignore if you're earning over $30K per annum because many companies exclusively use headhunters to fill their higher-level positions. Even if you're flush with great ads to answer and it's a seller's market for your skills, it's foolish to limit your target population of potential jobs by ignoring headhunters.

Where to Find the Headhunters

The best single source for locating and identifying headhunters is the *Directory of Executive Recruiters* published each year by Consultants News. The *Directory* is updated each year and usually contains the names and addresses of about 2000 to 2100 executive recruiters and recruiting firms. Consultants News is located on Templeton Road in Fitzwilliam, New Hampshire 03447. The telephone numbers are (603) 585-2200 and (603) 585-6544. They welcome telephone orders. The *Directory* is paperbound and should cost less than $20.

The *Directory* presents headhunters in two main alphabetical listings: contingency (paid only if they find someone) and retainer (fee plus expenses and commission). As noted in the Chapter 2 discussion of headhunters, this distinction is pretty much immaterial from the job seeker's point of view. The *Directory*'s value comes not only from the breadth of its listings but also from the additional information it provides on each headhunter's area of concentration. The *Directory* provides the approximate minimum salary level of jobs for which each headhunter searches, any industry or function specializations, and cross-indexes by industry, function, and geographical location. I've never found a better source of headhunters.

Don't try to get by with a shorter or more convenient list of headhunters. Many job search books include a short list of major headhunters that is supposed to help the reader. Don't believe it. These lists are worthless for two reasons. First, they're too limited to do any good. You're playing the odds when you contact headhunters; sending twenty to forty resumes out isn't going to do any good at all. The second problem is that the lists are usually badly out of date. If you use them, you'll waste a lot of postage and time. I recently conducted a test of a list that was provided in a new edition of a well-known job search book. I called directory assistance in each firm's city and asked for the phone number of each of the almost forty firms listed. I attempted to contact each firm and ask for its correct address. Twelve of the addresses were either wrong or the company was out of business. That's almost a 33 percent failure rate. I've conducted several mailing tests of all of the *Directory's* listings. The return rate for "addressee moved—no forwarding address" or "addressee unknown" was never more than 5 percent. (There's a lot of turnover in the industry because all you need to get started is a phone.)

Regional job search guides are no better than most of the lists provided in job search books. The lists they provide are generally taken straight from the phone book and consist of a hodgepodge of headhunters, personnel agencies, and career consultants. Such lists are worthless to a properly planned and executed job search.

How Many to Contact?

You should contact as many headhunters as you can afford that are appropriate to your search needs and budget. If you're going to contact any headhunters at all, think of one hundred as the absolute minimum number. Don't contact more than three hundred every four weeks unless you're out of work or in imminent danger of losing your job. You won't have time to handle the responses. (In the latter case, you'd just have to make the time.) If you can afford the lag time, it's better to space out your mailings so that the callbacks are more evenly distributed over time. If you're out of work, the sky (and your bank account) is the limit on the total number of headhunters you contact. As Chapter 3 estimates, you'll get only one interview per hundred launches; you'll have to get several hundred out there in order to assure yourself of a least one job offer.

Consultants News sells computerized address labels for all of the entries in the *Directory*, and it's not uncommon for job seekers to mail a resume to every one of them. In most cases that's not a recommended strategy, as it contacts a lot of headhunters who are low-probability prospects. The postage costs alone for one such mailing are about $450.

How to Select Headhunters

The *Directory* is valuable because it provides you with a means of selecting a target list that is much smaller than the entire list and, at the same time, more appropriate to your requirements. If you're going to use another source, make sure it contains the types of information you'll need to weed out the headhunters who can't help you. The following sections provide some of the criteria you should and shouldn't use for the selection of your target group, regardless of where you get your list of headhunters.

Geographical location

There's only a moderate relationship between the headhunter's address and the locations of the positions they're trying to fill. The smaller headhunting concerns usually concentrate more closely on organizations that are in the area of their office. Since most started as a phone in someone's spare bedroom, it's only natural that they concentrate on nearby businesses. As a headhunting firm and its reputation grows, the client mix becomes more diverse. The larger and more successful outfits work just as much with clients across the country as with those in their own city.

If you're looking exclusively for a position in a specific area, it's essential to exhaustively contact all of the appropriate headhunters in that area. If you're living in Los Angeles, contact (subject to the other selection criteria that follow) every headhunter in the Los Angeles–Orange County area. There are almost a hundred of them. If you're not familiar with the suburbs of a big metropolitan area, obtain a local map or zip code directory/map (at the library) and make sure to target every firm in the area. For example, if you haven't lived in or visited Los Angeles, you wouldn't realize that dozens of cities such as Newport Beach, Sherman Oaks, and Irvine are part of the Los Angeles–Orange County urban sprawl.

If you have any doubts or don't have much of a target population of headhunters to contact in the specific area you're interested in, hit every one of them in the state and perhaps the nearby states as well. For example, there are only about a dozen headhunters listed in the *Directory* for Kentucky. If you were looking for a job in Kentucky, you'd want to hit all of the headhunters in Indiana, Kentucky, and Tennessee, at least, in the hopes that one of the out-of-state firms might be handling a search for a Kentucky client.

There's a minor additional advantage when using local headhunters. It's a lot easier for them to bring you in for an interview because it doesn't cost them anything but time. They'll feel more confident about a local they've seen when compared to someone out of state whom they'll only interview on the phone. In addition, their clients are always happy to get locals for jobs because there are no expensive relocation fees, problems with the spouse's job, and so on. The trade-off you get from using more distant and perhaps larger headhunting firms is that they might have more and deeper client contacts.

Functional specialization

Many headhunting firms claim to specialize in searches for a specific function, such as finance or health care. Claims to the contrary, most headhunters are generalists who will recruit for any position they can handle. Some, however, do specialize. If you contact them and they actually specialize in a different area from yours, you're wasting your time and money. A good clue about the actual extent (and not just the claim) of specialization is to observe whether the firm claims a specialization to be a primary or secondary interest. In the *Directory*, for example, firms are described by functional and industry specializations. Probably just because they're surveyed in that manner, many claim to specialize in one area or another and then conclude by describing both their functional and industrial interests as "most." If you see a "most" in the *Directory*, send your materials to them if the other indicators are good. On the other hand, if they state that they're working in only one specific functional area, don't bother if you're not looking in that area. Headhunters who claim to specialize solely in the functional areas of medical, legal, finance, and data processing are generally very narrow in their functional interests. That's one advantage of the *Directory* versus most other sources of headhunters; other sources imply that all headhunters handle everything. Such an assumption can waste valuable postage and typing dollars as well as time.

Industry specialization

Many headhunters also claim to have industry specializations. If the claimed specialization is in a single industry, it's probably real; they probably don't handle much in other industries. If they claim a specialization and also work in "most" or "other" areas as well, the chances are that they operate across industries but derive some pride and marketing influence from the claimed specialization.

Salary ranges

For most headhunters, the *Directory* provides the minimum salary levels of the jobs for which they'll search. This is very important information if you're going to be contacting a comparatively small number—one to three hundred—of headhunters. Concentrate on those firms that search for jobs paying from $5K less to $10K more than you're currently earning. The firms that search for much lower-paying jobs than your target range will have fewer opportunities that you'd find attractive (but they'll still call you and waste your time). More importantly, as the salary level of the jobs handled by a headhunting firm decreases, the headhunters themselves are increasingly less experienced and have fewer and less significant contacts with client companies. Of course, there's always a statistical probability that you could hit something, so don't exclude all of the low-end headhunters if you're sending out very large mailings.

Meat-market operations

A number of headhunting firms seem to have offices in almost every city. Some of the best-known names in the business fall into this category. Don't solicit from them unless you're really desperate. These franchise operations spring up and die faster than summer weeds, if returned mail is any indication. They can't possibly have a solid base of client contacts. You'll discover if you send out a large mailing that the majority of returned mail will come from these chain-store franchises. They seem to spend most of their time trying to sell additional franchises instead of obtaining job orders and candidates.

After one large test mailing, I got calls from the managers of three different branches of one firm, each of whom asked if I was interested in starting up my own branch. All I needed was $70K. There must have been a special bonus on signups that month.

A related irritation is that after you've gone to the trouble to mail them a great, detailed *Inside Track* cover letter and a resume, a lot of these franchise operations will send you an application to fill out. They claim that if you fill out their application form, they'll have a better idea of how they can sell your skills. Most of the applications have only two or three lines for each job. Some even ask you to check off areas of experience or interest from a limited list. It's a joke. What they want to do is put all of your information on an easy-to-handle card so they can quickly spot a body if they get a hot call from a client. They also like to brag to clients about the uniqueness of their candidate-coding system. Their applications can't possibly tell them as much as your resume, which itself isn't enough to determine whether you're right for a specific job; they should call you and conduct a detailed interview. If you fill out a few of these "unique candidate tracking forms," you'll get calls from headhunters one to three years later asking if you're interested in a job they've got open. Many won't even bother to screen you beyond asking about your interest in the position.

Don't bother with such applications (or any headhunter applications); they're a waste of your time. Since most of the "chain stores" won't use your resume on its own, there's no point in sending them anything unless you want to bet on the remote chance that they'll have a hot, urgent job sitting on their desk when your resume arrives. It's not much of a bet.

How to Make Contact

The *Inside Track* method of contacting headhunters consists of sending an *Inside Track* resume and a cover letter. Do not call headhunters unless you're returning their call. If they don't call you, they're not interested in talking with you. If they do call, they've got something that might be appropriate for one of their job orders. A few headhunters will save your letter and resume if it looks like something they might use at a later date. A very few firms actually maintain large central files of submitted resumes for areas in which they do a lot of searching.

Occasionally, you'll get a "please update your resume form" from one of these firms. What's usually happening is that the research department just got a new person and they're making an attempt to clean things up. The majority of headhunters will hang on to your resume for a few days (in a big pile on the corner of the desk) before they toss it. Most often, they'll simply throw it out as soon as they've determined that they don't have a current job order for which you'd be appropriate. A few headhunters maintain small private filing systems (stuffing everything in a big bottom drawer) which they'll refer to once in a while before it gets so crowded that they've got to throw some out.

The Challenge You Face

The above discussion demonstrates that the challenge you face in contacting headhunters is different from the one faced in responding to ads. With ads, you're trying to show them that you're the one for the specific opening mentioned in the ad. With headhunters, you have two simultaneous objectives. The first is to make it easy for them to determine whether and how you'll fit any of their open job orders. The second objective is to demonstrate that you're an impressive and polished professional who would represent them well to the client (that is, get the job so they can collect the fee). The first objective is realized by means of a detailed, concise *Inside Track* cover letter. The second objective is accomplished by presenting yourself with an impeccable *Inside Track* resume and at least decent credentials for the jobs you're seeking.

The competition you face is also much different. Larger headhunting firms sometimes receive five hundred resumes in a single day, sometimes many more. Most of them are unsolicited; they're sent by job seekers who hope they can fit a current job order. A very small proportion are solicited (in response to ads placed by the headhunters). It's a major paper-shuffling exercise. A secretary or receptionist opens the resumes and, if he or she is an "administrative assistant," has the authority to throw out grossly deficient resumes. The remainder are then sorted into piles on the basis of each job seeker's stated qualifications and the assignment areas in which the various headhunters operate. Most of the unsolicited letters and resumes are confusing and poorly targeted. The only reason the headhunters even bother to read them is that they're afraid they'll miss a candidate for one of their open job orders. In the midst of this turmoil, your cover letter and resume will arrive, alone and without you there to guide and protect them. On their own, they will have to make it past the receptionist to the correct headhunter and then impress him or her so that you'll get a call if there's a job order that fits. The secondary goal, if there's no job order that fits your resume, is to get your resume stuffed into their bottom drawer in the hopes that maybe you'll get a call next month or next year (if they remember your resume and haven't thrown out the top layer lately).

In essence, you're not up against the competition of other peoples' qualifications as much as you're fighting it out against the confusion of an overcrowded system and the low odds that an open job order in your area will be on the headhunter's desk when and if your resume makes it. That's one of the reasons why you've got to launch a great many of them to get results.

The Inside Track Cover Letter

What it looks like

Figure 6.1 presents an example of an *Inside Track* cover letter to headhunters. It should be an individually typed (not photocopied), right-side unjustified (if word-processed) letter with an inside address as shown. It's going to take a lot of typing or word-processing support to launch a large mailing. Unless you're a highly skilled and patient typist, don't consider doing it on a typewriter. See Chapter 11 for a discussion of word processing. On the other hand, large word-processing jobs aren't cheap. As Chapter 3 points out, each letter could cost a dollar or more. That's a lot of money when you're talking about three hundred to two thousand letters. (A later section of this chapter presents an "economy model" approach for mailings to headhunters which is much cheaper but less effective.) The stationery and type style should match that of the resume. Keep it to one page if you can. It should never be longer than one and a half pages with ample open space and wide margins.

Its characteristics

The *Inside Track* cover letter shown in Figure 6.1 has several characteristics that distinguish it from cover letters sent in response to ads

John Jones
2333 Maple Leaf Court
Upper Creek, MD 21234
(301) 555-9999

September 12, 1986

Mr. I. V. Gotabody
Tightpack and Associates
345 Main Avenue
New York, NY 10116

Dear Mr. Gotabody:

I am seeking to make a positive career move. The titles of positions for which I am qualified include:

DIRECTOR OF TRAINING

DIRECTOR OF MANAGEMENT DEVELOPMENT

DIRECTOR OF ORGANIZATION/MANAGEMENT DEVELOPMENT

SENIOR MANAGEMENT DEVELOPMENT SPECIALIST

CORPORATE/INDUSTRIAL PSYCHOLOGIST

I am currently employed as a Training Manager for one of the largest plants of a Fortune 50 company. My responsibilities include management development, executive coaching, supervisory training of production managers, and coordination of the employee involvement program. I have extensive knowledge of current theory and research as well as comprehensive applied experience in two other business and industrial environments.

My qualifications include an M.A. in Industrial Psychology with a B.A. in Business Administration.

I am seeking a compensation package in the $40–45K range. I am willing to relocate anywhere in the continental U.S. for an appropriate opportunity.

I would be pleased to discuss my qualifications with you in the event that you have an open search for a professional with my credentials. My detailed resume is enclosed.

Thank you for your attention and courtesy. I look forward to hearing from you.

Respectfully,

John Jones

Enclosure

Figure 6.1 Example of an *Inside Track* Cover Letter to a Headhunter

(although many of the business courtesy and format considerations are identical to those described in Chapter 5 and won't be repeated here). Among the critical design elements demonstrated in the example are the following:

1. A list of the job titles for which you're appropriate. Nobody is going to take the time to analyze your letter and resume to see if they can figure out which positions you're interested in. If you think the headhunter will do that work, you're going to be disappointed. If what they need doesn't leap right out and bite them on the nose, you're out of luck. The listing of typical job titles makes it easy for them to relate your materials to what they need; they think in terms of open position titles, and they even talk that way. ("I've got a radar engineer still open, but I closed a compensation manager last week.") Your listing of titles will enable them to instantly decide if you're on their hot list. Don't give more than seven titles, and don't scatter them across several functions or industries. If they get the impression that you're shopping for anything, the good headhunters (the ones with contacts and clients who respect them) will toss your resume. If you're not sure of which titles to use, look at the ads for jobs in your area.
2. A brief teaser about your top two or three best qualifications. Just whet their appetite; don't feed them. This will make them more curious about the resume while at the same time demonstrating that you're organized and concise (because they won't see many such letters).
3. A brief statement about your educational or professional qualifications. Don't list everything; just drop a few crumbs so they'll be led to believe there is rich pastry in your resume.
4. A brief statement about your desired compensation levels and relocation preferences. Some experts would tell you to omit this, but that's just causing the headhunter more problems and possibly making it too much trouble to call you, especially if he or she has a candidate almost as good whose desired salary is known. If you want to enhance your prior salary levels in order to get more money on the next job, the headhunter probably won't be overly concerned as long as you appear qualified for what you're asking. After all, the more you get, the more he or she gets. But, whatever your circumstance, put down something about what you're looking for. If you don't put it in the letter, it will be one of the first questions they'll ask if they call. State your geographical preferences in general. If you're looking for something in your area, say so. Don't present an exhaustive list of areas you won't go to, such as "relocate to any major city except Detroit, New York, Chicago, Los Angeles. . . ." Negatives are never good, and you don't want to appear picky; it could signal that you'd embarrass

them with their client. If you've got something against big cities, use "Willing to relocate. Prefer a rural, small town, or suburban location." That gets the point across and makes you seem reasonable and objective. You can always get more picky when the location of a potential job is disclosed.

5. An "I would be pleased" statement exactly like the one shown in Figure 6.1. It's important to mention that you'd like to talk if they have an open search. This reassures them that you know how they operate (many people don't have a clear understanding of headhunters) and once again reminds them of their open search problems as they scan your resume.
6. Don't mention the enclosed resume until right before the "thanks" sentence. This reminds them that there's more great stuff just waiting to be read.
7. A final "thanks" and "I'm waiting by the phone" statement exactly as shown in the example. They expect it, and it's just good business courtesy.

Things to avoid

1. Do not state that you are looking for a "challenge" and are seeking a "fulfilling position" in place of specific job titles. To them that is worse than useless; it makes them sick. They see it hundreds of times every day.
2. Don't mention personal data in the letter. You want it to be hard-hitting and businesslike. They can find out if you're married by reading the resume (where such data are expected).
3. Don't mention specific company names in the letter; use "Fortune 50," "fast-growing manufacturer," and such to tease them into reading the resume.
4. Don't mention specific reasons why you're looking. Anything could be a turnoff. Be general and positive, as in "looking for a positive career move." Don't mention more money as your primary interest in a new job. It's 90 percent of what's on every worker's mind, but it's still forbidden to mention it in the open during a job search. If you're out of work, don't mention it specifically. State instead, "My experience includes. . . ." They'll see your job status on the resume if you're candid, but after reading that far they may be interested. Headhunters don't like to sell out-of-date goods, and that's how many employers view the unemployed, so try to conceal your out-of-work status for as long as possible. Try the consultant ploy described in Chapter 4.

The Economy Model

Few people who are out of work can afford to spend hundreds of dollars at one time in order to send a mass mailing of word-processed cover letters. Even many who are employed would be loathe to spend that much money. You can do it cheaper and still get the job done. It won't be as good, but you can save a lot of money that might be urgently needed for necessities later in the search. The economy model consists of the exact same letter content as that shown in Figure 6.1 but without the inside address of the headhunter. You simply space down four to six spaces under the date and start the letter with "Dear Sir or Madam:" (which is OK since it's not going to a specific individual). Have your original letter word processed onto plain white paper and then get as many copies as you need either offset printed or photocopied (on a very good machine) onto your own stationery. If you're going with the economy model, I suggest that you purchase somewhat cheaper stationery (but still good quality) than you'll be using for the other strategies. Use this economy stationery for the resume, cover letter, and envelopes.

There's no sense pretending that the economy approach isn't less effective than the full *Inside Track* approach. If you're only going to a narrow sample of two hundred headhunters, I'd try to use the full *Inside Track* approach. But it won't hurt you as much as you might think, based on the discussions of earlier chapters. The headhunters know that everyone is sending out hundreds and thousands of resumes, so they won't be as offended as you might imagine. Still, you lose the chance to make the impression that you're only contacting "a few choice and carefully selected executive recruiters whose reputations I know." (Never tell them how many you're really contacting; they hate it.) There's also the sacrifice of the nice associations a proper letter conveys about you. But money is money. And the headhunter is interested in finding someone for the open jobs. So even if he or she knows it's a mass-produced form letter, if you've got what it takes you'll get a call. The problem is that many will be put off by the form letter and won't want to look for the details. The unique appearance of the *Inside Track* cover letter list of job titles will help offset this tendency.

A word of warning

Don't consider trying to use a variant of the economy approach for strategies 1 and 3. In those strategies, a form letter will invariably bring the cold kiss of the trashcan to the sweet, soft, warm neck of your beautiful resume.

Chapter 7

Strategy Number 3: Direct Solicitation to Executives and Organizations

Direct solicitation techniques attempt to locate or create unadvertised jobs by means of contacting specific individuals within organizations. All sorts of so-called experts recommend direct solicitation techniques as an extremely effective job search strategy. Such recommendations get a lot of press and attention in general because they seem to make intuitive sense. "Taking it to the head shed," "going right to the top," and "seeing the man in charge" are concepts that seem downright American. As you should understand if you've read the previous chapters (especially Chapters 2 and 3), what seems natural and reasonable is often bad news in job searching. So it is in this case. At best, trying to contact executives directly is a low-probability approach.

Networking, which is the practice of contacting an executive (generally by phone) under the pretense of "just wanting to get your thoughts on business" and then trying to get him or her to refer you to other people, has fallen into disrepute lately. It's about time. It would have happened sooner, but the experts kept pushing it, some executives didn't catch on too quickly, and at first many executives were flattered to be asked for advice by so many sharp young tigers. Soon, however, the trickle of calls turned into a deluge as everybody started using the technique. Now executives are loathe to waste their time on legions of callers who are looking for jobs but who try to act like they're just visiting for advice. It's a shallow ploy and not a very good one. It also wastes a lot of your time that might be better spent in more profitable job search activities.

There are five basic variants of the direct solicitation strategy. One of them is, in my opinion, worthless. Three others can be marginally effective if properly implemented. One of the techniques is an outstanding career-building tool but isn't an effective way to find a job within six to eighteen months. If you've got extra time and resources that can't be effectively allocated to strategies 1 and 2 (Chapters 5 and 6), you may be able to increase your odds of success by using one or two of the techniques described in this chapter. Before you make any

DIRECTION SOLICITATION 115

selection decisions, read the entire chapter and pick only those techniques with which you're comfortable and which are best suited to your search situation.

Basic Guidelines

If you want the best results possible from any of the direct solicitation techniques, it's essential that you carefully follow a number of general guidelines. Direct solicitation techniques, by their very nature, make unannounced demands on the time of the persons who are the targets of the solicitation. They're not all that disposed to help you out in the best of cases. If you use less than perfect materials or conduct yourself in a careless manner, your solicitation will fall on deaf and irritated ears. Good technique isn't enough because there will be all sorts of fair to good competition doing the same thing. You've got to be outstanding in your approach, technique, and materials. If you follow the general guidelines below and implement the techniques presented later in the chapter, your materials and tactics will be better than those of anyone who hasn't bought this book.

Production values

It's essential to use high-quality matching stationery for all letters and resumes. If you're using a cheaper (but still good-quality) stationery for mass mailings to headhunters or for responding to ads, upgrade the quality of your materials for direct solicitation efforts. If you're going to be trying variant 4 ("Let's be friends"), use monarch-size (7 by 10 inches) personal stationery and matching envelopes with your name and address printed on them. The smaller stationery will increase the recipient's feelings of personal involvement and will serve to differentiate your letter from the hundreds that arrive on business-size stationery. Of course, others will be using monarch stationery, too. You shouldn't use monarch stationery for any direct solicitation attempt (such as variant 2, "Personnel end run") that involves sending a copy of your resume. The size difference between your resume and the letter would look strange. Worse, the obvious "what have you got" message that a resume infers would cancel out any positive warm feelings that might result from using the smaller stationery. Rather than sending a resume with your cover letter when trying variants 3 ("See my greatness"), 2 ("Personnel end run"), and 1 ("In before the ad"), you could send a letter resume on monarch-size stationery. Chapter 4 outlines the construction of letter resumes. A letter resume can be more effective than a cover letter with a resume for variants 3 and 1 but generally won't do as well for variant 2 because a letter resume isn't as easy to digest. When there are a lot of easily read resumes around, you don't want to be sending something that's harder to interpret. The typing of the letter must be perfect. If you can't do it perfectly, have it word processed. Be sure to use unjustified right edges on all letters. It's assumed that you'll be following all of the normal and expected courtesies of business correspondence that were detailed in the two preceding chapters.

Selecting, qualifying, and verifying your targets

The effectiveness of any direct solicitation campaign is limited by the accuracy and appropriateness of the target list who will be solicited. Before you send anything or make a single phone call, invest some time in your research effort. Go to the library and use the reference section. If you're unfamiliar with reference resources in the business section, ask the reference librarians for help. Tell them what you're trying to do ("I'm attempting to identify companies and executives in this industry, area, or profession. I need names, addresses, and phone numbers"). Tell them you're looking for a job. They've helped thousands of others find the same kinds of data; they know what you need. They can save you a lot of time and effort if you're not already familiar with the reference materials. Some of the sources you'll probably be using are the *Million Dollar Directory*, *Poors Register of Corporation Directors and Executives*, and the *Thomas Register*. There are many hundreds more. Each state usually has its own directories of manufacturers and businesses, industries have their own (the banking industry has the *American Bank Directory*), and professions have their own (the *Who's Who in Electronics* lists thousands of electronics manufacturers). There are even directories of directories such as the *Guide to American Directories* and the *Directory of Directories*.

Use the most up-to-date directories you can find. People switch jobs, are promoted or fired, and reorganizations take place. If you send something out with the wrong name, it's wasted. If you're sending out very large numbers of solicitation letters, you probably won't have the time or money to call and verify that each addressee on your list is correct. In that case, it's essential to use the latest source. If you were using the directories to research a narrower solicitation (such as a list of all of the directors of electrical engineering in your city), you could probably afford to call each listing and verify the correct name, title, and address. Do this if you can.

The Five Variants

The following sections will present the purpose, approach, and method for each of the five variants of direct solicitation techniques.

Variant 1: In before the ad

Purpose. The aim is to get the job seeker into an interview for an upcoming opening before the position is advertised, thereby beating the competition to the punch.

Approach. Variant 1 isn't unreasonable, but it has a low probability of paying off compared to answering ads and using headhunters. Very few organizations have empty slots just sitting there. Nature abhors a vacuum no less than any aggressive manager abhors an empty slot; if it's empty long enough, someone is apt to decide it's not needed. If a job hasn't been filled for a while, it's usually because of internal politics or the organization's inability to locate a highly specialized applicant. There's not much you can do about internal politics. If you're in a highly specialized field and you can target organizations and managers who have a high probability of needing your specific talents, direct solicitation is indicated (but if you're that specialized, you'd probably do just as well through carefully selected headhunters). If the slot's been sitting empty for a while, chances are that it's being advertised, is assigned to a headhunter, or is "on hold."

Method. The objective in sending an "In before the ad" letter (with your resume) is to present your qualifications to organizations and individuals who are most likely to have an immediate or shortly forthcoming need for someone with your qualifications. The letter you use must do the following:

1. Let them know immediately that you're looking for a job.
2. Present your qualifications concisely.
3. Make it easy for them to determine where you'll fit in best.
4. Demonstrate that you can make significant contributions in their area of operation.
5. Tease them into reading the accompanying resume.
6. Attempt to gain a commitment by mentioning that you'll be following up with a call.

Figure 7.1 presents an example of an "In before the ad" cover letter. The letter is an adaptation of the headhunter letter shown in Figure 6.1. Notice that the letter leads right in with the "I am currently employed" statement. If you are employed, use it right up front; it increases your apparent value. If you're not employed, substitute something along the lines of "My successful experience as a training professional includes" and then continue as in the example. The second paragraph explains the purpose of the letter once the qualifications hook has been dropped. That's followed by a listing of a few of the major accomplishments that should be most appealing to the reader. Don't use more than five; you don't want to make it difficult, and you want them to have to read the resume to get the whole story. Next come the obligatory and expected statements about educational qualifications (keep it short) and your confidence that you can make

John Jones
2333 Maple Leaf Court
Upper Creek, MD 21234
(301) 555-9999

September 12, 1986

Dr. John J. Johnson
Vice-President of Industrial Relations
Blech Industries
231 Smokestack Road
Piscataway, NJ 08854

Dear Dr. Johnson:

I am currently employed as a Training Manager for one of the largest plants of a Fortune 50 company. My responsibilities include management development, executive coaching, supervisory training of production managers, and coordination of the employee involvement program. I have extensive knowledge of current theory and research as well as comprehensive applied experience in two other business and industrial environments.

I am looking for a more demanding and challenging position which will provide me with an opportunity to make substantive contributions in all areas of training and development. I'm contacting you in the hope that you have a current or forthcoming opportunity for an experienced and successful training professional.

The contributions I've made to my present and past employers include:

*** Development of complete management development curricula for middle and senior managers in two organizations.
*** Establishment of an extremely successful employee involvement program in a 2500-person manufacturing facility which enabled management to improve quality 15% with a cost reduction of 13%.
*** Successful design and implementation of large-scale technical training programs which contributed to a 22% plantwide decrease in scrap and down time.

I can make the same type of substantial contributions to your organization. My qualifications include an M.A. in Industrial Psychology with a B.A. in Business Administration.

I would be pleased to discuss my qualifications with you in the event that you have a need for a professional with my credentials. I will call your office next week to determine whether we have any common interests. My detailed resume is enclosed.

Thank you for your attention. I look forward to speaking with you next week.

Respectfully,

John Jones

Enclosure

Figure 7.1 Example of a Variant 1 ("In Before the Ad") Cover Letter
---

great contributions. Only then mention that the resume is enclosed. Close with the expected statement that you'd like to talk with them about any potential openings, and then state that you'll call next week. The expected call will motivate them at least to glance at your resume; they know they might have to talk with you. If you're sending out hundreds of letters, keep in mind that you'll be making a lot of calls. Call them no later than a week after they will have received the letter. A follow-up letter about six weeks later will increase your odds, but such follow-up takes more time and money. If your campaign is large, you might want to forego some of the calls or any follow-up letters in favor of a larger initial mailing effort. I don't recommend follow-up letters or calls for all launches of large campaigns; you won't get the return for the investment. It's better either to limit your campaign to a more select target list which you can follow up or to expend all of your resources on a larger initial list and only follow up the really high-probability contacts.

Variant 2: Personnel end run

Purpose. For a job that's advertised, you attempt to contact the hiring manager directly and impress him or her enough to get an interview. This variant attempts to skip the first hurdle at the personnel department.

Approach. If the job you're after is already assigned to a headhunter or is being advertised, variant 1 becomes variant 2. The "Personnel end run" technique consists of simultaneously responding to both the personnel department and the hiring manager in response to an ad. Of course, it's only feasible when you can identify and locate the hiring manager. It's nearly impossible and not worth the trouble for blind ads. It's pretty expensive (for phone calls) if the employer is out of town. For normal local ads, however, it's relatively easy to determine the identity of the hiring manager. Simply call the organization and ask the switchboard operator for the name of the person who runs the function or department associated with the ad. I'm assuming you understand the structure of titles and departments in your specialty area. Start calling and asking questions about who's in charge of what. It's usually easy and takes only a call or two.

Variant 2 sounds good, and it would be a laudable enough practice were it not for the fact that the hiring manager will most likely be swamped with all sorts of resumes and applications received through personnel. He or she isn't just sitting there at an empty desk waiting for a great letter from you. However, a nicely written cover letter addressed and sent directly to the hiring manager in response to an ad will get delivered and does have a chance to make an additional positive impression. If you decide to try this technique, you'll have to decide whether the added benefit is worth the time and effort required to track down the identity of the hiring manager for each advertised position. If you're responding to a lot of ads, it could take a lot of time. You might consider using this technique for a small number of choice positions where you believe you're already one of the top candidates. In that case, send the usual letter to personnel and then send a "Personnel end run" letter directly to the hiring manager.

Method. The "Personnel end run" letter consists of a simple adaptation of the "face down through the cactus" cover letter (Figure 5.5) with an added supplementary qualifications section (Figure 5.4). Of course, unlike the blind ad situation shown in Figure 5.4, you'd know all the names, titles, and so on. All that's required is to alter the first paragraph to read as shown in Figure 7.2.

Variant 3: "See my greatness"

Purpose. Here you are trying to motivate the creation of a new position (or push someone already there out of the way) exclusively for your talents.

Approach. This variant is a joke, yet it's the solicitation technique we hear the most about in the job search media. The stories of job seekers

---

I am contacting you in regard to the recent advertisement you placed in the Wall Street Journal for a Nuclear Fuel Executive. I have responded to the personnel office (use the name of the contact if it's given in the ad) as the advertisement instructed, but I felt that my qualifications are such an ideal match that it would be appropriate for me to contact you directly. I have enclosed a detailed resume for your review.

Figure 7.2 Suggested First Paragraph for a Variant 2 ("Personnel End Run") Cover Letter.

who get great jobs simply because they impress an executive have been told so often that it seems as if we all personally know such a lucky one. Such events are 1 in 100,000 shots, with the 1 usually being a young manager who impresses an older chief executive of the opposite sex and is suddenly recognized as a great talent. Even if you wanted to try your hand at this type of job searching, you'll still have to find a method of making contact with the executives. Regardless of your skills or contacts, very few executives have the power or the motivation to create a slot out of thin air. Almost no middle managers have such authority.

This technique, at best, amounts to a watered-down and less effective version of variant 1. When you send an unsolicited job search letter to an executive, the best you can hope for in most cases is to have it end up in personnel. Those executives who have the power to create a spot for you are so high up the corporate ladder that you'll never get to them unless you devote weeks of effort to each one. And even then you won't get their attention without doing outrageous things that will alienate the executive or his or her secretary. If you doubt it, try right now to get through to the president of a major corporation on the phone. You could use the often recommended angry customer routine, but when you confess you're out of luck. If you try mail, you're no better off. Powerful executives don't read unsolicited mail unless one of their top people brings it to their attention. Their secretaries open all of their mail (including the ones that say "eyes only," "deeply personal," and "wired to kill if opened by other than the addressee"). Their secretaries open *everything*. If it's a solicitation of any kind, it goes in the trash or to personnel. From then on it's personnel's problem, not theirs. At best, you'll get the standard form letter about "keeping your resume on file."

Method. This technique isn't recommended, but that won't stop a lot of you who insist on learning the hard way. If you're going to try it, do it right. Figure 7.3 presents a sample "See my greatness" letter. Essentially, the letter is a hard-hitting restatement of portions of the summary of qualifications and achievements sections of the candidate's *Inside Track* resume. If the letter becomes outrageously hard-hitting, it becomes a nonstandard piece of correspondence and belongs with some of the techniques discussed in Chapter 8. The letter shown in Figure 7.3 is based on the Marlene Flabeaux resume example shown in Figure 4.23.

You'll notice that the letter is addressed to the president of the company. There's no sense trying this ploy if you don't go to the top. The letter begins with an immediate statement of outstanding qualifications and then lists a number of highlighted achievements taken right from the resume. Use achievements that have numbers in them. Then summarize in paragraph form the main features of the summary of qualifications section of your resume. It reduces your odds to state a

Marlene Flabeaux
P.O. Box 23506
Everytown, KY 40222
(502) 555-9999

September 2, 1986

Mr. Buford Kremple
President
Kremple and Sons Health Care, Inc.
One Anna Kremple Place
Kremple Park
Kremple, MD 21136

Dear Mr. Kremple:

I am a health-care executive with exceptional qualifications and an outstanding record of achievements in the health-care industry. I have:

*** Founded and profitably operated (18% before tax profits) my own home-health-care firm which I sold at a profit.

*** Increased the weekly billings of a branch of a major health-care provider from 800 to 2100 (262% increase).

*** Reduced staff 7% and cut nonstaff costs another 8% while improving service in a major hospital.

*** Planned and directed numerous sales and marketing campaigns including cold calls on physicians, direct mail, and media advertising.

My preference is to operate in a lean, "profits come first" environment. My experience encompasses operations and general management in a variety of health-care settings. I possess exceptional talents in leading, motivating, and developing professional and hourly staff.

My qualifications include an M.B.A. in marketing and a B.S.N. I have successfully worked in several corporate environments at the director and vice-president level. My resume is enclosed.

Although I am currently employed, I am seeking a more challenging position with an industry leader which will permit me to apply my entire range of skills and qualifications.

I will call you in a week in order to talk with you personally.

Thank you for your attention.

Respectfully,

Marlene Flabeaux

Enclosure

Figure 7.3 Sample of a Variant 3 ("See My Greatness") Cover Letter

specific position title in which you're interested. If you do, the letter will get sent to some manager who will do what all middle managers do with such hand-me-downs from the head shed: they throw it out. State the expected "looking for more challenge," mention that you're employed if you are, and then say that you'll call in a week. Good luck on getting through.

Variant 4: "Let's be friends"

Purpose. This variant aims to build a base for future communications and a possible professional relationship which could lead to a position or a significant referral to a position in the future.

Approach. This is the only purpose for which direct solicitation is reliable and appropriate. Yet it's hardly ever used by the individuals who could best utilize its power: successful, employed persons who are attempting to build solid long-term relationships throughout their industry or profession. The ultimate purposes of such relationships are as follows:

1. To obtain useful information on the industry or profession.
2. To benefit from proximity with persons of power and influence.
3. To locate talent and resources when they're needed.
4. To establish a circle of successful contacts who respect your abilities and who may assist you in moving up to a better position.

These purposes don't represent those of a job search technique, but this is networking in its best and most complete form. As such, it's not manipulative or one-sided. It's an attempt to promote long-term professional relationships that have the possibility of benefiting both parties. Of course, you hope to benefit in the form of a better job down the line, but the technique won't work if you even imply such a motivation in your activities. People do favors for and look out for the interests of business colleagues and friends whom they trust. Once you ingratiate yourself with a circle of influential managers and executives, any goodies that get thrown in your direction will be viewed by all concerned as natural and normal courtesies that are a by-product of the business relationship; what helps you helps them. Once you've established such relationships, you'll occasionally be expected to help out others if you can. Such assistance will strengthen the relationship. The down side is that it takes a lot of these relationships to increase the odds that the help you need will be there when you need it. No matter how close you get to a highly placed executive, most of the time he or she won't be able to help in a given situation because of other circumstances.

Getting a better job through this technique is something that can't be forced. It requires long-term business relationships built upon mutual concerns, assistance, and trust; it has to happen naturally. In order to apply it correctly, you must maintain contacts with follow-up letters, occasional phone calls, some socializing, and so on. It takes a lot of time, effort, and hard work. It's an outstanding way to build your career, but it's a lousy way to try to get a job in a short time. This chapter will provide some guidelines for implementing this technique, but don't use it until you're in a job, industry, or career in which you plan to stay.

Method. The best way to initiate such associations is through business and professional groups. Participating in community groups and projects is an even better way to meet a lot of influential executives. (Don't waste time with groups that don't have any high rollers.) Professional associations are good initial contact points.

If you're unemployed and already belong to some of these associations and groups, use them without hesitation. It isn't "Let's be friends," but you need all the help you can get. Ask around and call everyone you know, have worked with, or may have met in the course of any projects. Tell them you're out of work and what you're looking for, and give them some resumes to spread around. You can never tell whom they might know or talk to.

People enjoy helping those with whom they share some common interests, especially if it's a civic or community interest. If you don't have such contacts and prefer to use a more targeted technique, pick out the people with whom you want to establish a relationship and begin a correspondence. If they've made a speech or public comment, if they have written an article, or if their firm has done anything noteworthy, write them a letter and compliment them. Figure 7.4 presents an example of one such letter. The letter is the reaction of John Jones to an article written by Dr. Johnson. You'll note that Figure 7.4 contains absolutely no hint of "What can you do for me?" If it did, Dr. Johnson would see through it and toss it out. The letter does several things that are very important when attempting to establish a long-distance "Let's be friends" effort:

1. It flatters the reader ("leading executive").
2. It agrees with the reader's viewpoint ("obvious limitations," "scathing refutation").
3. It contains enough data to give the appearance that the writer understands the situation and has been following it.
4. It makes a suggestion about some technical or thought-provoking aspect of the situation that will assist the reader in remembering the writer as someone with possibilities. (In the example, it's the mention of "0 or 1 variables.")
5. It thanks the writer again and expresses a hope that they can talk together some time.
6. It will get through the secretarial screening because it appears to be a legitimate piece of correspondence (which it is).

The things a "Let's be friends" letter must *not* do are the following:

John Jones
2333 Maple Leaf Court
Upper Creek, MD 21234
(301) 555-2345

September 12, 1986

John J. Johnson, Ph.D.
Vice-President of Industrial Relations
Blech Industries
231 Smokestack Road
Piscataway, NJ 08854

Dear Dr. Johnson:

I want to compliment you on your recent article in Human Resources Management Magazine/Chronicler. Few leading executives have been willing to speak up about the obvious limitations of the Farfel-Diddly technique of smooth compensation regression lines.

It was a pleasure to read such a scathing refutation of the premise made by Mr. Levy in his article, "Farfel-Diddly: A technique to rescue job descriptions" which appeared in the June 1985 issue. I don't think you left any doubt as to the serious flaws of Farfel-Diddly when used in technical career ladder systems. It will be interesting to see if Mr. Levy replies.

I've often wondered if there might be any possibility of saving Farfel-Diddly by using a multivariate correlational approach in which the subjective factors are coded as discrete 0 or 1 variables. What do you think?

Once again, thanks for the great article. I hope we have the chance to meet in person and talk in the future.

Sincerely,

John Jones

Figure 7.4 Example of a Variant 4 ("Let's Be Friends") Letter

1. Mention anything about jobs, employment situations, or companies (unless it's directly relevant to the discussion, as in "We've experimented with this technique at Dorf, Inc., but we don't have enough sample size to tell if it's working").
2. Say anything negative about anything other than the reader's own statements. Who knows? Mr. Levy and Dr. Johnson may be buddies who play golf every week.
3. Ask for anything. Never ask for anything in the first contact. And never ask for anything that puts you in a position of inferiority,

such as asking for an autographed copy of the article. You want the association to be one of professional equals.
4. Ask for a meeting or tell them that you'll call. Either one is a dead giveaway that you're on the make for a job.

The letter should go out on monarch-size stationery and matching envelopes. Don't ever use business stationery. And, of course, don't even think about enclosing your resume.

Follow up with another letter in a few months. Use a related topic to jog the reader's memory. After two letters it's OK to make a call, but be careful not to ask for anything. It's still too early. Use the call to get advice about where to look for information or technical assistance on a topic of interest to the executive. Or ask the executive if he or she might know of someone for a position you might have opening up (for a job type in which the executive is interested). Make sure that you know enough about the topic of discussion not to be discovered. If you get a suggestion to call another executive, you can then start to build an additional relationship with the new contact. Follow up any phone calls with a brief two- or three-sentence thank-you note on personal stationery. If you're lucky, you might get something going that will pay off way down the road.

As you can see, this technique takes time and some effort. If you're willing to invest two hours per week (and if you can't find time on the job, you're in sad shape) in this type of activity, you can build up a solid base of contacts. If you happen to be traveling on business and are staying in a city where you have contacts, call them up and see if you can meet for lunch or breakfast. If you're having some big event in your area that's related to their professional interests, drop them a line and ask if they plan to come. If you find out they're going to be at a professional convention or meeting, arrange to meet them briefly. Don't hang around. Act like you have other pressing business.

Then, after at least a year and preferably two, when you next need a job or some other important help, go for it. Send them each a personal note explaining the situation and asking if they could please help you. Don't try to slick them; just honestly ask for help. Some of them will gladly give it if they can.

Variant 5: "Who da ya know?"

Purpose. The aim is to locate or create a position through an ever-expanding series of networking phone calls.

Approach. This is the direct solicitation technique that gave networking a bad name. It's the one to which most poorly planned direct solicitation campaigns usually deteriorate. It usually consists of calling executives and managers in an attempt to get them to see you in person. If they won't let you come in to interview for a job, you try to pump them on the phone for other contacts. You then start the process over with each new contact. If you do enough of it, you'll eventually get something. Enough in this case means many hundreds, maybe thousands of calls. Worse yet, few of the interviews will be worthwhile. As mentioned in Chapter 3, many will be guilt interviews given as a courtesy to the person who referred you to them. It's a waste of time in terms of the benefits you can expect.

As indicated in the discussion of variant 3, executives are getting fed up with poorly disguised calls from job seekers. When you do manage to get through, you'll most likely get a quick brushoff or a referral to the first person who comes to their mind. If you direct your efforts at middle managers, you'll get through on a larger proportion of your calls, but it won't help. They're not the ones who have what you need. Of course, if you spend enough time at it, you'll eventually find a position that's available, but then you're actually employing variants 1 or 2. Most of the time you'll simply be shuffled along from one disinterested caller to another, lost in a netherworld of "I wish I could help, but," "Why don't you call so-and-so?" and "We may have a position opening up in six months, but. . . ." You'll make dozens and dozens of calls, and you'll get nowhere. At best, you'll locate a few openings that are already being advertised. And to do it right you'll have to send follow-up thank-you letters to the most important contacts. That's a lot of work to invest in a low-probability effort.

Method. If you're going to try this technique, target the companies you want to go after and just start calling. Never give up. Call every single referral you get; you're playing the odds. This means that you have to follow every trail. Use as your starting line, "Ms. Frobish, my name is Bill Monroe, and I'm interested in finding a position as an accounts receivable manager. Mr. Doe suggested that I give you a call. When can I come in to talk with you?" If you can't get an appointment, ask, "Do you have any openings?" If they say no, counter with, "Whom do you suggest I call?" Get something from every call.

Once you make the first few calls, you'll have plenty of names to drop during future calls. Start with personnel managers, as they usually know a lot of people. Ask them, "Whom do you suggest I might call in your organization to find out what their plans might be for the next year or so?" Most will tell you a few names just to get rid of you. (If you think I'm being pessimistic about what you'll run into, wait until you start!) Work your way up as high as you can in every company you contact. Drop the names of the biggest fish you've hooked as often as you can.

"Hi, Ms. Jacobs. My name is Bill Monroe. Mr. Foggybottom, the president of Flashburn Electronics, felt that you might be able to assist me in locating a position as an accounts receivable manager. Can I come in and meet with you for a few minutes?" If you can't get in, ask, "Do you know of any opportunities anywhere else?" If that doesn't get you something, try, "Whom do you suggest I call?" If you've got the time, send thank-you notes to the high-level executives you talk to. Then follow up with another call a week or two later and ask for more help. Don't worry if they get angry; if they don't have a job for you, who cares?

When calling a high-level executive, you can increase your odds by attempting to contact him or her when the protective screen of underlings is thinnest. The best times are between 6:30 A.M. and 9:00 A.M., between 5:00 P.M. and 9:00 P.M., and on Saturday mornings between 8:00 A.M. and noon. At these times, they're often in the office alone and may pick up the phone.

If you're going to have any success with this variant at all, it's essential to avoid getting caught in the "Send me a resume and I'll see what I can do" trap when you finally make telephone contact with something that may have meat on it. That's generally a brushoff. You can't afford to waste time on calls that don't get you in to see them or at least get you a few more names, preferably higher up the ladder. You've got to work hard on every call. The best way to maximize your results is to construct a telechart for yourself.

A telechart is simply a script used to conduct telephone cold calls. It makes it much easier to deal with any rejections or barriers. All of the sophisticated telephone solicitation companies use them. Figure 7.5 presents a sample telechart for cold call "Who da ya know?" solicitations. Adapt Figure 7.5 to your own campaign. Imagine every possible rejection line and then write a response that doesn't take no for an answer. Have two or three responses to each rejection. When you get a rejection, don't think about it, don't take it personally, just read the line from the telechart. If they reject again, read the next response. Typically, after your return of service to a few rejections, they'll give in and agree to meet you. At the very least, if you can't get an appointment, you should be able to get a few names and addresses for future calls. If you get a new rejection, simply add it to the list and think up a few replies. Try them on your next call. Don't worry about flubbing a few.

At first it will be difficult. Very soon you'll learn not to think about your responses and not to worry about the content of the call. You'll just read a reply from the telechart and wear them down. Start your campaign on lower-quality leads for a few days in order to polish your telechart and build your confidence. As you develop your telechart and cold call skills, your response repertoire will grow in quality and number.

Summary

The techniques described in this chapter are tedious and time-consuming. They're also no fun. The returns you'll get will be low, but

Hi, Mr./Ms. _____. My name is Bill Monroe. _____, the _____ of _____, felt that you might be able to assist me in locating a position as an accounts receivable manager. I'd like to come in and talk with you for a few minutes. When can we get together?

If *yes:*   Date and place _____

If   *don't have time or really too busy:*

1. I'll only take a few minutes of your time. How about _____ at _____?

2. I understand that you're very busy. Suppose we get together at _____ for breakfast/lunch/dinner?

3. I'm willing to work it in anytime you say. How about _____?

If   *I'll be out of town:*

1. No problem. What time would be convenient when you get back? I'll only need a few minutes. How about _____ at _____?

2. I'll drive you to the airport. We can talk on the way. What time should I pick you up?

If   *no meeting possible:*

1. Whom do you suggest I could call who might be able to help me?

2. Even the name of one colleague in the area would be helpful.

If   *don't know anyone:*

1. I'd really appreciate any help at all. Anyone who might know of something would be a big help.

2. Just one name would be very helpful. How about someone in your own company who might be able to help me?

If   *don't have time now:*

1. I understand. Suppose I call back _____ and promise not to take more than five minutes of your time.

Figure 7.5 Sample Telechart for Cold Call Telephone Solicitations

you can increase them by careful preparation and consistent attention. Even the "Who da ya know?" variant can be tremendously successful if you're willing to sit at the phone and make hundreds of calls, ignoring the rejections, swallowing the humiliations, and enduring the rudeness.

If you practice with the telechart, never take no for an answer, and pound away without fail, you'll get results. Few people can handle that kind of rejection (or work). Few people have the time, skill, and perseverance to mount direct solicitation campaigns that are sufficiently focused and large enough (in terms of items launched) to get results. They get discouraged and turn to other strategies. If you aren't ready to stand toe to toe with the Father of Rejection, don't waste your time with a large phone solicitation campaign. If you've got the guts to do the work and if you do it properly, you can be successful with the techniques presented in this chapter.

Chapter 8

Miscellaneous Strategies of Passing Interest

The techniques described in this chapter are worthless for 9,999 out of every 10,000 job search situations. Some require basic violations of common business etiquette, appearances, and courtesy. You won't get many job offers by demonstrating that you're not properly regimented or may not fit in after you're hired. Some of the strategies are impractical and out of touch with the manner in which the business world operates and makes decisions. There's no sense asking the wrong people the wrong questions. And some of the strategies are nothing more than tedious, outrageously low-probability wastes of time, effort, and resources. You don't need exercise; you need a job. Unfortunately, many of these worthless techniques are, if not enthusiastically praised by so-called job search experts, at least given nods of approval.

Why You'll Want to Use Them

You'll be drawn to these techniques at some point in your search if it lasts long enough. You'll be losing patience with doing the right things and then just waiting. In your frustration and anger, you'll want to do more and you'll want to do it more savagely. Many of the more flamboyant techniques in this chapter enable you to release all sorts of pent-up psychological and physical energy as you make the big move. If you lose control and try the more far-out strategies presented in this chapter, you'll release energy but you won't get results. Then you'll just be more frustrated and angry. It's natural to want results and to get angry when things aren't happening (good things, that is). You'll just have to live with it. After you've read this chapter, you'll understand that off-the-wall and semicrazy techniques won't do anything but get pointless attention and waste your time. The less bizarre techniques won't even get the pointless attention.

These strategies are appealing because they offer a more comforting view of the job search world. They suggest that there's an easier way than harsh and often cruel reality. For example, it's appealing to believe that executives read all of their mail, that they're always looking for top talent at your level, and that if you can get them to notice you they'll hire you. If you've read the earlier chapters, you know all of these beliefs are false. Yet it's hard to resist the pull of the "This one's on me" strategy. We all want to believe that someone is out there waiting to notice us. Most of the time, the only notice you'll get in the job search world is something like, "Say, Fred, hand me a few of those resumes, will you? I just spilled coffee all over the floor." That's life. The strategies presented in this chapter are based on false beliefs, ignorance of the business world's operations, and depression-induced hopes. Read about them, understand why they don't work, and then forget about using them.

What They Are

This one's on me

This is the job search equivalent of the free samples of soap, toothpaste, and cookies that are occasionally mailed to your door by consumer products companies. In "This one's on me," the job seeker sends a clever, bold, or cute letter to an executive or manager. The letter makes reference to or is completely built around some noncorrespondence item that's also included. For example, one job seeker opened his letter with "I know you are probably tired of reading stacks of resumes. I hate to inconvenience you with another one. Why not relax and have a cup of coffee while you read mine? It's on me. Simply open the enclosed packet, add water, sit back, relax, and read my resume." The job seeker had enclosed a single serving packet of instant coffee with the letter and resume. Sure, it's cute. And there's no denying that it's fun to design, send, and (most of all) receive such letters; it's much more exciting than sending or receiving the typical job search letter. I know that hundreds of you are dying to try it as soon as you can. Don't waste your time (or coffee). The added attention you'll get will be counterbalanced by the negative effect of the cuteness. In most people's minds, professionals do not send packages of coffee or other goodies with their correspondence.

"This one's on me" has no end of ingenious possibilities. Don't be deceived into thinking that more dramatic displays of creativity, humor, or impact will improve this technique's chances. It's sad, but creativity, the spark of intelligence, and a good sense of humor are no longer welcomed in the business world. Any display of intelligence is threatening to a great many people. Humor is a thousand times more dangerous than incompetence. The display of either is a signal to the reader that you're not afraid to express yourself candidly on occasion, that you're recklessly creative, and that you'd probably cause more work for everyone if you were hired. Once, in his younger, more sanguine (and more ignorant) days, an associate of mine tried this strategy. His efforts and their lack of results are instructive. A prominent monthly anthology magazine had run an ad in which they said they wanted a tiger. The ad was strongly worded and even surrounded with tiger stripes. My colleague answered with the letter shown in Figure 8.1. A small can of cat food was packaged with the letter. He never even got a form-letter rejection. He thought the idea was clever, so he put together a direct mail solicitation that used a similar letter and the can of cat food. The letters were word processed and sent to the presidents or senior partners of approximately seventy consulting companies and advertising agencies in Los Angeles. The whole affair cost about $160 dollars. He got no responses, not even form letters. Keep in mind that the recipients were the leaders of some of what are considered to be the most creative agencies/consultants in the hype capital of the world. Yet his bold and cute effort got nothing from these cutting-edge bastions of creativity and innovation. It's the same everywhere. Play it safe, be boring, and avoid the "This one's on me" gimmicks.

Super tough talk

"Super tough talk" letters are those sent directly to chief executives in an attempt to impress them with your toughness and ability to solve problems. As explained in earlier chapters, the primary difficulty with such letters is that they don't usually get to the top person. If they do, there's not usually an opening, and who cares about you anyway? They get dozens of such letters every day. An ancillary difficulty is that most chief executives don't know they have any problems because everyone they see on a daily basis is justifiably afraid to tell them about problems; they don't want to be forced to use this book. Lastly, chief executives have gotten where they are by playing the rules (although their rules are a lot more fun than those that lower managers have to follow). One of the most important rules is to maintain appearances and not complain. A "Super tough talk" letter about the problems you can solve will violate the rules by alluding to problems. You'll be branded as a potential troublemaker before they finish reading the first page.

An inventive colleague of mine once found an article that described a corporate type termed a "gunslinger." The gunslinger was described as a fast-moving, get-the-job-done type who doesn't care what people think; he or she just comes in, does the dirty work, and then packs up

Dear _____:

I am responding to your recent advertisement in which you solicited the services of a TIGER. You said you were looking for a "take-charge TIGER" with the aggressiveness and energy to "handle the tough jobs and get things moving." You can stop looking. I've got the fangs to bite off huge chunks of rich, red responsibility. And don't worry about the food bill; unlike the common M.B.A. business house cat, I don't have to be pampered and fed from a can. It will only take me a few days to learn the layout of your jungle. After that, I'll hunt, track, and kill my own challenges. All you have to do is tell me what color problem you want killed. Of course, as a real TIGER, I not only hunt like one; I've got the broad, bright stripes that strike fear into the hearts of all challenges. Take a look at these stripes for yourself; my resume is enclosed.

I've got to admit that I'm a little concerned about your ability to handle a real TIGER. Everybody thinks TIGERS are pretty to look at, and everybody thinks they'd like to have one around the office. They think TIGERS are just slightly bigger versions of the typical M.B.A. house cats they keep around to warm their laps. It's a lot different living with a real TIGER. You see, TIGERS must have large herds of challenges to hunt and huge amounts of fresh responsibility to eat. If your actual supply of challenges is low, the feeding of a real TIGER could cause problems. TIGERS sometimes eat M.B.A. house cats for fun or diversion if there's not enough real challenge.

Another potential problem with TIGERS is processing the kill. House cats only occasionally drag a mouse or two onto the doorstep. It's easy to clean up. TIGERS, on the other hand, drag back large amounts of freshly killed challenges. Many organizations find they have to put on extra skinners and butchers to process the problems that have been solved. A lot of the people who've been spending their time petting cats, shampooing them, opening cat food cans, or filling litter pans get alarmed at all the activity and increased work.

So give it some thought. If you really want a TIGER and you have enough challenges to keep me fed, I'd be pleased to talk to you about thinning out your herds. On the other hand, if you decide to stick with house cats, I understand. In fact, let me buy their next lunch. It's enclosed.

Figure 8.1 Example of a "This One's on Me" Letter

and rides off into the sunset, looking for another range war. Inspiration struck (simultaneously with poor judgment), and my friend decided on a mailer. He located a pen-and-ink drawing of the side view of a gunfighter's torso and upper leg, showing a gloved hand drawing a huge Colt .44 out of a tie-down holster. He took the drawing to a printer and had stationery made in which the drawing was boldly printed off to one side of the paper. The typing on each letter was left justified to the right edge of the drawing. It was a real eye catcher. The letter referred to a copy of the gunslinger article, which he included with each mailer. He had a secretarial service word process letters to a mailing list of a thousand chief executives in three states. It was an expensive project. The letter content is shown in Figure 8.2.

Out of a thousand launches, my friend received a total of thirty-seven replies. Thirty-two were form-letter rejections from personnel departments. Two were custom notes from personnel types in which they said they had found the letter amusing and they'd keep the resume on file. Two executives responded with personal notes. One of them was nasty, a cheap "what's your problem" shot, and the other was a "thanks for the breath of fresh air." The final response was from a career development type who offered to help my friend develop a more effective search campaign! From a thousand launches, over $1400 in expenses, and endless envelope stuffing and stamping, my

---

Dear _____:

I'm not going to beat around the bush about who I am or what I want. I'm a gunslinger, plain and simple. I solve the tough, nasty, and dirty jobs your staff hasn't been able to handle. The attached article, taken from _____, describes my temperaments and skills exactly.

Gunslingers don't want gratitude, thanks, or warm feelings. I'm not looking for a soft touch or a career with your organization. I'm looking for a year or two of knuckle-busting, hard-riding range wars. I work because I like the challenge of winning the hard fights that most managers can't face up to. All I want from you is the names of the problems you want solved, nobody in my way (that you care about), and good money.

If you've got a division that's in trouble, send me and I'll clean it up. I've done it before. If you've got a sloppy operation that can't keep its costs in line, I'll weed out the problems and straighten things out. The bigger the mess, the better I like it. When the job's done, I won't hang around to bloat your staff and create problems. I'll simply saddle up and ride into the sunset.

I've been in a lot of rough spots for a lot of employers, and I've come out on top every time. The enclosed wanted poster (clod busters call 'em resumes) describes some of the Fortune 50 "towns" I've cleaned up. I'm ready to saddle up and ride out for you. Just tell me when and where.

At your service,

Figure 8.2 Sample of "Super Tough Talk" Letter

friend got not one interview, much less a job offer—a typical result for a talk tough mailer.

The effort was bound to fail because it violated too many rules. Occasionally, an executive will be amused by the tough talk. Impressed is another story. And if one executive in a thousand is impressed by such a ploy, what are the odds that he or she will also have an opening for you? The odds are too small to justify any effort at all. If you're inclined to take the talk-tough approach, use the more restrained "See my greatness" technique outlined in Chapter 7.

Position wanted ads

Position wanted ads are ads in which job seekers solicit employers to call them. It would be great if it worked, but it doesn't. When employers want to recruit, they want a range of candidates from which to pick. They also want to set the standards for qualifications by specifying salary levels, asking for resumes, requiring years of experience, and so on. If they simply call a job seeker whose ad they see, they have no way of knowing what they'll get. So they don't waste their time. You shouldn't either. Job search publications occasionally run special sections in which job seekers are encouraged to send in their position wanted ads. If it's free, give it a shot if you're out of work. (Don't do it if you're employed; you don't want a present employer to see it.) If you have to pay for it, forget it.

Master or mistress of printing technology

This strategy attempts to dazzle the recipient with the latest in modern printing, origami, or packaging technology. The object is to impress the reviewer with the job seeker's creativity and intelligence. As noted in "This one's on me," creativity and intelligence, if used to do anything but be traditional, are dangerous. Employers, headhunters, and executives expect to see restrained, formal, and dignified business correspondence. Multifold resumes, resumes in the form of booklets (printed on all four sides of a single 11 by 17 inch sheet which is then folded in half), fancy bordered paper, pictures of the applicant, and so forth are totally inappropriate. Nobody wants to see what your printer, origami counselor, and you can come up with. All of these things are dangerous wastes of time and resources. Job seekers have tried pop-up story booklets, wall calendars with some of their qualifications on each month, cardboard cubes that alternated their picture and resume data on the sides, and pens and pencils with their names on them. All are clever; none will get you a job. If you're trying for a job as a graphics artist, these techniques may be appropriate for design positions in small, aggressive organizations. For any other purpose, they're useless.

Stunts, stunts, and double stunts

Stunts are bold actions in which the job seeker attempts to draw attention by means of personal action. On a slow news day in any but the largest cities, you can get your name in the paper by means of a carefully planned job search stunt. On real slow days, you may get a picture in the paper or even a few seconds of TV coverage. But you won't get a job offer. The most common job search stunt involves standing on a busy freeway overpass or next to a heavily traveled city street and attempting to attract attention by means of outrageous clothing, signs, helium balloons, and so on. Sandwich boards are often used with the message "Hire me" or "Hard worker available." In recent years, this sort of thing has become more common, but you can still get quite a bit of attention if you carefully plan your location and signs. This message technique is useful for laborers and college students seeking part-time work. As mentioned in Chapters 4 and 7, everyone expects college students to be a little more outrageous because they're still green. Laborers can get away with these techniques because they're selling not their image but their muscle; nobody perceives that they're compromising their value by advertising. It's different with managers and professionals. The stunt reduces the perceived worth of the person performing the stunt. The impression is, "If this person has to do this, how good can he or she be?" Many people find the stunts embarrassing because they imagine how they'd feel if they were reduced to such actions. Seeing the stunt makes them feel uneasy, and as a result they try to avoid the stunt performer. They won't generally want to interview someone who uses a stunt.

The same is true of all stunts. My favorite, planned to the point of execution and then wisely abandoned by two friends of mine, would be sure to obtain TV and newspaper coverage if properly handled. As they envisioned it, a job seeker in a big city (the bigger the better) would have a very brief resume printed in green ink on one side of paper cut in the shape of dollar bills. The reverse side would have as close a facsimile of a twenty-dollar bill as possible without breaking the law. The job seeker would have several thousands of these bills made and would take them to the top of a big office building near the city's busiest intersection. It would be important to select an area with many businesses that would have positions relevant to the job seeker's objectives. Prior to the stunt, the job seeker would call all of the radio and TV stations and tell them that "something big" was going to happen at a certain time. At that time, preferably during the noon hour with good weather, low wind, and lots of people and traffic, the job seeker would throw the bills from the top of a high building. Can you imagine the chaos below as people thought twenty-dollar bills were raining into the street? Few people's resumes would get read by so many in so short a time. Unfortunately, there would probably be massive liability for car wrecks, injured pedestrians, and littering violations. Like all stunts, there would be plenty of attention but not the correct type.

In less public spectacles, job seekers have had themselves delivered to executives in shipping crates, have posed as caddies, and have established relationships with executives' family members. All of these strategies are totally worthless for the majority of job seekers. The last-mentioned may be feasible for a lucky few who have the opportunity, but the chances are small that a specific executive would have an opportunity in the appropriate field at the right time.

In-depth research and proposal

It's often proposed that job seekers target an organization and then learn everything about it that they can. The goal is to learn enough to propose a solution to one of the organization's pressing problems. This approach ignores the way the real world operates. First of all, it's going to be extremely difficult to learn enough about any organization to make a meaningful proposal. Second, if they have serious problems they can't handle on their own, do you think they'll take kindly to having an outsider point them out? They won't.

In fact, most organizations tolerate very little discussion of problems by the employees themselves. If you know a lot about a certain area and you know that an organization has a need for what you've got, you're facing a consulting sales problem rather than a job search challenge. It's hard enough for a big-name consultant to get an organization to buy what he or she recommends. A low-status, hat-in-hand job seeker isn't going to have much influence on anyone. If you want to ingratiate yourself slowly into an organization over time, fine. Use the "Let's be friends" approach recommended in Chapter 7.

Career planning counselors, consultants, and firms

These organizations place ads in or near the classified sections of newspapers or in the *National Business Employment Weekly, National Ad Search, National Job Market*, and similar publications. They claim to be able to help you find a good job. What they do is give you a little advice, put together a semiadequate resume, and charge you a large fee. Chapter 2 discusses these firms and what they do. Avoid them at all times.

Employment agencies

Unless you're seeking very low-level or temporary work (such as summer work for college students), don't use employment agencies. Chapter 2 discusses the many reasons why they're not appropriate for most professional and managerial jobs.

Job clubs

Job clubs are a recent phenomenon. They usually consist of informal groups of job seekers who get together to trade tips and leads. Their size varies from two to two hundred people, with the membership constantly changing as people get jobs and drop out and new job seekers join. Often a college or state employment department will sponsor a club by providing a meeting room and minimal support. The premise is that these large numbers of unemployed people can learn from each other and benefit by pooling their knowledge of techniques, leads, contacts, and so on.

These clubs are a dangerous waste of time for any but the most limited, ignorant job seeker. They can't do anything for you that you can't do better yourself now that you have the *Inside Track* and know what to do. Most of the people in these clubs are seeking the support and comfort of the group because they're depressed. If you're interested in the ministry, they'll sign you up tomorrow; your search is over. If you're looking for a job, you don't need to hamper yourself by wasting time giving succor to a bunch of depressed and confused job seekers. The people in job clubs don't know how to write resumes and cover letters, don't know how to solicit executives and headhunters, and don't know much about effective interviewing. If they knew these things, they wouldn't be wasting time in the job club trying to figure out what to do next; they'd be out fighting for a job. They join the clubs to get help, not give it. If you join to get advice, you'll get watered down, bad advice. If you join and already know what you're doing, they'll be on you like starving vampires, sucking your knowledge and wasting your time.

The bigger danger is that you'll get sucked into the group therapy syndrome. When in therapy, the patients spend most of their time sitting around and whining about the injustice of the job search and trading anecdotes about how the last interview went. This type of malarkey is a waste of time. You'll improve your technique only by knowing what to do (that's what *Inside Track* is for) and then by practicing. Whining about job search problems and wallowing in self-pity won't help.

It's sometimes argued that job clubs can be a valuable source of leads. The odds of getting decent leads are low. The club members come from too many different backgrounds and industries for there to be much of a chance that you would stumble onto anything decent in your area. If there was a nugget, everyone in the club in your area of interest would be after it, thereby reducing your chances.

Chapter 9

Somebody's Got to Do It: Administration and Recordkeeping

It's absolutely essential to maintain a well-organized recordkeeping system of your job search efforts. If you don't, you're risking serious problems, particularly if you're responding to large numbers of classified ads or talking with a lot of headhunters. You can't possibly remember what each and every ad said, what you talked about in a particular phone interview, or what specific things you mentioned in the cover letter. Without a proper recordkeeping system, you might have doubts about what, if any, salary levels you claimed in a given response to an ad. You might forget to send a thank-you letter for a phone interview, or perhaps you'll send two. There's no end to the problems that can be brought about by failing to maintain a job search recordkeeping system.

Why Job Seekers Fail to Maintain Recordkeeping Systems

They think the search will be a short one.

Since it takes so little time to maintain a complete and easy-to-use recordkeeping system, at first glance it seems amazing that so many job seekers don't do it. Those who don't are falling prey to some common self-delusions. Many don't keep records because they're kidding themselves about how long the job search will last. To set up any kind of a "job search command center" or recordkeeping system is, to some people, an admission that things might not work out as well as their most optimistic estimate. It's the same sort of mechanism that operates on people who, when they know they're running short of funds, delay balancing their checkbooks. They don't want to be reminded. Unfortunately, problems don't go away by avoiding them. In fact, they usually get worse. Without proper records, you risk blowing a few phone interviews, forgetting to follow up contacts with thank-you notes, and so on. You can't afford to compromise your efforts; each

141

contact with a potential position is a valuable asset that must be protected. Proper records protect.

It's too much work.

If the burden of establishing a recordkeeping system was large, it might make sense to delay the investment in time and effort. But it's easy to set one up. You can establish the *Inside Track* recordkeeping system in ten minutes with some paper and a notebook. For every ad you answer, you'll only have to spend about one minute to write down the essential information. After each phone and personal interview, it will only take a few minutes to jot down notes on how it went, attach any business cards, and enter notes on future actions you need to take. Weighed against the possible dangers of not having such a system, the effort is minuscule.

The Inside Track Recordkeeping System

The entire *Inside Track* recordkeeping system can be kept in a single three-ring binder. Truly heroic searches may require an additional binder after several months. You could use file folders, but they invite misfilings and aren't as easy to handle. If you're frantically trying to locate a cover letter while you're on the phone with an interviewer, you don't need to be juggling a handful of slippery folders. It's much easier to turn the pages of a notebook. The *Inside Track* notebook system is organized into fifteen sections. Not all searches require all sections; some job seekers will not be using every strategy. I suggest that you use labeled dividers to separate the sections. You can use either plain or lined paper. The fifteen sections of the complete *Inside Track* recordkeeping system are:
1. Classified ad log sheets
2. Cover letters used in response to classified ads
3. Headhunter mailing log sheets
4. Lists of headhunters
5. Cover letters used in headhunter mailings
6. Headhunter feedback records
7. Direct solicitation log sheets
8. Direct solicitation lists
9. Cover letters used in direct solicitations
10. Direct solicitation feedback records
11. Phone solicitation tracking sheets
12. Phone solicitation telecharts
13. Resume versions

ADMINISTRATION AND RECORDKEEPING

14. Expense log
15. Thank-you and follow-up letter log

You may not be using all of the sections listed. For example, if you're not planning on using mailings to headhunters, you won't need sections 3, 4, 5, and 6. However, I suggest that you provide a divider and a few blank sheets of paper for every section in your notebook when you set it up, even if you don't plan to be using one or more of the strategies; at least the sections will be there if you need them. While there aren't explicit sections provided for the strategies discussed in Chapter 8, they can be tracked with the above sections, as most of them are derivations of direct solicitation efforts.

Section 1. Classified ad log sheets

These log sheets are the heart of the classified ad tracking system. For each ad you answer, you'll prepare one log sheet such as the sample shown in Figure 9.1. The log sheet functions as a single reference document which tells you everything about the ad, your response to it, and any follow-up information you obtain at a later date. As displayed in Figure 9.1, the log sheet records the exact name and address of the

---

November 14, 1986   34

Mr. John Bloblannon
Personnel Manager
Lamont Industries
1123 Iron Road
Blast Furnace, PA 99999

November 11, 1986   Pittsburgh Chronicle

45K   39K   28K

Resume 4   Cover letter 34

```
        ┌─────────────┐
        │   Attach    │
        │             │
        │     Ad      │
        │             │
        │    Here     │
        └─────────────┘
```

Figure 9.1 Example of Classified Ad Log Sheet

person and organization to whom the response was mailed. (It might not always be the same as the one in the ad if the applicant is doing a little research.) The number at the top right ("34") is the log number. It's simply the next available sequential number assigned to the ad. It will enable you to quickly cross-reference between ads and cover letters. The date at the top ("November 14") is the date on which the cover letter was typed. The lower date ("November 11") was the publication date on which the ad appeared. The name of the publication that ran the ad ("Pittsburgh Chronicle") is shown to the right of the publication date. You may elect not to use the publication date of the ad in your cover letter (for instance, when you substitute "in your recent advertisement" for "your November 11, 1986, advertisement").

Record the actual publication data anyway; you may need it for later reference. The "45K," "39K," and "28K" entries were salary levels the applicant claimed for three current or past jobs (by penning them in on the resume). When you don't reveal salary data, put in zeros so there will be no doubt that you deliberately did not provide the data. You'll have as many entries on the salary line as jobs for which you reveal salaries. Record salaries from left to right, starting with your most recent (or current) position. This procedure, coupled with the resume code number, makes it unnecessary to write down the job names next to the salaries in order to keep track of claimed salaries. Of course, if you're always stating the same salaries, all you have to do is write "Yes" or "No" on the line to record whether you revealed salaries or not. The next line denotes the code number ("4") of the resume version sent and the code number ("34") of the cover letter that was used. The ad is stapled or taped below this information, as far to the left as possible (leave room for the binder rings) so that the right side of the sheet (and the back) can then be used to record any data on calls, interviews, and so on. If the ad is large, staple or tape one end and then fold it up.

When you're about to reply to some ads, first cut them out and trim them. Place them in a pile with the best bets on top. (You want to be freshest for them.) Before you do any letters, check the last log number in your log book and then consecutively number (on the top right border) each one of the new ads, starting with the ad on top. Attach (with tape or staples) each ad to an empty log sheet and record the log number on the log sheet's upper right corner. You'll then have a pile of numbered log sheets with ads attached. As you answer one ad at a time, record the appropriate data on the log sheet. If you create a custom cover letter that differs in more than the addressee, company, and job-specific data from an existing letter, label a copy of the cover letter with the log number of the ad and put the copy in section 2. Be very careful to keep things organized when you're making copies of your letters; a mix-up could cost you at a later date. In the Figure 9.1 example, the code for the custom letter is "34." When you refer to a cover letter code on a log sheet, you'll know immediately that you used a custom letter if the cover letter code number matches the log number. If you use the content of an existing cover letter, assign the appropriate code. In the example, if the letter sent to ad 34 was identical (except for names, dates, etc.) to a letter that had been custom-made for ad 21, the cover letter code shown on log sheet 34 would be 21. This system enables you to track exactly what you said in the cover letters to each ad without having to save redundant copies in section 2.

The log sheets are also used to record information about phone and in-person interviews. Make notes on the right side and the back of the page concerning the dates, names, places, and major points covered. Attach any business cards you obtain right to the log sheet; if they call again or you call them, you'll have their names and titles right at your fingertips. When you send thank-you letters, record the thank-you letter code number beneath the resume code number with the date it was sent (as in "Thank you 5 sent on 12/4/85"). Make similar notations about any other correspondence. Your goal is to have the log sheet either contain or quickly refer you to everything that's happened in regard to the position.

Section 2. Cover letters used in response to classified ads

This section contains one coded copy of each basic version of the cover letter you've used. Put the code number in the upper right corner of each version for easy reference. Since you may be using a standard cover letter for many ads, you'll have many gaps in the sequence of the cover letters. For example, let's say you use your standard bare-bones cover letter (see Figure 5.1) to answer ads with log numbers 1 through 7. If you were then to create a custom letter for the ad with log number 8, you'd label the new letter with code number 8. Your section 2 would then have two letters, one coded with a "1" and one coded with an "8." Don't try to cheat and make minor changes in stated qualifications on an existing letter without creating another custom letter by assigning it a new code number and placing a copy of it in section 2. You don't need to have any doubts about what you think you said if you get a call.

Section 3. Headhunter mailing log sheets

These sheets are to headhunter mailings what the section 1 log sheets are to ad responses. Figure 9.2 presents a portion of a headhunter mailing log sheet for a job seeker who had made four mailings to headhunters between June 4 and August 27. Each line of the log sheet records the relevant information for one mailing effort. Each line

1. June 4, 1986	List 1	Letter 1	Resume 3	75
2. July 5, 1986	List 2	Letter 1	Resume 1	54
3. August 3, 1986	List 3	Letter 2	Resume 1	105
4. August 27, 1986	List 4	Letter 3	Resume 4	45

Figure 9.2 Portion of a Headhunter Mailing Log Sheet

presents six items of information. None but the most homeric job searches will require more than one headhunter mailing log sheet. The numbers on the extreme left are the sequential numbers of the mailings. The dates are the dates on which the mailings were sent out. The list entries identify the mailing list that was used (coded and placed in section 4). The fourth column identifies the code numbers of the cover letters that were used in each mailing (coded and placed in section 5). The fifth column identifies the resume version that was sent (coded and placed in section 13). The last column records the number of headhunters contacted.

Section 4. Lists of headhunters

This section contains separate lists of the names and addresses of the headhunters contacted in each mailing. For example, the job seeker whose log sheet was shown in Figure 9.2 had made four mailings. That job seeker would have four separate lists in this section. If you're using a word-processing service, they can generate a typed list for you. In fact, they'll probably give you a list of the typed names and addresses to proof before they put the variables into the letters. Ask them for the list back after they've done the letters. If you're doing the typing yourself, you don't have to type or handwrite a list of contacts for each mailing. Simply photocopy the pages of your basic list sources, check off the headhunters used in that mailing, and put the photocopies in this section. Staple the list together and write the list code number on the upper right corner of the first sheet.

Section 5. Cover letters used in headhunter mailings

This is essentially the same as section 2. Maintain a coded copy of each different letter version used.

Section 6. Headhunter feedback records

This section initially consists of blank sheets of paper. When you get a call from a headhunter, turn to the next available empty sheet, enter

ADMINISTRATION AND RECORDKEEPING 147

the date, and take notes. Get the headhunter's name, address, firm, phone number, and the nature of the position. Write down everything. Don't be reluctant to ask them to repeat the information. Make notes of everything they say about the job. Write down the main points of what you emphasize about your skills. If the same headhunter calls again, turn to the original page, draw a line across it, enter the date, and proceed as before. Use a separate sheet for each headhunter. When you get feedback from a headhunter, turn back to section 4 and put an asterisk next to the name. If you use the list in the future, you can personally address the letter. (Chances are the headhunter will have moved on, but it can't hurt.)

Section 7. Direct solicitation log sheets

This section is similar to the headhunter mailing log sheet shown in Figure 9.2. If you're sending highly personalized direct solicitation letters, where each one is unique, you won't need this section because your section 9 will contain copies of all letters sent. However, if you're using a mailmerged basic letter for many contacts, set up this section in the same format as described for section 3. Assign the mailing a number, record the date the mailing went out, and list the code numbers of the mailing list, the cover letter, and the resume. Complete each line with the number of pieces launched. Make sure that coded copies of the cover letters and resumes you use are placed in the appropriate sections.

Section 8. Direct solicitation lists

This record is maintained in the same manner as section 4.

Section 9. Cover letters used in direct solicitations

This record is maintained in the same manner as section 5.

Section 10. Direct solicitation feedback records

This record is maintained in the same manner as section 6. Be sure to make notes about any thank-you letters sent and include coded copies of the letters in section 15.

Section 11. Phone solicitation tracking sheets

If you're going to try phone networking, prepare for each phone call by formatting a new sheet of paper. At the top of the sheet, write down the name, title, company, and phone number of the person you're about to call. As you conduct the call, write down new information below the first name. If you get information about another contact, draw a line across the page and record the name, title, company, and phone number of the obtained contact. If you receive information about the organization of the person you're talking to, record the information below his or her name, but don't draw a line across the page. Proceed down the sheet and use additional sheets if needed. When you review your sheets, you'll be able to spot new contacts quicky by looking for the lines across the page. When you get ready to call one of the obtained contacts or a previously targeted contact, start a fresh sheet and write their information at the top. As you talk with them, proceed as described above. Keep all of the phone sheets in this section so that you'll be able to identify new leads and trace old names for future or repeated use.

Section 12. Phone solicitation telecharts

This section consists of all of the current and past versions of the telecharts (see Figure 7.5) you'll be using to make direct contact with executives and organizations. Don't throw the old ones out; you might want to refer back to them in designing new ones. Keep a few copies of the most current ones in front of this section in case you run into a new rejection or stumble upon a great new line and want to pencil it in for future use.

Section 13. Resume versions

This section contains one copy of each of the resume versions used in all aspects of the search. If you make any change in an existing resume, create a new version by assigning it a new code number and putting a copy of it in this section. For every contact you must know exactly what version you've sent. After several months and perhaps two to ten different versions, you'll no longer remember who got what if you don't religiously use this section and the various log sheets.

Section 14. Expenses

As of the date of this book's publication, federal tax laws allow for the deduction of job search expenses as long as you are not attempting to change careers (such as an accountant trying to switch to commercial airline piloting). Save all receipts for postage, paper, typewriter ribbons, photocopying, typing, and other secretarial support. Keep a record of mileage to and from interviews.

Create one sheet in this section for each one of these major expense categories: stationery and general supplies (ribbons, paper, tape), postage, printing and secretarial support, travel expenses (keep a separate sheet for personal mileage with date, destination, and company name), and miscellaneous (books, mailing lists, computer equipment). Log in each expense on its appropriate sheet by writing the date of the receipt, the name of the vendor, and the amount. Store the receipts in separate envelopes labeled with the same names as the log sheets. This system will enable your tax preparer (or yourself) quickly to compute your job searching expenses without having to sort through a jumbled pile of mashed-up receipts.

Section 15. Thank-you and follow-up letter log

This section is maintained in the same manner as sections 2, 5, and 9.

Where to Keep It

The purpose of the *Inside Track* recordkeeping system is to enable you to conveniently determine the status of each of the leads you're following. If you get a call, whether it's the first one or a postinterview follow-up, it's imperative that you be able to find out what you said, when you said it, and whom you said it to. You've got to sound as if the only thing that's been on your mind is their call, as if their organization's opportunity is the only one you care about. If you've launched a five-hundred-piece mailing to headhunters, have been answering five to ten ads per week, and have been doing some direct solicitations, you probably can't recall what you said yesterday, much less what you claimed in a letter sent four weeks ago. The recordkeeping notebook will serve as your instant recall. If it's going to serve that function, the notebook must be easily accessible whenever there's a chance that you might get a call (6:00 A.M. to 11:00 P.M. your time). If you've got an answering machine (I very strongly recommend that you get one if you don't have one), it's not quite so critical to have the log at arm's reach. With an answering machine, you can take the message and then call back after you've researched the notebook to see who it might be and what you should be ready to say.

If you don't have an answering machine or if you're not inclined to pay for all of the return calls you'll have to make (if you elect to listen to the call, do the research, and then call them back), you'd better have the notebook right next to the phone. If you answer and it's a job search call, talk for a minute to get a little data that will help you locate the right log page; then excuse yourself for a moment. Use "Hang on; I've got to close the front door," "Give me just a second; I've got to turn off my computer printer" (such "high-tech" references are always good), or "Let me put the phone down for a second and put the dog in his run," and then try to locate the ad so that you can talk from a position of knowledge.

A Final Word

If you've never maintained a job search log, the fifteen sections of the *Inside Track* recordkeeping system probably appear excessive. That's a false impression. It takes less than one minute per ad to log in the necessary data in sections 1 through 3. You can log in an entire head-hunting mailing of a thousand pieces (or a direct solicitation effort of similar size that uses a standard letter) in less than thirty seconds. Even if you're sending out custom direct solicitation letters, all you've got to do is put a copy of each one in section 9. The system doesn't require any extra work for tracking your phone efforts; you'd have to take notes in any case. The *Inside Track* system simply organizes them for you. The time needed to log in expenses, resume versions, and thank-you letters is so small that it's almost beneath mention. The *Inside Track* recordkeeping system isn't a drain on your energy or resources.

Time and resources aren't the barrier to maintaining the *Inside Track* or any other recordkeeping system. It's the self-discipline that's the problem. Make yourself do it whether you like it or not, and you'll soon find that maintaining the notebook will become a very reassuring and calming part of your job search duties. Not only will you have the peace of mind of knowing exactly what's going on with each lead at a moment's notice, but the very presence of the notebook will also be comforting. It will be just about the only tangible evidence of your job search efforts prior to an actual job offer. You'll have the reassurance that you're doing something and doing a lot of it. Such a guilt-reducing comforter may not seem important now, but it will be when you're a few months along in your search. Start your recordkeeping system right from the start by putting the notebook together and entering your first resume version. You won't be sorry.

Chapter 10

Hand-to-Hand (and Phone-to-Phone) Combat: The Interview

All other activities in job searching point to the interview. It's the moment of truth. No matter how good the resume, no matter how piercing and concise the cover letters, no matter how well researched the mailing list, the job will be won or lost in the interview. Good materials and strategy can improve your odds of winning an interview, but it's a new ball game when you answer the phone or walk into the interviewer's office. If you don't handle interviews with skill, you won't get many job offers.

Most job seekers see the interview as a complex, bewildering, and frightening situation in which they are pretty much at the mercy of the interviewer. This is a false and misleading perception. While there's not much that can be done to salvage interviews with totally incompetent interviewers, a skilled job seeker can move onto the *Inside Track* in the majority of interviews by remembering and applying a number of basic guidelines in all interviews. Once the job seeker knows these techniques, his or her interviewing effectiveness is limited only by the effort devoted to preparation and practice. With dedicated attention and study, even totally inept interviewers can dramatically improve their technique after two or three interviews.

There are two types of interviews: phone and face-to-face. In some ways they're alike, but the differences between them are more significant. Phone interviews are preliminary and more or less objective, checklist screenings of applicants. Face-to-face interviews are more intense and subjective appraisals of a candidate's total persona (personality, qualifications, appearance, character). In the typical search situation, you'll have to win a phone interview in order to get an invitation to a face-to-face interview. Your technique in each must be superb.

General Guidelines for All Interviews

A number of principles of effective interviewing apply to both phone and face-to-face interviews. Before you attempt to develop more sophisticated aspects of your interviewing skills, you must know and follow these guidelines in every interview.

1. Don't say more than the minimum required.

In most interactions, the central message is usually straightforward and easy to understand in theory. In practice, many interactions turn into arguments, frustrating stalemates, divorces, wars, and lost job opportunities because the central issue is complicated by unnecessary and irrelevant information that one of the parties volunteers. Excess information does several things to a job interview, all of them bad:

1. It makes it more difficult for the interviewer to perceive or understand the few simple points you're trying to make. For example, if you're trying to demonstrate that your experience as a proposal writer is outstanding, a mention of your skills in the area of production management may confuse the interviewer or cause him or her to downplay the weight of your writing experience.
2. It may set off one of the interviewer's unique and very subjective "hot buttons" about which you couldn't possible have any foreknowledge. Since you don't know what these hot buttons are, you must avoid mentioning anything that isn't essential to the central issue.
3. It may lead the interviewer to ask off-base questions which then take the interview totally away from the central issues you're trying to address.
4. It may overwhelm an interviewer who's less than intellectually gifted. If the interviewer wants to know whether you're a good accounts receivable type, why complicate the issue by mentioning your abilities as a master of financial modeling and forecasts? If it's in the resume, the impression has been made. If the topic comes up in the interview, acknowledge it, connect it to the basic issue under discussion (the accounts receivable job), and then abandon the topic. If you dwell on it, you take the fire away from the central issue and may bewilder the interviewer.

Keep your interviews as lean and sparse as you can. Be comprehensive in your answers, complete, and responsive, but don't volunteer anything that's not directly related to the issue at hand. If they want to know about something you don't think is important, they'll ask.

2. Act like a winner.

Status and power are inherent positive values in our social structure. Nobody wants to associate with losers, people of low status, or people who need something. Everybody wants to be with the winners, individuals with an aura of achievement who can do something if they want to. It's no different in job searching. The more you want the job, the less attractive you'll appear as a candidate. If you appear desperate, you'll be viewed as a powerless person who needs something done *for* you, rather than someone who can *do* something. Research has repeatedly shown that applicants who need the job are seldom hired. Typically, it's found that applicants who already have a good job, who are "practice interviewing," or who can just about pick their next spot are the ones who get the offers. In fact, follow-ups with the applicants immediately after their interviews routinely show that the applicants who don't want the job get subsequent offers more often than the applicants who express the greatest desire for the job or those who need it most. The desperate ones are sending out "help me" signals which the interviewers are sensing.

You must act as if you don't have to have the job, as if you're interested in a positive career move and are looking for just the right spot. If you come across as sincere but not easily bought, you'll be perceived as an attractive candidate simply because you're successful enough not to have to take just any job. If you're perceived as desperate, no one will want you. If you are desperate, hide it well. With a little practice, you'll become a more self-assured interviewer, and you'll more readily project the right attitude.

3. Exude enthusiasm and optimism at all times.

Everything you say must be unabashedly optimistic, cheery, and positive. As far as the job selection world is concerned, things couldn't be greater for you, everything is fine, and you are happy and content. If this all sounds disgusting and ridiculous, you're right, it is. Unfortunately, it's a reality of the job search world. People who are less than beacons of light and joy look particularly bad because so few candidates ever say anything that's less than totally positive. Your problems or negative views may be realistic, but they'll cause you to be perceived as a problem. If you let on that you have any disagreeable qualities such as wanting more money, have doubts about the future of the industry, or don't expect to be president of the company in twenty years, you'll be seen as a problem and not a valuable asset to be pursued. You must never suggest fatigue, disrespect, depression (even if you've lost your house, spouse, and career), anger, aggression, or any other natural human emotions. You must seem positive, happy, and confident regardless of how you really feel. If you're discovering that you're not turning your own stomach with phony optimism and good cheer during interviews, beware; you're not laying it on thick enough.

4. Never be negative about anything except safe targets.

Negative words create bad impressions in and of themselves. The words "I don't," "you can't," and "no" set off emotional reactions in most of us. The reactions stem from the implications of control that such words signal. Negative words and opinions or evaluations are dangerous for an additional and more important reason: if you're willing to be negative in the confines of a formal interview in which tradition and etiquette demand optimism and sunshine, how much trouble will you cause when you get into the organization and begin to feel at home? No smart interviewer wants to bring in a troublemaker. You're signaling that you're a potential rabble rouser if you bad mouth past employers, other organizations, industry practices, or your profession. Don't say anything negative about anything but safe issues, and even then, be charitable. The safe issues are employees who don't work at a white-hot heat for sixty hours a week, workers who don't love the company, foreign competition, government regulation, and related concerns that the industry views as evil. However, even when you're being negative about safe issues, you've got to be measured and charitable. Always phrase your criticism as a challenge that you recognize, as in "Yes, I think ax-murdering child molesters are sick people, but it's a challenge to us to find out why they go bad." Appear as if you regard every negative in life as just another challenge.

5. Keep your manner formal and reserved.

At the same time that you're being courteous, optimistic, and positive, you must also be slightly reserved, formal, and a little cool or aloof. Everyone expects candidates to be on their most formal behavior in job interviews. You must act as if the interview is one of the most prestigious appointments you've had in years. They don't have to know that you've had five interviews and three offers in the past four days or that you're about to starve if you don't get the job. The way to convey the proper impression of respect and professionalism is to be formal and just a little reserved. You want the interviewer to feel that you're taking things seriously, not desperately but seriously. This will flatter the interviewer and increase your perceived worth as someone who will fit in if hired.

6. Be firm but reasonable and understanding of others' problems.

No one but an idiot is going to hire someone who may cause trouble. In an organization, trouble can be caused just as much by someone who inflexibly pursues excellence (or regulations) at the expense of all other things as it can by someone who never does any work. It's a big mistake to give the impression that there are some things that you just can't tolerate. At the same time, you have to participate in the charade that everybody in the organization wants nothing but hard work, challenge, and achievement. You can successfully walk the middle of this road if you watch the traffic. State your beliefs in the motherhood issues of hard work, adherence to policy ("for everyone's good") and eliminating incompetence, but then qualify everything with the caveat, "But, of course, it's important to work within the system and give every employee a chance to develop." Whenever a problem is mentioned, express rueful sorrow and then state, "It's just something that has to be continually watched and worked on. Personally I regard it as a challenge." You'll be recognized for what you'll sound like: someone who will fit in without making any trouble.

7. Never give an honest answer about why you're looking.

Never say why you are looking unless the truth is that you want more challenge, more work, longer hours, and don't really care about money. Your actual reason for looking for another job may seem reasonable to you and may be morally correct, but it may turn off the interviewer. If you say, "My present company is a family operation, and the boss's sons and relatives get all the top jobs, so there's no room for someone like me to grow," you may be unpleasantly surprised to find that your interviewer is the chairman of the board's nephew and is very sensitive about how he got his job. Never admit or intimate that you're looking solely for more money or status. These are the first things that come to people's minds when they think "new job," but they're unmentionables during initial interviews. As far as the interviewers are concerned, everything is great where you are (or were), but things weren't challenging enough; you're looking for more challenge and growth. Once they get down to the stage where they've decided they want you, you can talk about money, and everyone will view it as a natural and expected part of the business transaction.

8. Don't intimidate the interviewer.

Since most of your interviews will be with personnel people, headhunters, and typically limited middle managers, it will take considerable control for you to avoid appearing more intelligent or dynamic than they are. Nonetheless, it is critical that you leave them with the impression that you are just a little less knowledgeable and intelligent than they are. Don't worry about them arriving at the conclusion that you're not good enough for the job if you appear to be less scintillating than they are; nobody's making that type of objective analysis of your skills and suitability during the interview. They're forming impressions. The impression that you want to leave is that you're pleasant and skilled and will fit in if you're hired. If you come across as arrogant or spend the entire interview pumping up your achievements, the interviewer is going to get the impression that you're self-centered, egotistical, difficult to deal with, and could be a threat (if you'll be working for or with the interviewer). Whether or not you can do a great job will be irrelevant at that point. They're hiring people, not skills, and you must appear to be an acceptable person. You'll help develop that impression by appearing to be just a little less vibrant and creative than they are. If you come across as too qualified, an overachiever (something everybody says they want but few hire), or someone who is not a team player (which you demonstrate every time you show that you don't need a team to get the job done), you won't get the offer.

The paradox is that you must also leave the interviewer with the feeling that you're special. It's a matter of presentation style. You must quickly size up the confidence level and intelligence of the interviewer. You must then adjust the confidence and mastery you project. If the interviewer is a gifted, intelligent person, you must demonstrate just a little less so that he or she will not feel threatened; you want them to feel you're awed by their brilliance. You can present a list of achievements and credentials as long as the interviewer's leg without intimidating him or her if you keep your tone and manner a little more subdued and less confident than his or hers. If the interviewer is a total clod, you must leave the impression that you're just a bit more of a clod, but an eager, proper, hard-working clod. Interviewers won't make the logical assumption that anyone with a long list of achievements must be better than they are. Credentials get you into the interview; after that they're not very important. Sending the proper signals is the issue. The interviewers expect you to try to impress them. They won't be impressed if you don't. On the other hand, they don't want to be intimidated and reminded of their sorry lot in life. You must balance the two, with slightly more emphasis on the latter concern. You may have to switch roles several times during a series of interviews. It's not as tricky as it sounds; you'll do a good job if you are reasonably intelligent, practice a lot, and pay attention to the signals during the first few minutes of each interview.

9. Avoid humor at all times.

Humor is extremely dangerous in all types of interactions with people you don't know very well. We've all had the experience of having told one of the funniest jokes we've ever heard to a group of strangers and, when we dropped the punch line, everyone just stood there with blank expressions. You never know what some people will find offensive, blasphemous, or in poor taste. You're at even more risk in a job interview because everyone's expecting you to be more reserved and formal than normal. Stick to the safe, straight-laced, and formal presentation they expect. If they start to be humorous and to make jokes, laugh but don't make any jokes of your own; they'll love you even more for recognizing their wit and not attempting to steal the stage.

10. Never assume that you understand the interviewer's value system.

You can never be sure you understand what the interviewer likes, values, and respects. Don't assume that you can. Just because you think productivity and creativity are the only two things that count doesn't mean the interviewer does too. You can blow an entire interview by making one bad assumption about the interviewer's values. A friend of mine was once asked the hackneyed old saw, "And where do you expect to be in three years?" The friend, who should have known better (and does now), replied with the also hackneyed but dangerous, "I expect to be sitting in your chair," thinking such a reply would be a good way to demonstrate the aggressive talk every organization wants. It wasn't a good way. The interviewer was shocked. His face got white, and he asked my friend, "Where will I be if you get my job?" The guy was dead serious; he planned to be in the job for a long time and had never thought of moving anywhere. We all laughed when we heard the story, but my friend didn't ever hear from them again. The safer answer to the above question is, "Well, I've never been afraid to let my work speak for itself. I just want an opportunity to do some meaningful work in a stimulating environment and be rewarded for my efforts if they help the organization." The key is to use only safe, remote examples such as "let my work speak for itself" and "be rewarded for my efforts if they help," which don't require mention of specific actions or people. You'll sound positive and healthy to all interviewers, and you won't be offending any of them.

11. Never admit any but the most harmless personal flaws.

Any normal human frailty you admit during the job interview will be blown totally out of proportion. Remember, the selection process is not a search for excellence. It's a search for problems and defects, and the winner will be the one who demonstrates the fewest number. When you're asked the overused and stupid question, "What is your biggest drawback?" say something like, "That's a good question. (They will actually believe it.) My biggest problem is that I have always thrown myself too completely into the job. I really enjoy my work, and I don't mind working nights and weekends because I love the work. I have to control myself and realize that others who work with me might have outside interests."

Of course, for most of us, this is a total and complete, raging and gaping lie, but it's the only type of frailty you can admit. Other types of acceptable frailties include admissions of tendencies to attempt to be too parsimonious with salary increases and admissions of having neglected to pay enough attention to family life because of all the weekends spent at work. Never admit actual "shortcomings" such as that you're sometimes unmotivated, you sometimes actually become aggressive, or you hate to work for stupid, out-of-date bosses. Never admit or intimate the slightest normal human condition, no matter how small. People will be screening out problems, any problems, and they'll interview many people who will present super-polished images. Faced with that competition, any tiny, we've-all-got-'em, common human frailty will bring the curse of the form-letter rejection upon your mailbox.

12. Use plenty of current jargon.

Jargon is the crutch of a weak mind. You're going to be dealing with a lot of weak minds, so get handy with this orthopedic device of the job search process. I once lost out on a senior-level management position because I didn't know a jargon item from a worthless book on quality circles. It didn't matter that I was expert and articulate in all of the background theory supporting the "new concepts" that the author of the book had dreamed up to make his book appear to be different. Unfortunately for me, the interviewers didn't know enough to realize that the book was a simplistic ripoff of more substantial existing techniques. Every field of endeavor fosters and supports such jargon generation. It's a crock, but it's a crock you'll have to deal with if you want to optimize your chances of success in impressing weak minds. If your field is heavy with jargon, use it where appropriate. Keep up with the hot new terms during your search (and when you're working as well). If you talk like what they expect, they'll think you are what they expect. When you hear a new bit of jargon in an interview, remember it and use it in your next interview. The more jargon you use (which they can understand; don't get too technical), the more knowledgeable you'll appear.

13. Let the interviewer do as much of the talking as possible.

A skilled interviewer will attempt to have the applicant do 80 percent of the talking. If the interviewer is skilled, you won't have to take control of the interview. It will most likely go smoothly; you'll be able to pack all of your goodies into your answers to his or her questions. The interviewer will be looking for certain things that you'll be able to

supply by handling the questions properly. If interviewers aren't skilled, you must do two things:
1. You must put them at ease by allowing them to talk about themselves and what they know about their company. Ask a lot of questions, such as "What's your assessment of this organization's management style?" and "Where do you think the industry is headed, and how is this organization preparing to deal with it?" These types of questions solicit the interviewers' opinions. Even if they don't have any information, they'll tell you all about it, and they'll be flattered that you asked. This will put them at ease.
2. You must skillfully work to present your qualifications and achievements in such a way that the interviewer doesn't feel that you're trying to fight for control of the situation. You can easily do this by observing the instructions in the following sections.

14. Have a rationale for everything you've done.

Very few people are in their present situation as the result of a carefully planned life strategy. Most of us have taken entirely unexpected twists and turns to get where we are, seizing opportunity when it's noticed, changing course as we recover from setbacks, making mistakes, and taking chances. That's life for almost everyone. Such admissions won't impress interviewers. They've heard too many renditions of "I laid out my life plan when I was six, and I'm now at step 154 of 212." You've got to create a logical reason for everything significant that you've done. You want the interviewer to believe you're in the interview because you've decided that his or her organization could be the logical next step in your plan. You'll be seen as a serious, heads-up businessperson rather than a desperate job seeker who will take anything. Such an approach also makes any irregularities appear less significant because your entire story will seem to be well planned, consistent, and organized; it will look more impressive than it is.

15. Give the impression that you're constantly working on a self-improvement plan.

Many interviewers look for evidence that the candidate is hard at work on a plan to improve himself or herself. Don't disappoint them. Whenever you admit a slight acceptable flaw, immediately follow with a plan you're working on to fix it (such as "I used to be a little worried about speaking in front of large groups, but now I'm going to Toastmasters on Monday, Wednesday, and Friday nights and I've made some big improvements"). Your self-improvement efforts will demonstrate that you're humble, still eager to learn (which means they can teach you to accept their outdated systems), and flexible enough to admit errors.

16. Have a detailed plan for the future.

No interviewer is going to be reassured if you give the impression that the length of your stay will be influenced by chance, your mood, the job market, and so on. Interviewers are comforted by the belief that their organization will endure. Help them be comfortable by demonstrating that your life plan calls for you to be with them for a considerable time in order to reach your next carefully planned career step (which sounds as if it will be with them). This will make you look like a safe candidate.

17. Demonstrate a rock-solid traditional set of values.

There are a number of candidate assessment systems around that rely heavily on data concerning the careers of your parents, whether you were the first-born child, and similar demographic variables. Ignorant employers are seduced by these systems because they're looking for easy answers to their selection problems. There are no easy answers, and these systems are worthless. It's true that there are some correlations between variables such as parents' job types and childrens' work attitudes, but these correlations are only moderate, with values of $r = 0.25$ to 0.40. A correlation of 0.40 contains 84 percent error, far too much to be of any value in predicting individual cases. Unfortunately, employers know little about statistics. Therefore, you must demonstrate a conservative, traditional set of values if they start asking about your parents, your upbringing, and so on. As far as they're concerned, your parents were both professionals who instilled in you a love for hard work, careful planning, and honesty. The smart job seeker remembers home life as being secure, warm, and firmly rooted in respect for home, flag, and hard work.

18. Never argue or disagree.

If the interviewer says, "You seem to have had a pretty disorganized career path up to this point, don't you think?" the smart job seeker says, "You're absolutely right (even if he or she isn't); it does appear that way at first glance. Let me explain what I've been doing." After this the candidate explains how the messed-up career is actually a carefully planned professional development program. The key to this guideline is never to state that you disagree with the interviewer. Agree and then tell the poor misguided fool why he or she is wrong. They won't see what you're doing because you will have first told them they're correct. Whatever they say, agree, don't argue, and then tell them why they're wrong.

19. Give the impression that you consider all problems and difficulties to be nothing but exciting challenges.

It's essential to give a lot of lip service to the glory of overcoming challenges simply for the exhilaration of it. In reality, problems and difficulties turn most managers' knees to jelly and reduce the majority of executives to indecisive wafflers. While you may fit in nicely with these types after you're hired, you won't be hired if you don't give the impression that challenge is your middle name. It's the aura of energy and the refreshing chill of "no problem, can do easy" that makes talk of overcoming challenges so effective on interviewers. The job seeker seems like a properly enthusiastic, eager, and dedicated worker. The converse side is that since many job seekers already talk fervently about how much they love challenge, those who don't will look twice as bad. No matter what the problem or circumstance, toss in lines such as "I personally see _____ as a challenge" or "When _____ strikes, I try to look at it as a personal challenge to my skills and determination."

20. Liberally spread around lots of gratitude and praise.

Many short-sighted job seekers (and workers in general) feel they're short-changing themselves when they share the credit or kudos for a job well done. Just the opposite is true. When you give others credit for helping you, when you openly praise them for all of the assistance they've provided, and when you talk about how you couldn't have done it without them, you not only make everyone concerned happier, but you also make yourself look better. People who share the limelight are seen as team players, workers with the right attitude, and positive and enthusiastic employees. Take advantage of this perception by liberally praising everyone who has had anything to do with your background. You'll be showing the interviewer that you're the type of employee who makes everyone look good. Praise your parents for teaching you solid values, past employers for giving you opportunity and instruction, and past colleagues for making your jobs pleasant and stimulating. If it moves, did move, or will move, talk glowingly of at least some aspect of it. ("Well, yes, Mr. Ajax of Ajax, Ltd., did fire me for accidentally parking in his spot one day, and I did lose my home as a result of being out of work. But you know what? I learned a lot from that experience. Mr. Ajax showed me that I should take executive parking spaces more seriously. It's a lesson that I needed to learn, and I thank him for that.") You'll look doubly good by doing this in job interviews because most applicants will be spewing forth such a constant stream of *I's*, and *me's* that your charity and good sense will appear refreshing.

How to apply the general guidelines

A later section of this chapter presents lists of the key questions you'll have to answer to succeed in the interview. Each question is referenced to those of the above guidelines that are most critical in developing an appropriate response. Study the guidelines well. Then, after you've explored the dynamics of phone and face-to-face interviews in the sections immediately following this one, practice incorporating the guidelines as you develop your answers.

Phone Interviews

The phone interview is almost always the first "real time" encounter with a potential employer. Before the phone interview, you're in total control of the impression you present. You can work at your own pace to design your resume and cover letters, select ads, and orient your presentation style. Once that phone rings, however, you're going to be forced to act and react without the benefit of time to contemplate and ponder. If you're going to be successful, you'll have to prepare in advance and then practice and learn from your mistakes.

Purpose

An employer's goals for a phone interview are entirely different from those of face-to-face interviews. The phone interview is a preliminary screening which attempts to thin out the candidates to those who will be called in for face-to-face interviews. Most of the time, organizations will do as many phone screenings as necessary (usually ten to thirty) to come up with four to ten people who will be asked to come in for an interview. Once the phone rings, you know that they're interested in you on the basis of the materials you sent. Their hope and purpose in calling you is that you will be what you appear to be on your resume. You've already got them half sold before you say hello. With careful

HAND-TO-HAND COMBAT: THE INTERVIEW 163

attention and a little effort, you can easily lead them to invite you to a face-to-face interview.

Preparation

Keep your records handy. Chapter 9 discussed the *Inside Track* record-keeping system. Keep your log book right by the phone at all times if you're not using a telephone answering machine.

Telephone answering machine. A telephone answering machine is essential. You can't afford to miss messages, particularly if you're out a lot or don't have someone who's there to take messages. A lot of personnel types and headhunters will call once or twice and then give up on you if they can't get through. Never use a phone number at work (unless you have an absolutely private line). An answering machine has a number of other advantages. Get one that allows you to listen to the incoming call (call monitoring) before you have to decide if you want to answer it. This can be valuable if you're unprepared for a call. For example, you might get a call from a Ms. Jones of ABCX Computers in reference to an MIS director position. If it was a blind ad or you've been sending out a lot of resumes, you won't know or remember the company name. And you couldn't possibly remember any details about what the ad said and the past salaries you claimed. In that case, you would let the machine take the message. You could then review your records and dig out the ad. You'd know what the ad said, how much you said you made in previous jobs, when you answered it, and the resume version you used. Only when you're so informed are you ready to call her back. On the other hand, suppose you listen to the caller start to give the message and you remember the ad perfectly. You pick up the phone in midmessage and say, "Hello, I just came in the door." You'll never get caught unprepared and risk blowing your chances by being flustered as you try to collect your thoughts.

When you use an answering machine, avoid cutesy outgoing messages. Be professional and formal. There's no need to risk making an offense right at the start. I recommend the following message: "Hello, you have reached (area code and number). No one is available to take your call right at the moment. If you will leave your name, phone number, and a short message, your call will be returned as soon as possible. Wait until (machine-specific instructions about when they can talk) before you leave your message. Thank you for calling."

An added nonsearch benefit of such machines is that you don't have to talk to a lot of people selling newspapers and appliance warranties during the evening.

Never take a call if you're not ready. If you can't give a good interview at a particular moment, don't try. If you're not sure you can give a good interview, simply say something like, "I'm sorry but I was just on my way out the door to speak at a professional dinner meeting," or, "I'm sorry, but my husband just cut his hand very badly and we're on our way out the door to the hospital. Could I call you tomorrow?" Never try to perform when you're not prepared. If you don't have an answering machine and have to take the calls unscreened, don't be afraid to make up an excuse such as the above. Use your imagination. If you don't want to try a "call me later" ploy, simple excuse yourself for a moment so that you can run to your records and skim them. A good excuse here is, "Could you hang on for a minute? I have to put the dog in his run (baby in her crib)." You can then take thirty to sixty seconds to review your records. If you use the dog ploy and don't have one, be careful to keep your story straight if they ask about your dog later. A reply of "What dog?" wouldn't help your chances.

Conducting the interview

Presentation style. All you've got to work with in the phone interview is your voice. The interviewer won't be able to see your great-looking smile or your "power" suit. You've got to project your entire personality with your voice. Most people don't use the phone correctly because they don't consider the voice to be a tool with which they create an impression; they think it's merely an information carrier. You've got to use it for more than that if you want to win more than the average number of interviews. Speak a little more loudly and slowly than you normally do. Avoid contractions such as "don't"; use "do not" with an emphasis on "not." You'll project authority and expertise. Be carefully courteous at all times, using "Yes, sir or ma'am" and "Thank you, sir or ma'am" for all answers to yes-and-no questions. Use the caller's name as often as you can, with the appropriate Mr. or Ms. in front of it. Smile as you talk; it will come across on the other end as enthusiasm and interest. Although it's technically against the law, some job seekers use a tape recorder with a suction-mounted jack to tape all of their phone interviews for later review and assessment. There's no better way to improve your technique than hearing yourself under actual field conditions. No matter how good you are, you'll be shocked at how bad it sounds. If you're not inclined to break the law (it's only legal to tape if you tell the other party, and you can't do that to an interviewer), read the later section of this chapter on questions and then practice by answering them into a tape recorder.

Qualifying yourself. Once the phone rings, you're going to get an invitation to interview in person unless you disqualify yourself. If you need the job very badly, don't admit or volunteer any but the most glaring deviations from what they want. If you can afford to be picky, your purpose is to qualify them just as much as they're qualifying you. Very seldom will they be interested in detailed explanations of your experiences. If the caller is from the personnel department, the questions will be more general and will attempt to verify that you possess the qualifications described in the resume. Many of the questions will ask you to repeat what's on the resume or cover letter. The interviewer wants to hear it in your own words, to be assured that you can talk about it as well as you can write about it. Often, job seekers have such disorganized and vague resumes that it's hard for the screener to tell when and where the applicant worked. Your *Inside Track* resume will obviate that need, but the interviewers will still want to hear it in your voice. If the caller is more of a technical expert, perhaps the hiring manager, then you'll get more specialized and detailed questions. Most often, these questions will attempt to take your resume claims down to the next level or two of detail. If you've claimed to have "reduced sales cost by 15 percent," the caller will want to know exactly what you did to get that 15 percent savings. Have answers prepared and rehearsed for every claim you make on all of your materials.

If the caller makes a statement that you don't have an important qualification or essential item of experience, don't argue or contradict him or her; that's an immediate turnoff and will lose the interview for you. Agree with the caller, and then point out your additional qualifications that render the one that's lacking less important. For example, suppose the interviewer says, "Well, I was hoping your experience had included work in automated robotics. We really need someone with that experience." Don't argue. Say, "You're absolutely correct, Mr./Ms. _____. It is important. I have robotics knowledge. I served on a number of project evaluation teams that put together large technical proposals for robotizing our plant." Note that the applicant doesn't say, "I don't have it *but.* . . ." Always agree with them and then continue to demonstrate that you're amply qualified. You want to leave them with a positive impression of your assets after every comment you make. Don't worry about them seeing through your steamroller; if they don't like your qualifications, you're out of luck anyway. You've got nothing to lose by putting the full-court press on them the minute they focus on a weak area.

Ending the interview. As the phone interview winds down, the caller will be getting ready to do one of four things: drop you from consideration, ask you to come in for an interview, put you on the back burner until he or she sees what else is out there, or arrange to have someone else call you for another phone interview. Any of the last three mean that you will have moved onto the *Inside Track* within a smaller group of candidates. As the interviewer tells you the next step, thank him or her for his or her trouble, say that you enjoyed the talk and that you're very excited about the opportunity (unless it sounds absolutely horrible). Tell the interviewer that you look forward to meeting him or her in person and that you look forward to hearing from him or her. If the caller says that someone else will be calling, enter that person's name and title in your log book so you'll be familiar with the name when the call comes through. Always ask for the caller's name, title, address, and phone number. Don't be embarrassed to ask. Simply say, "Could you spell out your name and give me your title, phone number, and address?" Write it all on the log sheet if it's not already there.

If an invitation for a local face-to-face interview is made, get detailed instructions on how to get there. If you're planning to drive to the interview, you're expected to pay for the expenses if you don't have to stay overnight. If you must drive more than a hundred miles or pay for parking expenses, you should ask the interviewer on the phone, "Whom should I submit my mileage and parking expenses to?" The caller won't be offended and may be impressed with your straightforward, businesslike approach to such a minor (to them) matter. If they are offended by the question, they're not the type of organization you need to work for.

If the interview is out of town, inquire about expenses by asking, "Will you be arranging airline tickets through your travel agency?" Ask what you should do about local travel once you get into their city. Do they want you to take cabs or would they prefer to have you rent a car? If it's a large company, they usually have very well-established procedures. If it's a smaller company, there's always the risk of getting stiffed for part of the expenses, so take nothing for granted.

Follow up. If you're still in the running when you hang up, summarize the main points of what was said in your log book (Chapter 9 discusses the details) and then send a follow-up thank-you letter (outlined later in this chapter).

Face-to-Face Interviews

Once you make it to the face-to-face interview, you're only inches away from a job offer. It's an intense few inches which will require careful preparation and execution. Unlike the phone interview, where your voice must do all the work, you've got to use your whole body to get your message across in the face-to-face interview. Face-to-face, the interviewer will be watching every gesture and every movement and listening to every quiver and waver in your voice. Few interviewers conduct these observations in a planned, objective manner. For most, it's a subconscious activity that incorporates all of their own idiosyncrasies. As a result, you can take nothing for granted. You must orchestrate every aspect of your face-to-face interview technique so that it presents a safe and positive picture of yourself.

HAND-TO-HAND COMBAT: THE INTERVIEW

Purpose

The purpose of phone interviews is to select a pool of candidates who appear approximately suitable for the job. The face-to-face interview will pick the person who gets the job. The emphasis switches from general screening to hunting for the specifics they want in the person they'll select. The specifics are not merely technical qualifications; they're going to be evaluating the total person in an attempt to find the best fit to their organization. Fortunately, organizations are generally looking for the same things. If you present an image that corresponds to the general guidelines given earlier, you'll be giving them what they want.

Preparation

Several days before. If you get enough advance warning, attempt to gather some information on the organization so that you'll be able to sound more informed. Refer to Chapter 7 for reference sources that can help you. If you've got a couple of weeks, call the company and try to get annual reports and anything else they'll send. Check your interview clothes and get them cleaned if necessary. Get your hair cut or done.

The day before. Make sure you know exactly where the appointment will be held. If you have the slightest doubt, call and get detailed instructions. Don't call the person who arranged the interview; you don't need to let them know you're having even the slightest problem. Call the switchboard, the shipping department, or the sales department if you need directions. Check your clothing for the interview. Make sure it's in good shape. Much too much is written about what to wear to interviews. It's very simple: play it safe. Men should wear conservatively styled dark (blue, black, or gray) suits (three-piece suits are best), white shirts, subdued ties, very little jewelry, and well-shined shoes. Hair should be neatly trimmed, cut or styled at least every two weeks during a job search. Women's clothing is much more critical; they must appear businesslike and feminine at the same time in order to make the correct impression on mostly male interviewers. Women should wear skirt suits (never pants suits) in dark blue, gray, or black with white or light-colored pastel blouses, very little jewelry (earrings, watch, wedding rings and no more than one other ring, and perhaps a simple necklace), and well-shined high heels. It doesn't matter what you like, these are what interviewers want to see. Sport coats, loud ties, too much jewelry, and unkempt hair are losers for men. Dresses, pants, loud patterns, too much jewelry, and avant-garde fashions aren't going to make the best impression for women. The proper accessories are also important. A high-quality leather briefcase or folio is essential, as are an attractive pen and pencil set and a good watch. You must exude an aura of professionalism and success; accessories help a lot (and they help once you're on the job too). Pay attention to details such as fingernails. It's almost embarrassing to have to mention that neatly trimmed and clean fingernails and cuticles are mandatory, but a glance at a random number of fingernails in the average office makes it clear that people don't give them a second thought. If you want to optimize your odds of success, pay attention to these details. For women they're even more critical.

If it's an out-of-town interview, carefully pack your interview clothes and wear something else while traveling unless you're going directly to the interview when you arrive. Don't check your baggage; carry your garment bag with you. If you're arriving the night before, leave a wake-up call at least an hour earlier than you think you'll need, and lay out your interview clothes for the next day. If anything is wrinkled from the trip when you unpack, hang it in the shower and run the hot water with the shower curtain closed for twenty minutes, and the wrinkles will come out.

The day of the interview. Always bring along extra copies of your resume. Make sure you give yourself plenty of time to get to the interview. If you think it will take thirty minutes, allow an hour. You can use the time to rehearse and review your records as you sit in the parking lot. Don't go to the interviewer's office more than ten minutes early; it gives a too hungry impression. If you're in a strange city and using a rental car, allow at least an extra hour in case you get lost or the rental car dies. Buy as detailed a map of the city as possible. (You can usually pick one up at the airport or train station when you get in or in the hotel gift shop.)

When you get to the interviewer's office, announce yourself to the receptionist and then sit quietly (don't "visit" with the secretary) and browse through any company literature that's available. This is particularly important if you hadn't been able to do any prior research. You can learn enough in five minutes to sound like a twenty-year veteran if you reach the right things. Look through annual reports, company newsletters, and such for information related to the positions you're after. If you find something relevant, work it into one of your answers or questions during the interview.

Conducting the interview.

General demeanor. The first few minutes of the interview will determine 95 percent of the impression you make. Conduct them carefully. When you first meet the interviewer, smile, shake hands, introduce yourself, and don't hurry in your answers or comments. Don't feel obliged to fill in all of the empty spots in the conversation with chatter. It's not a good idea to smile constantly, but make sure that you flash a warm smile at appropriate times, such as when the interviewer comments that the job is a "wonderful opportunity." Nod your head occasionally when the interviewer speaks, and smile when he or she completes a topic. Always look the interviewer straight in the eye as much as you can. This will demonstrate attentiveness, sincerity, and honesty. Most interviewers don't think people can look you in the eye and lie, so they'll be doubly impressed by whatever you say if you do look straight into their eyes. Don't use a continuous glare; break your eye contact occasionally to glance about the room, particularly when you're pretending to be in deep thought. After some practice, you'll have ready answers to everything, but it's a good idea to pretend to think about an occasional answer; the interviewer will be flattered that he or she came up with a good question. If you do get stumped by a question, don't be afraid to say that you'll have to think about it for a minute.

If you interview during a meal (which will invariably occur on out-of-town interviews), watch your table manners carefully. Order easy-to-eat and nonmessy food to ensure that you don't spill anything on yourself. Eat lightly so that you won't be lulled into the sense of false security that a full stomach brings. Never, under any circumstances, drink any alcohol, even if the interviewer does. You can't afford to have your judgment or reactions dulled, however little.

Posture is an extremely important interview tool. Always sit up very straight, and don't fiddle with your hands, hair, or jewelry. Keep your hands resting in your lap, and use them to make small gestures as you talk. By not moving around a lot, you'll seem more stable, less nervous, composed, and in charge. If you sense the interviewer warming to you, begin to lean closer to his or her desk. This is a particularly good move when coupled with phrases such as "Look, let me be honest with you" or "I'm glad to hear you say that. Here's how I feel." In social situations, people move closer as feelings of intimacy develop, as they begin to feel empathy with someone, or if they like someone. Your moves toward the interviewer after a decent interval will signal your acceptance of the interviewer and lead the interviewer to like you more without knowing why. All of these things usually happen subconsciously, but you can use them very consciously. If you're a male interviewing with a male, a pat on the shoulder or arm when you're leaving can be very effective if the interview has gone well. A two-handed handshake is also good for male-to-male interviews. Women should never attempt any touches other than a formal, "man-style" handshake (palm to palm with firm grip, not a caress with a few fingertips) with either men or women.

Be particularly sensitive to the interviewer's preferences toward your demeanor and responses. If you're giving an answer to a question and the interviewer starts to fidget, you're taking too long; make your future answers shorter. If the interviewer is continually asking you to elaborate, make your initial responses longer. If the interviewer is very serious and somber, stay very formal. If the interviewer is more genial and wants to be more relaxed, act more relaxed (but remain detached and objective).

Bad scenes. Once in a while, you'll be in an interview that is going totally wrong. The interviewer will be rude, nasty, and constantly badgering you. Nothing you say will work, and you'll know you're wasting your time. Once things get that bad, the interview is lost; you might as well face it. When this happens, don't waste more time and inflict suffering on yourself that you'll brood about for weeks. Simply say something to the effect of, "Excuse me. It's clear that neither one of us is getting anything out of this interview. You're being rude and inconsiderate, and you're not a particularly good interviewer. I'm leaving." You'll feel much better if you limit the amount of abuse you take from such losers.

So-called stress interviews used to be popular but have even lost the limited appeal they once enjoyed among narrow-minded and abusive tough guys. The stress interview consists of marginally insulting, intimidating, or accusing questions peppered at the interviewee without giving him or her adequate time to respond. Often, the interviewer will encourage or permit interruptions to see how much you can take. If you practice as this chapter suggests, you'll be able to handle anything in the normal range of interview abuse. If you think it's getting excessive, state your concern and ask what's going on. Call them on it if you have doubts.

Group interviews. These don't happen often, but if you're not prepared they can be real disasters. In fact, they can be real disasters even when you are prepared, especially if you're not used to talking in front of groups. If you have such difficulty, it's a good idea to join some groups where you get that type of experience. While you may never need these skills for interviewing, they'll be invaluable to your career in general. Managers who can speak well are perceived as being professional and dynamic. Group interviews are bad for more fundamental reasons. In one-to-one interviews, it's fairly easy (with practice) to size up your interviewer and play to his or her personality and needs. In group situations, there are usually too many different personalities to appease. If you're showing just enough confidence to one person, someone else is going to feel you're coming on too strong. If one of the group likes humor, you can be sure someone else will not. Even worse, their evaluations of you are going to be heavily influenced by the political struggles within the group. If person A sees that person B is warming to you and person A hates person B, guess who's going to give you a rough time? Even if such backbiting doesn't surface in the interview itself, you'll probably get shafted when it's vote time. It's a messy situation. Avoid these types of interviews if you can, but if that's what the organization wants you have no choice. The only thing you can do is play it as straight as you can. Show them as little of your personality as you can. Be even more careful than under normal conditions. Stick to the facts, and give only direct, concise answers to their questions. The less you show, the better your odds of not offending anyone. In these group situations, it is even more important than usual to present a smooth answering style to all questions. Any pauses or uncertainties will stick out like a shocking pink resume. This is just one more area where extensive out-loud practice will be helpful.

If the schedule changes. Countless job seekers have had the experience of showing up for a series of interviews and then having the whole purpose of the visit destroyed by improper substitutions or last-minute emergencies. An oil company once flew me to Dallas for a day of interviews in which I was supposed to meet and talk with eight people. I was sent typed itineraries ahead of time and even received an update by mail before I left home. When I arrived on the morning of the interviews, the schedule was down to three people as the result of "last-minute changes and emergencies." I ended up talking to two lower-level managers and a personnel guy who told me about benefits for an hour. I missed all the top brass. Needless to say, I didn't get the job; I never interviewed for it. The same sort of thing may happen to you. Face it with equanimity. At the worst, it's a good opportunity to practice your interview skills. Don't try to get even while you're there by complaining about it; you'll only ruin any small chance that's left. If you must have revenge, zap them for an extra dinner on the expense report.

Empty spots. As you gain experience in interviewing, you'll find that the majority of interviewers are incredibly inept. After their canned spiel about the company, how great it is, where it's going now that it's ready, and the smug discussion of how great the benefits are, most interviewers don't have much else to talk about. If they were skilled, they'd get you to talk about the relevance of your skills and interests to the job. Most of the time this doesn't happen. In order to help the interview move along pleasantly, you must have a large number of questions ready for use in filling the inevitable dead spots that will occur when the interviewer is lost and doesn't know what to do next. This will save the interviewer from being embarrassed and associating the discomfort with you. Even with a competent interviewer (you may meet one if your search lasts long enough), your arsenal of questions will be invaluable. They'll help you give the impression that you think the organization is fascinating. Questions can range from the tried and true but always good "Why is this job available now?" to "How would you describe the general management style of this organization?" Let your imagination be your guide.

Even if the interviewer does not require your extensive support to get through the interview in good shape, you'll need to ask several questions when the interviewer pops the inevitable "Well, now, are there any questions you would like to ask me?" I've been in interview situations that lasted twelve hours per day over two days and involved five personnel managers, all of my prospective colleagues, three levels of management in both directions, and a number of miscellaneous people from the organization at large. After endless hours of meetings and mealtime briefings, after I had learned more about the organization than most of the people who had been there twenty years, they asked me, "Well, now, you must have a lot of questions. What can we tell you?" If it happens to you, you must, as I did, excitedly ask a few more questions. If you don't, they won't think you're interested. Prepare your questions, rehearse them, and hang in there.

Concluding the interview. When you sense that an interview is about to end, take control. Tell the interviewer that you enjoyed the meeting, that you know they'll need some time to consider your qualifications and evaluate other candidates, and that you'll get back to them in a week or so to see how things are going. This enables you to maintain the initiative about getting in touch with them. It's also a good time to get in any qualifications that might be important but weren't mentioned. Don t try to force in a lot of extra details; you'll appear too hurried and hungry. It's better to say a little less than to come on too strong. If you're interviewing with a number of people, don't make your official concluding remarks to anyone except the person who's running the show. Make sure that you get a business card from everyone you talk with. Conclude each interview with a firm handshake and a smile.

Following up the interview

Once you get home from the interview (or hang up from a successful phone interview), prepare and send a thank-you note to everyone who interviewed you. Keep it short and formal. It's only a courtesy, but it's one they won't get from many people. It will keep you in their thoughts and high in their esteem while they're evaluating the candidates or interviewing more people.

Many people don't follow up with a thank-you letter. It's a big mistake. The letter will demonstrate that you are professional and courteous enough to know the formal business graces. It will also provide you with an opportunity to demonstrate that you liked the interviewer. A sample follow-up letter is shown in Figure 10.1.

Keep it short and to the point. Don't get cute, and don't volunteer anything that doesn't relate directly to the interview's topics. If, as in the interview that preceded the Figure 10.1 example, the interviewer mentioned she had a cold, say that you hope it's better. Don't make any

Dear Ms. _____ :

It was a pleasure to meet with you (talk with you on the phone) yesterday. The position of Director of MIS sounds exciting and challenging. I'm doubly excited about the possibility of joining an industry leader such as ABCX Computers.

As I explained, my background is an ideal match for the position's current and future requirements. In the key area of telecommunications, I've had extensive experience in the administration of a system similar to the one ABCX is about to install.

I look forward to meeting you in person. I hope your cold is better.

Figure 10.1 Example of Follow-Up Thank-You Letter

assumptions; if she didn't say anything about a cold, that may be the way she always sounds. Any little personal touch is good to show that you were paying attention to the person and not just the job. They will be flattered. Use stationery that matches your resume. Monarch-size stationery is best, but standard is OK. If you're going to be sending references on 8½ by 11 inch paper, use the same size paper for the letter.

References

The topic of references will most likely come up during the phone interview if they think you're a good candidate. You'll always be asked for them in face-to-face interviews. Have a standard reference sheet prepared. If they ask for references, send a copy with your follow-up thank-you letter. The sample shown in Figure 10.2 matches the *Inside Track* resume format. The style, spacing, and production requirements are identical to those detailed in Chapter 4. The similar appearance of both the resume and the reference sheet enables your materials to present an image of organization and consistency. If references are requested during the face-to-face interview, have a copy ready to hand out if the references are the ones you'll be using. The interviewers will be impressed that you've got a prepared sheet. Make sure that you call all of the references as soon as you can to let them know what they'll need to say if they're contacted.

Job offers

No matter how great things go during the interview, don't expect to get an offer. There are several reasons to avoid getting your expecta-

555 Luckawanna Place (202) 555–5555
Washington, DC 20018

REFERENCES
of
SALLY CANDOEZE
Administrative Manager

Mr. Marvin Dreck   Past supervisor, Dreck
President   Industries
Dreck Industries, Inc.
12334 Loading Dock Way
Potowski, NJ 65701

Home (888) 555–8888
Work (888) 555–9999

Ms. Euphemia Jackson   Past supervisor, Jackson
Executive Vice-President   Pig Belly Processors
Jackson Pig Belly Processors, Ltd.
998877 Spleen Street
Potowski, NJ 65701

Work (777) 555–4444

Dr. A. C. Ademic, Ph.D., M.B.A.   Academic advisor,
Director   Bronski State College
Bob Bronski Memorial School of Business
Bronski State College
Ivory Tower
4562 Headin Clouds Avenue
Potowski, NJ 65701

Work (666) 555–2222

Figure 10.2 *Inside Track* Reference Sheet

---

tions up. The most important is that if you start to think you'll get an offer, you'll start to send body language and verbal cues that will indicate how badly you really want the job. This is not the type of signal you want to send. The more you want it, the less valuable you'll seem to the interviewer. Secondly, no matter how badly they say they want you, you can't even begin to imagine the possible foul-ups that could ruin your chances. Remember, you're not dealing with the flower of the business world. For all you know, someone else might have just been offered the job in the next room. Don't compromise your cool objectivity and emotional energy by setting yourself up for a big letdown. You'll need the reserves for the long struggle ahead if you don't get the job. Don't expect; do the interviews. If it works out, fine. If it doesn't, it was good practice.

No matter how anxious they are, no matter (and because of) how excited you are, never accept an offer on the spot. There are several reasons for this. First, it's not professional or businesslike. They sure wouldn't do the same for you. You've probably been hanging on for weeks, suffering through interview after interview waiting for the offer. They view the delay as proper business procedure. So you must show the same business acumen and professionalism. Second, at the very moment of the offer, too much is going on in your head for you to be able to make a rational judgment, particularly if you've been out of work for any length of time. The offer represents acceptance and reaffirmation of your value as a person and a businessperson, deliverance from possible economic hardship, and the end of the debasing and humiliating job search. No matter how hard you try, you won't be able to avoid this type of reaction when you see an end to the horrible quest. Give yourself a little time to get your emotions together. Third, if you are married and you don't give your spouse the courtesy of discussing it with you, you are asking for major domestic problems. Even if you've been out of work for two years, are destitute, have children who are starving, and the job pays two hundred grand per year, save yourself a lot of trouble down the way and talk it over at home first before you accept.

But how do you do it? How do you tell these nice people who want to hire you (finally) that you are so ungrateful you won't say yes right away? You simply flatter them shamelessly. Try something along the lines of, "I'm very excited and pleased about the prospect of working for your organization. I can't make an objective decision until I get my feet back down on the ground. I'd like to take a day or so and talk it over with my family. (This will make you seem even more solid.) Is it OK if I get back to you on Friday?"

If they really push you, I would be a little suspicious, unless there's a good reason you can trust. If you're not happy with some dimension of the offer (such as money or perks) simply tell them you need a day or so to think about it. Give them a day or two to worry, then come back with your reservations and a counteroffer. After they've had a day or two to think you're in the basket, they'll be more inclined to make concessions. If you're desperate and will take anything, tell them you'll need a day or so, and then call them the next morning and accept. You want to preserve some dignity. Even if you're not desperate, you do need the time. The job is different when it's finally offered. Rather than being just an abstract job search challenge, rather than being just a job title and a bunch of interviewers, it's about to become a part of your life. Make sure it fits in at least marginally. It should represent the best available opportunity for you to advance your career. It's a value judgment, and you'll never know the absolute, objective best answer to the problem, but you've got to try. Turning down a not really bad job offer because it doesn't fit is a real character builder. Don't be afraid to do it if you feel the job's not right. Of course, feeding the family and making the car payment are very "right" things, so don't be foolish; the basics come first.

In some rare cases, you may get some unconscious (or overt if they're strong enough) signs that you'd be jeopardizing the offer if you were to tell them you need time to think. There are all sorts of inadequate personalities out there who can't handle any rejection at all. If you're in a spot like this, tell them you'll take it. You can always call later and change your mind. If you've been successfully interviewing and expect to get two or three offers in the next few weeks, don't compromise your interests. Many job seekers feel compelled, if they can't keep the first offer on hold long enough, to accept it and then turn down the others. Forget that nonsense. If you get one offer, you're not sure it's the best one, and you're waiting for others, accept it if you have to. You don't owe them anything; they haven't paid you a nickel yet. Then, if you get a better offer, tell the first organization you've changed your mind. Don't feel guilty. After all, how bad did the other two hundred organizations feel about not picking you? Nobody lost any sleep. Don't let parentally instilled morals coerce you into making shortsighted decisions based on guilt. Accepting offers and then changing your mind and even starting a job and quitting after a week to take a better one are not bad things to do; they are rational business decisions which you may have to make. You must manage your career and job search with the same calculating and ruthless objectivity that organizations use to further their interests.

Once they make you an offer, ask for a written offer letter. Most larger companies will provide one automatically. Ask for it anyway. It will enhance your professionalism. Don't do anything about your current position until you have the offer letter in your hands. If you should resign your current job and then something should happen to the person who hired you, you could be in big trouble without an offer letter. With the offer letter, you have at least some protection against any last-second disasters and changes in the hiring organization (although the offer letter isn't a contract and the employer can still back out with impunity at any time). The offer letter will also serve to reduce possible problems concerning salary, vacations, or relocation benefits.

Sharpening Your Interview Skills

There are no magic secrets to developing good interview technique. It takes knowledge and then hard work to make the proper responses a habit. *Inside Track* provides you with the knowledge; you'll have to do the hard work if you want to develop superior interviewing skills.

Never turn down an interview.

No matter how bad a prospective job seems, no matter how shoddy the organization is or how incredibly rude or ignorant the phone interviewer is, never turn down a face-to-face interview. Even if you know you can't take the job and wouldn't take it even if you were starving, go for the interview. Even if you have two other firm offers and you're going to take one of them, go for the interview. Things are not always what they seem. No matter what you think you know, you may be wrong. If you don't go, you may lose out. Consider what happened to an acquaintance of mine. He was working in a dead-end laboratory job and reluctantly went to an interview for a similar job in a state-run laboratory that had even fewer opportunities. The job turned out to be terrible. However, the head of the department was impressed with him. The department head was also on the admissions committee of a local medical school. You guessed it; the laboratory assistant who hadn't been able to get into medical school is now a physician. And all because he went to an interview he thought was worthless. Of course, that was a one-in-a-million shot, and nobody has any reason to expect similar luck.

There's a more important reason for going to as many interviews as you can: practice. After a few months of interviewing, you'll think you've heard every stupid question, met every type of totally ignorant personnel manager, and been subjected to the rudest behavior possible. You'll be wrong. After only a few months of interviewing, you won't have even begun to scratch the surface of cutting-edge stupidity, rudeness, and ignorance. Each interview will teach you a little more about the darkest side of human potential. Such exposure is invaluable; you couldn't buy it at any price. It will help you develop incredible skills for keeping a straight face when they tell you the salary, extemporaneously orating on any topic at the drop of a question, and kissing up to even the most limited intellects with finesse. In addition, you'll increase your skills in assessing the stupidity level of the interviewer in the first few minutes, you'll improve your ability to embroider fictional past experiences, and you'll further develop your repertoire of canned responses to stock questions. Most important of all, you'll become a little more at ease with each successive interview.

After enough practice in real-world situations, you'll become a confident and relaxed interviewee. Few people can reach this stage of performance without extensive practice, so don't ever turn down an opportunity to interview (unless it would jeopardize a current job by taking you out of the office too often).

Have some answers ready.

The following lists present some of the commonly asked interview questions. If you don't have a great stock answer prepared for each question, you're not ready to interview for any job. Read each question and then rehearse your answer to it out loud. Don't kid yourself that you can simply read the question, think "Oh, yeah, I can answer that one," and then read the next question. The point is not whether or not you can come up with an answer to it; anyone can answer it. The person who gets the job is going to be the one who answers it smoothly, the one who can concentrate on making the right impression of sincerity, candor, and reflection while reeling off a well-rehearsed stock answer. In order to do that, you've got to say the actual words and make them sound great. Rehearse out loud, preferably into a tape recorder. Once you hear yourself, you'll realize why practice is necessary.

The following lists are divided into loose categories, but whatever the category the interviewer is searching for answers that reflect your observance of the general guidelines given in the beginning of this chapter. Each question is referenced to those specific general guidelines for interviewing that should be emphasized in developing the answer. For example, the question "What motivates you?" is followed by the numbers 19, 17, 3, 10. These numbers indicate the general guidelines you should emphasize in formulating your answer (10 represents "Never assume that you understand the interviewer's value system"). Where the necessary or most common answer is apparent, the main point or key expression is given in parentheses. After each group of questions, a short summary will outline critical points for you to consider in formulating your answers to the preceding questions and will present a sample question and answer in which the use of the various general guidelines is demonstrated.

Questions about you and your family and personal affairs

Tell me about your home life (when you were growing up). (17, 20)

What did your father (mother) do for a living? (17)

How were you influenced by your upbringing? (17, 20, 15)

What's your family like? (17, 20, 11)

HAND-TO-HAND COMBAT: THE INTERVIEW

What type of discharge did you get from the service? (1, 11)

Does your spouse object to your working long or late hours? (3, 11)

Is frequent travel a problem for your family? (3, 1, 11, 19)

Would you have any problems with relocation? (3, 1, 11, 19)

What kind of transportation do you have? (3, and what it is)

Have you ever had credit problems? (no)

Have your wages ever been garnished? (no)

Do you own your own home? (yes or no)

What jobs did you like when you were a child? (17, 19, 3)

What's your personal net worth? (your choice)

Do you get alimony (child support)? (yes or no)

Do you find it difficult to work with men (women, blacks, whites, gays, etc.)? (have never had trouble working with anyone, and 3, 11, 17)

Where were you (your parents, wife) born? (tell them)

How involved are you with your children? (3, 10, 17)

What is your spouse going to say about this job? (3, 11, 1)

Is your recent divorce a problem? (no and 1)

Are you planning on a family? (haven't decided yet, and 1)

Who's taking care of your children while you're at work? (3, 1, 17)

Do you plan to get married? (haven't decided yet, and 1)

Why aren't you married? (haven't met the right person, and 1)

What kind of shape are you in physically? (great, and 1, 3)

Do you have any trouble keeping up with men (younger people)? (they have trouble keeping up with me, and 1, 3, 2)

When did you get your first job? (17, 20, 3)

Do you have any trouble getting to work on time? (never, and 1)

How good is your health? (excellent, and 1, 3)

Do you get sick often? (hardly ever, and 1, 3)

When was your last operation? (tell them, and 1)

Strategy

Many of the above questions are illegal. Many will be asked anyway, particularly of women and minorities. Whatever the question, you must answer it completely and with dignity and without alarm or you're not going to get the job (which you may not want after they ask some of the questions, but that's a choice you can make when they offer it to you). Your strategy must be to show no problems. You should characterize yourself and your family as possessing firm, middle-class values of discipline, hard work, and a solid home life that supports your job efforts.

Sample question and answer

Question: "What's your family like?"

Answer: "My family is very important to me (17). We're all very independent in our interests, and everyone is always very busy on their own projects (3), but we make the time to get together and help each other (17). I guess it's something our parents taught us when we were young (20, 17): get the job done no matter what it takes (19), but be sure to take care of the family (17)."

Questions about your schooling and education

What was your grade point (favorite or most difficult subject) in school? (1, 3, 19, 14)

How did you get along in school? (3, 19, 11, 14, 1)

Tell me about your extracurricular activities in school. (3, 11, 14)

What honors, offices, and awards did you hold in school? (have a few handy, and 2, 3, 17)

What proportion of your education did you pay for? (about half, unless it's more, and 17)

What were your SAT (GRE) scores? (3, 14, 15)

What was your social life like in school? (1, 3, 9)

Why did you go to college? (16, 19, 14)

Why did you pick _____ as your major? (16, 19, 14)

Did you do as well in school as you could? (14, 15, 3)

Why didn't you do better in college? (18, 14, 1)

How many times did you change your major? (truthful answer if low, and 14, 1)

Strategy

The interviewer is looking for solid values and a sense of planning and goal setting that extends back to your college days. It's ridiculous to

HAND-TO-HAND COMBAT: THE INTERVIEW

expect eighteen to twenty-five-year-olds to have such a plan, but you've got to make it look like you did. Characterize your educational efforts as a time of hard work and personal growth. Come up with a number of extracurricular activities to show that you're well rounded. If necessary, you can admit a certain amount of youthful indecision but not if you're recently out of school.

Sample question and answer

Question: "Why didn't you do better in college?"

Answer: "You're right, I should have done better (18). My problem was that I was eager to learn everything (14). I sometimes spent too much time on extra projects (17, 19, 3) and not enough time working for grades (11). If I had it to do over, I would concentrate on getting the grades first (14) and try to limit my special projects to a more select group (15)."

Questions about your personality, goals, and achievements

What new goals have you set for yourself lately? (15, 19 16, 3)

Where do you plan to be in five (ten) years? (16, 15, 3)

If you could start your career over, what would you do differently? (3, 2, 11)

What are your long- (short-) range objectives? (16, 15, 14)

Are you happy with your career progress to this point? (3, 7, 14, 2, 20, 11)

How come you're not further along in your career? (18, 14, 2, 3, 1)

What self-improvement programs are you working on now? (15, 14, 3, 1)

What other jobs are you trying to get now? (1, 3, 7, 10)

Are you planning on more education? (16, 15)

What do you see as the best opportunities in your field? (3, 16, 7, 3)

Why are you trying to change careers at this point in your life? (16, 14, 3, 2)

What motivates you? (19, 17, 3, 10)

What types of people do you like (dislike)? (4, 5, 6)

What do you think causes some people to fail in (job title)? (4, 6, 12)

Describe your closest friend, and tell me how you and he or she differ. (4, 10, 11, 1)

Describe how you work under pressure. (19, 17, 11, 3, 2)

Do you think stability is more important in a job than challenge? ("I've always felt that if a person can handle challenges, they create their own stability," and 10, 3, 16, 19))

What types of friends do you have? (17, 11, 3)

How would your friends (enemies) describe you? (2, 4, 3, 11, 1)

What's your temper like? (3, 6, 1, 5)

What is your major strength (weakness)? (3, 11, 15)

What is your biggest achievement (failure) in life (recently/last job/last five years)? (11, 20, 2, 3, 14)

What kind of people do you find it difficult (pleasant) to work with? (6, 20, 2, 3)

What do you do to get along with difficult people? (19, 20, 4)

Tell me something that supports your claims of being a self-starter. (1, 19, 2, 17)

Describe what you mean by success. (17, 2, 3, 12)

What do you get out of work besides money? (17, 19, 2, 3)

What would you do if you didn't have to work for a living? (17, 2, 3, and "I couldn't imagine not working")

How do you react when you're criticized by a supervisor? (15, 20, 3)

Are you sensitive to criticism? ("No, I appreciate the feedback," and 3, 20)

What does cooperation (teamwork) mean to you? (3, 20, 17)

How important is money (service to humanity) to you? (17, 19, 3, 2)

Describe how you feel in a group of people. ("It's great to be able to trade ideas and concepts; I feel renewed," and 3, 11, 10)

Describe your decision-making abilities. (2, 3, 11, 15)

What do you do when you make a mistake? ("I try to learn from it," and 3, 20, 15, 11)

What are your hobbies? (reading, team sports, and 2, 3, 15)

How do you spend your free time? (same as above)

Describe your personality (yourself). (2, 3, 19, 11, 15, 16, 17)

What do you do best (worst)? (2, 3, 11)

What's your opinion on women (alcohol/gays) at work? (5, 1, 11, 3)

How do you feel about abortion (religion/extramarital sex)? ("I hate to pass judgments on others who may be having problems," and 10, 6, 11)

What was the last book you read (movie you saw)? (2)

What was the last thing that made you really angry? (11, 10)

Who is your hero? (Lincoln is safe)

What qualities do you admire in a leader? (determination, enthusiasm, ability to provide feedback, appropriate direction to employees, and the ability to see the big picture)

What makes a good employee? (hard work, loyalty, creativity, and a refusal to accept less than the best product, and 3, 19, 17, 10)

Describe your leadership qualities to me. (2, 3, 11, 15)

Strategy

The above questions are beginning to get to the core issues: what type of employee or supervisor you will be. Interviewers expect motherhood and apple pie on these questions. Admit nothing but acceptable flaws. ("Sometimes I expect too much from people who aren't as devoted as I am," and "I get darned impatient with people who don't take work seriously.") Keep all of your opinions evenhanded and distant. You must appear to be a hard-working, career-bound, farsighted planner who leaves nothing to chance. You're a great leader, you love constructive criticism, you look for challenges, and you can deal with and work with all types of people under any circumstances if that's what it takes to get the job done. You've got your career planned out in detail for the next twenty years, but you're flexible if something develops. You're continually improving yourself through self-help, education, and taking on more challenges at work.

Sample question and answer

Question: "Tell me about yourself."

Answer: "Well, I'm a pretty straightforward person (1). My career is very important to me, and it's the one thing that really provides me with a sense of accomplishment (17). It's how I prove myself to the world (19, 2). If I didn't have my work, I'd be a totally different person (17). In terms of personality, I enjoy other people and the interchanges of enthusiastic groups (3), but I also need time by myself to think and recharge my batteries (5). I enjoy having a lot of complex projects to work on so that I can stay challenged (29, 3, 17). If I have one fault, it's my willingness to take on just about anything for the challenge (19, 3). Sometimes I end up with too much work and not enough time to enjoy it as I do it (11). Then I know how people who don't like their work feel (4, 6)."

Questions about past jobs

What kind of recommendations (references) will I get from your past employers? ("I'm sure they will be outstanding," unless they're terrible, and 3, 20, 11)

You've been out of work a long time. Why haven't you found something sooner? (18, 11, 19, 14, 3)

What's your professional reputation like? (2, 11)

What would your past bosses (employees) say about you? (2, 20, 11)

Have you ever been fired? (14, 11, 1)

Why did you leave your last (a specific) job? (19, 7, 11)

Why are you leaving (what's wrong with) your present job? (4, 11, 20, 7, 3, 1)

Tell me about your employment history. (3, 2, 20, 14, 11, 12)

Why have you had so many jobs? (18, 14, 16, 3, 1)

How have you been treated by past employers? ("I've been fortunate to work for some great organizations who have always treated me very well," and 20, 4, 3)

What single thing did you like most (least) about your last job? (20, 19, 4)

What changes would you make in your last job to make it better? (19, 4)

What working environment do you like best? (19, 16, 3)

How did your military service go? (great, and 19, 14, 3)

What are some of the toughest parts of your present (last) job? (not enough challenge, and 20, 4, 6, 2)

What was your biggest frustration (satisfaction) in your last job? (4, 20, 6, 2)

What have you done to change things for the better in your past (present) job? (19, 10, 4, 6)

Why did you fail as a consultant (private businessperson)? (18, 14, 10, 3)

What were your supervisors' best (worst) points? (20, 1, 4, 6)

Tell me about a typical day in your _____ job. (1, 3, 19)

Which of your jobs did you like the best, and why? (19, 20, 3, 10, 1)

What have your supervisors done to help you develop? (plenty of feedback and good advice, and 20, 3, 10)

HAND-TO-HAND COMBAT: THE INTERVIEW 185

Strategy

You must not have anything negative to say about anyone in any job. As far as the interviewer is concerned, you've been helped by everyone, you're grateful for it, and you want more. Portray your job history as an odyssey of great jobs working for great people with the only problems being that there were sometimes not enough growth opportunities and challenge. Of course, you don't hold a grudge for that because it wasn't anyone's fault. You feel fortunate to have gotten as far as you have. You might have come along faster but you've tried to take the time to develop your skills rather than moving too fast. Now, however, you're ready for the big time with this next job. If there have been any problems, they're only minor setbacks that have only sharpened your resolve to succeed, which is your only goal.

Sample question and answer

Question: "Why did you leave your last job?"

Answer: "I was very sorry to have to leave JBI. It was a great place to work, and everyone there was outstanding (20, 3). I learned a lot there (20), but things eventually got to the point where I didn't feel that I was learning any more (14). Of course, I enjoyed the work and would have stayed anyway, but I just wasn't getting challenged enough (20). Once I learned the job and cleaned up most of the problems I was assigned to work on (2), there wasn't much to do. I wasn't happy taking their money for less than I can give (17), so I looked around."

Questions about working conditions

How long will you stay with us? (16, 3, 4, 17)

How many hours a week should a person put in on a job? (as many as it takes to get it done right, and 19)

How do you feel about company policies? (3, 1, 17)

How long would it be before you'd be making some major contributions here? ("I like to think that I would be able to make some major contributions in a very short time," and 2, 3, 19)

What unique contributions can you make? (2, 3, 16)

Are late hours a problem? (no, unless they are, and 19, 3)

You're overqualified for this job. Why do you want it? (14, 16, 10)

So, what do you think of our little company? (4, 6, 1)

This place is a pressure cooker. Can you handle it? (yes, and 3, 11)

Do you think you want (can do/would like) my job? (with the proper help, experience, and guidance, and 2, 8, 15)

Are you going to be out to take your boss's job? ("I expect to open up opportunities for myself through hard work," and 10, 8, 3)

Are you willing to relocate to anywhere the company needs you? (yes, unless you're not, and 1, 3)

Do you like to travel? (love it, if there's a lot of it and you don't mind, otherwise 1, 3)

Do you like big or small companies? (whatever they are, and 3, 16)

How much money do you want? (tell them)

Why do you want to work for us? (16, 7, 14, 3, 1)

What is it about this job that interests you? (16, 7, 14, 3, 1)

What do you think (your field) is all about? (12, 8, 16, 3)

You've been moving around (with one firm) for so long, what makes you think you'll fit in around here? (16, 14, 7, 3)

How long do you think it's reasonable to wait for a promotion? ("As soon as I prove myself and an opportunity opens up," and 15, 3, 2, 1)

What do you know about our company? (have something to say, and 1, 5, 10)

Strategy

You must convince them that your interest in their company is motivated by your objective assessment of their wonderful characteristics and the unique fit of their organization to your skills, plans, and interests. If there's a problem with long hours, overtime, travel, or future relocations, you'll have to decide whether to be candid and risk losing the interview or to tell them what they want to hear and worry about the problems later. If you're hard up for a job, you don't have much choice but to live with the grief until you find a job. The topic of salary levels has already been dealt with in Chapter 5. You must show a healthy amount of aggressive talk about how fast you expect to move up, but temper it with statements about how you're always willing to let your work speak for itself and that you realize that the system has a certain amount of inertia that keeps things on an even keel.

Sample question and answer

Question: "So, what do you think of our little company?"

Answer: "Frankly, I'm more impressed than I thought I would be (4). The most obvious thing is that a lot of people are doing a lot of very hard work on some very exciting projects (17). The management here has obviously done a lot (20). I'm sure there are challenges to be worked on, but they probably require minor adjustments rather than major changes (2). For example, I noted in the parts control area there seemed to be a little congestion. I think my routing experience might come in handy in contributing to a more efficient flow of traffic (3). Of course, I don't know what constraints that department has to work under (6), but I'd be excited to tackle that issue (19). All in all, you've got a very impressive operation here (3, 20)."

Questions about job skills

What single thing do you do best? (2, 5, 19, 20)

Have you hired (fired) people before? (yes, unless you couldn't handle it, and 1, 6, 11)

How do you feel about firing people? (1, 6, 11, 19)

How have you increased profits (sales) in the past? (examples, and 2, 12, 14, 19, 20)

Explain how your lack of (some qualification) isn't going to be a problem for you. (2, 3, 16, 14, 19)

How have you reduced costs (overhead/staff) in the past? (examples, and 2, 3, 10, 19, 20)

How do you rate yourself technically? (very high, and 15, 16, 20)

How do you think your skills will stand up to the other professionals we have here? (very well, and 5, 4, 15, 19)

What are your best (worst) qualities as a manager? (2, 11, 17)

What unique contributions have you made in the past which we can expect here? (examples, and 2, 3, 16, 19)

What's your philosophy of management (employee supervision/team building)? (3, 6, 10, 17)

Describe a situation in which your management skills were put to the test. (example, and 19, 4, 10, 14, 1)

What areas as a manager do you need to improve? (11, 15, 17, 1)

What do you look for in potential employees? (loyalty, willingness to work hard, enthusiasm, and desire to succeed, and 3, 17, 19)

How do you motivate your employees? (3, 6, 10, 17, 19, 20)

Are you a leader? (a natural leader, unless you're a total washout as a leader, and 2, 3, 15, 16, 17)

Strategy

Have specific examples ready for all of the above questions. You're a great natural leader, you love to work closely with all employees, you need to work on having more empathy and not driving them so hard, and you've made incredible contributions in reducing costs, sales, and so on in past jobs. Your approach to management in general must be characterized as bottom-line oriented but with an understanding that people are important in the productivity equation.

Sample question and answer

Question: "How do you feel about firing people?"

Answer: "Nobody likes to fire people (4). I certainly don't (11). But sometimes it's part of the job, and it's the only fair thing to do for everyone concerned (4). I look upon it as a last resort after rehabilitation efforts have failed (5). When an employee is having a performance problem, I think it's in everybody's best interests to try to fix the problem (3, 20). If the rehabilitation succeeds, the employee benefits (6) and the company saves money and lost productivity (3). On the other hand, if the employee doesn't come around, it's not fair to the remaining employees to make them do extra work (6) by keeping the employee with the problem. I take it as a personal challenge to develop and monitor my employees so that I can head off trouble before it gets to the firing stage (20, 3). But if it gets to that stage, well, then it's just part of the job, and I do it the best way I can (17, 20)."

It's Not As Hard As It Looks

If you're not a great interviewer already, this chapter may appear intimidating because of the vast array of questions you'll have to master. Don't worry about it. If you begin to rehearse the above questions aloud as you're driving, walking the dog, or taking a shower, you'll quickly discover that there's a smaller number of key phrases that can be used over and over in dozens of questions. With moderate amounts of out-loud practice, you'll quickly learn to weave these phrases together in novel and appealing ways. More important, you'll devote a mental set for approaching each question in which you'll immediately recognize the key elements that must be included in your answers. You'll then find that you have to force yourself to pay attention while you're in an interview giving an answer; it will be so automatic that your mind will wander. It only takes ten to fifteen hours of practice to get that good. But do it right. Practice out loud and give complete answers. Use a tape recorder to listen to your answers if you can. If they don't sound right, change them and do it over. When you get back from an interview, rehearse answers to questions that you didn't handle as well as you would have liked.

Finally, don't be deceived into believing that the content of your answers is the absolute bottom line. Content is important, but your presentation style and manner are much more important. With practice, you'll be able to devote more time to sizing up the interviewer and tailoring your presentation style to his or her needs and less time to sweating over what you're going to say. If you work at it, your interviewing skills will become excellent in a short time. Don't push, and don't worry about it. Just practice, be honest with yourself about your problem areas, work on them, and you'll turn into an interviewing tiger. Your *Inside Track* resume and letters will get you into the interviews, and then you'll finish them off with your interviewing finesse. They won't have a chance. Be gentle with them; they're only trying to do a job.

Chapter 11

Using Your Personal Computer As a Job Search Aid

A personal computer (PC) with the appropriate software and hardware can be a tremendous asset to a comprehensive job search effort. Properly equipped, a PC can speed up your flow of first-rate correspondence, provide you with the capability to generate custom-appearing correspondence from mailmerged form letters, and permit you to make numerous and speedy changes to your resume if you wish to tailor it to specific ads. This chapter will provide you with guidelines for getting the most job search assistance from your PC.

Basic Equipment Requirements

In order to obtain any benefits from a PC, you've got to have access to a properly configured computer system. The basic equipment you'll need to generate useful resumes and correspondence is:
1. A PC with enough internal memory to handle the word-processing package you'll be using.
2. A word-processing (WP) software package. This item will permit your computer to function like an intelligent typewriter. A very basic package will permit you to do all sorts of labor-saving procedures. More sophisticated packages will save you even more time and effort. It's my experience that you get exactly what you pay for in terms of WP software. It doesn't make sense to save a hundred dollars now if you're going to have to use an extra hundred hours (or more) of time over the next six months to make up for the more limited capabilities of a cheaper package.
3. A letter-quality printer. If you're going to generate effective correspondence and resumes with your PC, you absolutely must have a letter-quality printer. Matrix dot printers are worthless for generating business correspondence. If you can discern the difference between your printer's output and the quality you'd expect from the typewriter of a corporation president's secretary, your printer isn't good enough to use for correspondence and resumes. And that also goes for any typewriter you plan on using.

Money, time, and knowledge

Just having the necessary equipment isn't enough; you've got to be able to use it effectively. If you don't already have the equipment in your home or office or you don't know how to use it right now, forget about a PC as a viable job search aid for the near future. If you were to go out and buy the necessary equipment solely to assist you in your job search, you'd be spending far more money than you could cost-effectively justify. If you don't already have a PC or need one for other work, you'll be able to produce your job search materials more economically by paying for WP and secretarial support from outside services on an as-needed basis.

Aside from the expense involved in buying a PC, there is the issue of the time involved in learning how to use one. The computer industry is notorious for underplaying the difficulties of becoming computer literate, even if you're just trying to learn a new software package. If you aren't already familiar with your PC and a WP software package, chances are that you wouldn't be able to learn what you need to know fast enough to help you with a job search (or anything else) in the near future. Even if you had the time for a crash learning program and were willing to mount one, you'd end up spending more time getting familiar with the software than you'd save by doing things through a secretarial service. Worse yet, you'd end up delaying far more important job search activities. Your job search is in a position to benefit from the assistance of a PC only if you already know how to use the software you'll need and you either have or are about to get a PC that you already know how to operate. If your situation is anything other than this, forget about using a computer to help on any near-term or current job searches. Instead, get busy finding a job, and worry about computers later if you're still interested once you've completed your job search.

What a Personal Computer Can Do for You

A PC can assist you in performing a number of job search functions. These functions, in ascending order of importance to your job search, are listed below.

Recordkeeping

The *Inside Track* recordkeeping system for keeping track of ads answered, resume versions sent, names, phone numbers, and so on, is described in Chapter 9. If you're going to be using a software package with a mailmerge capability, you can save a little time by having the computer assist you in recordkeeping. The computer can generate a data sheet for each job in much the same way that it generates a cover letter. But don't get excited about computerized recordkeeping; it's the least tedious and time-consuming aspect of your job search activities. If you can't implement the computerized recordkeeping system described in this chapter, don't worry about it. If you aren't going to (or can't) do more than keep records with your PC, forget the computer and do it by hand. You'll save time.

Resume construction

If you've got a letter-quality printer and a WP program that you know how to use fairly well, you can produce excellent resumes without going to a secretarial service. The minimum features or capabilities your WP software should have are right justification, underlining, file copying, and file editing. In order to follow exactly the *Inside Track* resume format, you'll also need boldfacing capabilities (striking over the same letters two or three times, each time slightly off center), but you can get along without this feature if you have to.

Generating correspondence

Here's where a PC can really save you some time, effort, and money. A major time-consuming portion of any job search involves the generation of correspondence. You've got to send cover letters with your resume in response to ads (discussed in Chapter 5), you've got to send thank-you letters for interviews, you might be sending cover letters and resumes to headhunters (covered in Chapter 6), and maybe you'll be soliciting directly to executives and organizations (as described in Chapter 7). A great deal of the letter writing is repetitive, boring, and tedious. If you're not a good typist, it can be infuriating to try to crank out a respectable-looking letter that has less than two pounds of correcting fluid on it (and the appearance of such letters will drive a sharpened pencil eraser into the heart of your resume's chances with most employers). A basic WP package can be a big help. A sophisticated WP package can make it almost laughably easy to crank out custom-appearing correspondence with a minimum of effort (although any typing is a nerve-wracking ordeal if you're not good at it). A sophisticated package with a mailmerge capability can generate large numbers of form letters that appear custom but are nothing more than the same old letter with a different name and address on each one. If you're contacting large numbers of headhunting firms, this function can be a tremendous asset.

Databases

Computers (although not yours) can play an additional but very minor role in your job search. There are a number of so-called computer services that solicit your resume and offer to put it into their system either for free or for a very nominal fee. They then sell access to their database to employers who are looking for candidates. So few job candidates and companies participate (statistically speaking) in these systems that they don't offer a high probability for finding job leads. However, if all you've got to do is fill out an application and send it in, you've got little to lose if you're not planning to change your story in the near future. There's always a slight danger of a security leak (your present employer finding out that you're looking) if you use a database service, but you face that probability every time you send out a resume. Most of the computer search firms claim to be able to prevent your current employer from viewing your data in the rare event that both of you are using the service. I have my doubts about such security, but the risk is probably very small. If you have to pay a fee, don't waste your time.

Word Processors

From this point on, I'm going to assume that you're computer literate with a WP package and your PC. Many WP packages will do an acceptable job of generating job search materials. They can be separated into two groups: (1) those that have a mailmerge capability (such as WordStar/Mailmerge and Easy Writer II/Mailer) and (2) those that don't (such as Bank Street Writer). In terms of generating resumes and unique single-copy correspondence (such as a letter to a friend), the two groups function in exactly the same manner. The generation of a basic resume or a unique, one-time letter doesn't benefit a great deal from a mailmerge capability. The additional power of the mailmerge capability comes into play when you're sending out numbers of documents that are more or less standard except for a few variables that change in each document (such as the employer's name and address and the title of the job in a cover letter for an ad response).

Generating Resumes

General approach

Using a WP to generate resumes is fairly straightforward. The basic approach is the same regardless of the type of WP you have. You'll be using your WP to design and compose an original copy of your resume. You'll run off a copy on plain white paper and then take it to a photocopying or printing outfit to have copies made. Don't use your printer to make copies for general use; you'll wind up burning out the printer, wasting time standing around while things are printing, and using up a lot of ribbons and stationery. The one exception is when you want to make some last-minute changes to a resume for a suddenly scheduled job interview; in that case, you might not have the time to get an original photocopied. Don't underestimate the amount of time it will take to start from scratch and turn out an error-free, photocopy-ready version of your resume. If you can do it in less than two hours of aggravation and frustration over missed errors and typos, you're doing great.

Create a separate file for each page of each resume version. This will permit you to make changes on one page without affecting the spacing and margins on other pages. If you have versions with and without objectives (as recommended in Chapter 4), you'll probably have more first pages (with objective, summary of qualifications, and so on) than second pages. With each page in a separate file, you won't have to duplicate a lot of extra pages.

File names

If you' going to have a number of resume versions, be extremely careful with file names; it's easy to get them confused and waste a lot of time. I recommend that you entitle each resume file as RESX.Y, in which the X represents the resume code number and the Y represents the page number. Thus, the file RES3.2 is the second page of resume version 3. The first page of resume version 3 would be in a file named RES3.1. Start your numbering scheme with a low number and then assign each subsequent modification or version a consecutively higher number. You won't have a lot of confusion when you're trying to figure out which files hold your most recent resume versions. As mentioned earlier, maintain a hard-copy file of all resumes (and other correspondence) in which each hard copy is labeled with the file name of the document. It's easier to sort through paper copies than to open and read ten different files.

Rough drafts and edits

When you're first typing the resume into the system, don't worry too much about the exact spacing of margins and spaces between sections of your resume. Enter each page in rough form and then print the file out. Once it's on paper, you'll get a better sense of what you have to work with in terms of space and format. Make your corrections on the hard copy and then open the file and modify it. Once you think you've got things pretty much under control, attempt to put in the correct margins and spacing, underlining, and boldfacing. When you've got it as close as you can, print off another hard copy and give it a careful proofreading (with some help if you can get it). I can't emphasize the importance of using a spelling checker on all of your search correspondence. There's no end to the way typos can elude you and your proofreaders and then explode in the face of personnel types or headhunters the instant they open your envelope. If your WP doesn't have a spelling checker, get one; it could be the best investment you make in increasing your odds of getting interviews from correspondence. I recommend a checker named Microspell, which works with many WP packages. It contains artificial intelligence heuristics that suggest correct spellings, and it's easy to use.

When you decide to make later changes in a completed resume, don't make the changes on the original file unless your software makes a backup copy (as WordStar does) when you open a file. Make a copy with a different name and modify the copy. You don't want to risk ruining the original if you wind up unhappy with the new version. This may seem like a lot of trouble, but so many surprising things (all bad) can happen when you're working on your only copy of a file.

Generating Letters and Correspondence

Once you've mastered the use of your WP to produce a resume, you'll have an easy time with letters and correspondence. There are basically three ways to generate correspondenc with a WP.

Create an original document from scratch each time

This approach is much the same as using a typewriter. While it's an acceptable (but somewhat inefficient) approach for short thank-you letters, it's clearly not appropriate for situations that require even a modest amount of correspondence.

Using a word processor without a mailmerge capability

This approach is to create a basic document and then copy it and modify the copy each time you need it. You'll have to use this approach if your WP doesn't have a mailmerge capability. This strategy eliminates a great deal of repetitive typing. Figure 11.1 displays an example of such a cover letter in response to an advertisement (Chapter 5 covers this topic in detail.) Once this letter is entered into the system, it can be readily adapted for use in responding to different ads. The areas that are boldfaced in Figure 12.1 indicate the information that would have to be changed if you were to use the same letter in order to respond to a different ad. Most of the letter could be used just as it is. Simply copy the letter's file, give it a different name, and then open the new file and edit it to meet the requirements of the ad. If you're only going to edit and send one letter, there's no need to copy

---

                                                    Joseph Jones
                                                    22 Main Street
                                                    Glendale, CA 91207
                                                    (818) 555–9999

June 23, 1986

Ms. Mary Quitecontrary
Personnel Manager
ACME HUMMINGBIRD MEAT PACKERS, INC.
9999-B Brand Boulevard
Glendale, CA 91206

Dear **Ms. Quitecontrary:**

I am responding to your **June 21, 1986,** advertisement in the Los Angeles Times in which you solicited candidates for the position of **Supervisor of Packing Operations**. My qualifications are an ideal match to those outlined in the advertisement. My resume is enclosed.

My qualifications include a M.S. in avian meat packing from Bird University. I am currently employed by Nadir Sparrow Packers, Inc., of Bellflower, CA, as Supervisor of Feet Processing. I am seeking an increase in challenge and responsibility.

I would be pleased to discuss my potential contributions with you in detail at your convenience. Thank you for your attention.

Respectfully,

Joseph Jones

Enclosure

Figure 11.1 Cover Letter in Response to an Ad—Shows (in Boldface) Portions That Can Be Edited for Reuse

it and change the name (as long as you've got a backup copy of the original. I suggest that you give all copied letter files the name adlet.XX where XX is a numerical code. The "adlet" will tell you that the file is a letter in response to an ad. You can put the letter code number on the ad's page in your log book (see Chapter 9).

You can use the same technique for addressing envelopes as well if you use your printer to address them. You could use a typewriter, but it looks better to have the same type style on all pieces of the correspondence. (Some employers actually keep the envelope attached to the letter.) Simply construct a master envelope file by formatting a file the size of a business envelope ($9^1/_2$ inches by $4^3/_{16}$ inch or about ninety-five 10-pitch characters wide by about twenty-six lines high). Each time you need another envelope, copy the original file, give it another name, open the new file, and then edit the addressee data.

Using a WP with a mailmerge capability

This is where you're going to save a lot of time and effort. The basic approach of all WPs with mailmerge capability is to create a single data file which will then be used to fill in empty spots, called variables, in a variety of target documents. The data file can contain hundreds or more sets of variables. The target documents can be letters, envelopes, or your recordkeeping log sheets. When things are organized in the proper fashion, you can have your WP crank out custom-appearing documents without ever having to open the document files themselves (although you may have to open some documents in order to add custom material such as the supplementary qualifications section discussed in Chapter 5).

For example, let's take another look at the letter that was shown in Figure 11.1. Figure 11.2 displays the same letter from the date through the end of the first paragraph. This portion of the letter contains the data that must be changed if the basic letter is to be edited and sent to other people. Note that each piece of boldfaced information has a variable number assigned to it. By using the mailmerge capability of your WP, you can automatically insert specified information into the variables.

The real power of this approach is that you don't have to open the document files or manually edit the variables one by one. Further, you can use the variable information, once it's typed into a data file, over and without having to rekey it. For example, an envelope for the above file could be generated by creating a document file that would specify variables 2 through 6 for insertion into the spots reserved for the address. The information would be taken by the mailmerge program from the data file and used for both the letter and the envelope (as well as your log sheets).

June 23, 1986 (variable 1)

Ms. Mary Quitecontrary (variable 2)
Personnel Manager (variable 3)
ACME HUMMINGBIRD MEAT PACKERS, INC. (variable 4)
9999-B Brand Boulevard (variable 5)
Glendale, CA 91206 (variable 6)

Dear **Ms. Quitecontrary:** (variable 7)

I am responding to your **June 21, 1986**, (variable 8) advertisement in the Los Angeles Times (variable 9) in which you solicited candidates for the position of **Supervisor of Packing Operations** (variable 10).

Figure 11.2 Cover Letter to Ad with Variables (in Boldface) Labeled

In order to take full advantage of this capability, you have to plan a complete mailmerge approach for generating letters, envelopes, and recordkeeping logs. Figure 11.3 displays the variables I recommend that you include in your master data file. Note that the figure presents a number of variables that wouldn't appear in the letter shown in Figure 11.2 or on the envelope that would accompany it. Variables 2 through 13 would appear on the letter as it's designed in Figure 11.2,

Variable number	*Alphanumeric name*	*What it is*
1	n	Log number
2	datea	Date letter sent
3	adda	First line of name and address
4	addb	Second line of name and address
5	addc	Third line of name and address
6	addd	Fourth line of name and address
7	adde	Fifth line of name and address
8	addf	Sixth line of name and address
9	addg	Seventh line of name and address
10	salutation	Salutation name
11	dateb	Date ad appeared
12	paper	Publication that ran the ad
13	job	Position title in ad
14	salarya	Salary of current/last job
15	salaryb	Salary of prior job
16	salaryc	Salary of next prior job
17	resume	Resume version sent

Figure 11.3 Recommended Variables for Mailmerge Job Searching Document-Generating System

YOUR PERSONAL COMPUTER AS A JOB SEARCH AID 199

variables 3 through 9 would be used on an envelope (shown in Figure 11.5), and all variables would be mailmerged onto the recordkeeping log (shown in Figure 11.6). I recommend that you name the master log file "adlog." Always add new log entries directly to your master file (adlog) and then copy the data files you've just added from adlog to a file called something like "run.log." This will enable you to maintain one large master list (in adlog) and not have to worry about accidentally mailmerging letters to ads that you've previously answered. Figure 11.4 displays the letter of Figure 11.2 with the variable numbers and names (within parentheses) inserted into their respective positions.

Figure 11.5 presents the envelope format and the variables that mailmerge software would read from the data file and insert into the envelope file. Note that both the letter and the envelope have seven available lines for the addressee's name and address. Most of the time you won't need them all, but you'll occasionally run into quasi-governmental organizations that have titles, departments, sections, mail stops, and so on. If you don't provide sufficient name and address lines in the design stage, you might end up having to modify your entire system for one letter. I've never run into a situation where more than seven lines were needed.

Your WP may not have an option that will enable you to specify that certain variables can be skipped and their spaces closed up. Such an option can skip empty variables (which don't have any data) so you don't have a lot of empty lines when the name and address uses fewer than the seven you've reserved. If that's the case, you'll have to put together several mailmerged systems, which differ only in the number of address lines. Don't try to get by with a system that leaves empty

---

(2 - datea)

(3 - adda)
(4 - addb)
(5 - addc)
(6 - addd)
(7 - adde)
(8 - addf)
(9 - addg)

Dear (10 - salutation):

I am responding to your (11 – dateb) advertisement in the (12 – paper) in which you solicited candidates for the position of (13 – job).

Figure 11.4 Mailmerge Ad Response Letter with Recommended Variable in Place

Joseph Jones
22 Main Street
Glendale, CA 91207

                              (3 - adda)
                              (4 - addb)
                              (5 - addc)
                              (6 - addd)
                              (7 - adde)
                              (8 - addf)
                              (9 - addg)

Figure 11.5 Mailmerge Envelope Format with Recommended Variables in Place

spaces; it will be a dead giveaway that you're using a WP, and your letter will get trashed.

Figure 11.6 displays the recommended variables on the recordkeeping log. The format displayed is the same as the one recommended in the Chapter 9 discussion of recordkeeping systems (except for variable 10 which is inserted here as an aid for proofreading your data entries). The recordkeeping log sheet would take up a whole sheet of paper. The mailmerge data would be run onto the top third of the page, and

(2 - datea)   (1 - n)
(3 - adda)
(4 - addb)
(5 - addc)
(6 - addd)
(7 - adde)
(8 - addf)
(9 - addg)

(10 - salutation)

(11 - dateb)   (12 - paper)

(13 - job)

(14 - salarya)   (15 - salaryb)   (16 - salaryc)

(17 - resume)
              (Clipped out ad is placed here)

Figure 11.6 Recommended Layout of Mailmerge Recordkeeping Sheet

the remainder of the sheet would be reserved as a spot to attach the ad and for making any notes about interview calls or results.

Once the variables listed in Figure 11.3 have been keyed into your adlog file, print your recordkeeping sheets before other correspondence and use them to proof your data. Mark minor corrections on the sheets and then open the master data file and make your edits. Unless the errors are large and ruin the continuity of the log sheets, there's no need to run the log sheets again. Simply put them in your notebook as they are. If you run the letters and the envelopes before you run the log sheets, you'll risk having to run them again when the inevitable typos appear.

Don't Go Computer Crazy

If you meet the requirements set out at the start of this chapter, you can use your PC as a very effective job search tool. If you don't have a properly equipped computer, you can probably get the job done through a secretarial service for less money than it would cost you to upgrade your system. Don't fall victim to computer mania and start to devote a lot of time to computerization. *Inside Track* is a job search book, and you're in a job search, not a system upgrade effort at a Fortune 100 company. Your first goal is to get a job. If you're not "systems ready" now, concentrate on the job search for the present time and worry about computers later.

Appendix

Facing the Dragon: How to Handle Being Fired

Many job searches are the immediate consequence of an involuntary termination or firing. Such searches operate under a tremendous burden. The job seeker is shocked, angry, perhaps depressed, and generally caught completely off guard. For many who have been fired, the shock takes months to wear off. The sense of disorientation, the anger, and fears about the future all combine to reduce the fired job seeker's ability to function in the cool, calculating, and objective manner that *Inside Track* job searching requires. The more quickly the job seeker can regain his or her equilibrium, the sooner an effective job search can be launched.

If you're currently conducting a search as a result of having been fired, you know how devastating such a termination can be. It's imperative to adjust quickly to the shock and get your job search under way as soon as possible. The purpose of this appendix is to provide before-the-fact guidance and advice so that you can prepare yourself to deal with a future firing. Such information will be helpful to you in three ways:

1. *The best job search is one that doesn't have to be conducted.* A detailed discussion of the mechanics of being fired will provide you with a more balanced viewpoint about jobs and work. If you haven't ever been fired or if you've been securely ensconced in one job for a long time, you've got a utopian viewpoint about your tenure and work in general. You're at some risk. Once you more fully appreciate the tenuous nature of any employment situation, you'll more objectively watch your step and keep your eyes open for hints of trouble on the horizon of your present job.
2. *Properly informed, you may be able to delay an imminent termination by taking the appropriate steps.* Such delays may be critical to a resultant search. All job searches are horrible, but the horror is attenuated to a degree if you're still employed. If you can delay a threatening termination, you may be able to find something else before the ax falls.
3. *Sometimes, there's no delaying a termination.* Perhaps everybody is being laid off; perhaps the department has been chopped; perhaps you've just had too many problems and it's too late to save it. (If this is a pattern for you, I once again recommend my book, *Conduct Expected: The Unwritten Rules for a Successful Business Career.* It will help you survive and prosper in your present or next position.) If it's to late to avoid it and too late to significantly

delay it, you'll have to make the most of it by getting the best deal you can. This appendix will tell you what to try for.

It happens to everyone.

There are few people who haven't been fired from at least one job. Getting fired is as much a constant and natural part of the business world as office furniture. This fact is small solace when it's happening to you, but you should prepare yourself by considering the possibility every now and then. Believe it; the same people who fawned over you will just as enthusiastically throw you out the door with not so much as an explanation if and when it suits their purpose. Bringing this to mind occasionally will make it easier for you to swallow the day-to-day insults, boredom, humiliations, and incompetence every job presents. It may seem bad, but it's not as bad as dealing with the more extreme day-to-day insults, boredom, humiliations, and incompetence you'll encounter in any job search. Sometimes, however, no amount of hard work, groveling, maneuvering, or delaying tactics will save you from a termination. Odds are, if you haven't been fired yet, your turn will come. It happens to everybody, and it's nothing to be ashamed of. (Personally, that is; it's not a good thing to disclose to potential employers.)

It's not the end of the world.

At the moment when it's happening, it may seem like it. The first thoughts that will run through your head will be thoughts of your ruined career, your dire financial straits, and ways to get even with the organization. These thoughts are natural and will help bolster you during the roughest period right after the initial shock wears off. Enjoy your plans for vengeance, but don't do anything other than fantasize about them. Your financial position is the only immediate and pressing item to worry about. Your career cannot be ruined by one termination, however terrible, if you handle it right. The largest part of the shock and emotional turmoil of being fired is related to lowered self-esteem and loss of identity. Most people define a large part of their self-worth, value, and identity in terms of their jobs. When the job goes, they feel they are less capable, less valuable, less worthwhile, and less important as a person. This is, of course, total nonsense. A job doesn't have any intrinsic meaning to your life. You could be in a thousand other jobs and be just as happy or miserable. Your value as a person is the same whether or not you're employed. However, this rational view will be clouded right after you're fired, so don't be surprised if you find yourself reacting emotionally. Just don't let it take control of you.

Plan ahead for the inevitable termination.

Hardly anyone (statistically speaking) buys grave sites on what the funeral industry likes to call a pre-need basis; people don't want to think about their own death. In much the same fashion, most workers don't give much thought to the possibility that their organization may pull the plug on their job's life-support systems. Such denial thinking will not change the probability that you'll be fired. Every year, hundreds of thousands of good workers are fired for all sorts of reasons. In almost every case, the person fired did not think it would happen to him or her. You probably feel the same way about your present job. Are you familiar with and in possession of a copy of your organization's termination policies and procedures? Do you know if and how much severance pay you'd be qualified for? Do you know how many verbal and written warnings are required for termination? Do you know what the termination grievance procedure is? Do you have a current resume prepared? Have you responded to any attractive-looking job advertisements in the past two months? Or have you said to yourself, "Hey, I don't need to worry about another job, I have this one?" Face it, you don't have any job; they're just letting you use it for a while.

Believe me, you'll be too confused at the moment of termination to deal with all of these questions if you haven't planned ahead. And if you're not out there at least browsing in the job market, it'll take four to six weeks just to get a job search cranked up. You better get to work now. Get a copy of your organization's termination procedures and read them. Put them in a file, along with copies of everything you might conceivably want to take with you if you're fired. You won't be able to gather everything up in the last few minutes as they throw you out. Update this file periodically so that you'll have recent copies of your best work. Consider this information to be your termination file. Keep it in the back of your desk drawer. If things are getting a little strange or you get a reprimand that you have to sign, read the procedures again and determine whether they're starting to ease you out. If so, start to work on the recommendations made later in this section. If you get the ax suddenly, take the file with you.

You should always have a current resume in circulation. Look through the classified ads, and send a resume to the best job you see every week. You aren't obliged to change jobs, but there's nothing wrong with looking. Best of all, when you're always scanning the opportunities, you'll find you have a much healthier perspective on your own job; you'll realize it's not forever.

HOW TO HANDLE BEING FIRED 205

If you get an early warning, make them suffer.

You're in a very special position if you know you're about to get fired, especially if they don't know you know. When you know it's only a matter of time (a short time), you'll be in the business world's counterpart of heroic last stands like the Alamo, the Little Big Horn, Wake Island, and Islandhwana. Once you know you've had it and there's no hope, your only satisfaction can come from taking as many of them with you as possible. Your goal is to make your firing appear as if it's the worst management decision they ever made. There's also the very slight possibility that you could delay or avoid the termination. It's small, but what else have you got? As soon as you think you're vulnerable for the ax, let loose with everything you've got. Send out memos about the great projects you're about to start. Set up meetings and committees to begin work on the projects. Visit a few of the brass to thank them for the opportunities they've given you and how great you think it is to work for them. Send out thank-you memos to anybody who has helped you on anything. Your goal is to make yourself look as good as you can so they'll look like ruthless brutes for cutting your throat. Talk up the organization to everybody who will listen; tell them how great it is and how you're looking forward to an exciting future. Tell them about the way the organization's leader called you into his or her office the other day to tell you about your great future. (Of course, you probably haven't ever been in his or her office, but who's going to quibble at this point?) If you're really into hardball guilt, you can get serious and try a tactic dreamed up by a past colleague of mine.

He heard a rumor that he was going to be fired in a week or so as part of an economic cutback. Totally unprepared to launch a job search, he rolled out the heavy stuff and managed to delay the inevitable final result by six months. The first thing he did was to tell one of his employees confidentially that his wife had cancer. Of course, he knew full well that the secret would spread like a prairie fire in a wind storm. Luckily for him, nature took its course and everybody knew within two hours. The outpouring of emotion was incredible. Management knew it couldn't make a fire move at that point without looking real bad. So they delayed. My friend knew he had them on the ropes. While the tears flowed, he started his job search in earnest. Two months later, he felt management was about to make another try. He then announced that his wife was pregnant and that all they wanted was for her to make it long enough for the baby to be born. The pregnancy ruse pulled him back from the brink once again. Those few of us who knew what was going on wondered what the next step would be. We felt he might have escalated a little too fast and might have run out of terrible stories. But no, he had one last ploy. When he felt they were moving in for the kill again, he told everyone that his wife had a miscarriage. I didn't see a smile around that place for a month. Fortunately for the tear ducts of his employees, he managed to find another job two months later and was able to resign with dignity. Before he left, he did the noble thing and announced that his wife had had a miraculous remission from the cancer and was pregnant again.

In situations where workers have felt that they're being more than brutally shafted, they have taken more drastic actions. There have been cases where workers have started rumors about layoffs, shutdowns, management shakeups, drugs, sex, and liquor scandals about the brass. Workers have called charities and made appointments for them to come and make presentations to obtain aid or have actually promised corporate donations (notifying the newspapers at the same time). Other workers have volunteered all sorts of resources to community groups. They've even committed top executives to various speeches, appearances, and engagements that will occur long after they've gone. Enough said about these shoddy practices.

Make it hard on them in the termination interview.

Often, employees fail to read the signs ahead of time and don't realize they're on the way out until they're in the termination interview. If handled properly, all is not lost even at that point (especially the opportunity to make them suffer). It's hard to believe, but a firing is almost as rough on the person doing the firing as it is on you. (Of course, their discomfort only lasts a few minutes; yours will last months at least.) If your boss is the one handling the ax, he or she no doubt feels guilty over the miserable level of feedback and guidance you've been getting. Of course, knowing they're guilty and paying for it are two different things. So, if you get the chance, help them atone for their sins. When you realize you're only seconds from the end, make them work for it.

You can generally tell if it's a termination interview by reading a few simple signs. If you get called into the boss's office first thing in the morning or last thing at night, you're in trouble. If you go in and the desk is spotless, you're in big trouble. If the boss won't look you in the eye and seems to be ill at ease, forget it at that job. If the boss asks you to close the door and that's not a typical practice, get your resume ready. The most famous and reliable sign that it's all over is when the boss starts out the interview with "We know you're not happy here." Millions have heard it. It's important to read these signs as accurately and quickly as possible so that you can inflict a maximum dose of guilt and suffering. As soon as you think you're on the chopping block, pull out all the stops.

Notice how Fred correctly reads the signs and makes it rough on Ms. Jacobs as she attempts to fire him. It's 8:00 A.M. Monday morning, and Ms. Jacobs has asked Fred to drop by her office. Fred immediately

HOW TO HANDLE BEING FIRED 207

suspects trouble since she hardly ever sees anyone, much less him, that early. Another bad sign is the timing. As many peole are fired early on Monday as during the more well-known "last thing on Friday" terminations.

Fred: "You wanted to see me, Priscilla?"

Ms. Jacobs: (doesn't look Fred in the eye) "Yes, Fred. Please come in and close the door."

Fred's blood runs cold. He knows this is it. Ms. Jacobs wouldn't look him in the eye, her desk is perfectly clear, and she asked him to close the door. He's now eye to eye with the dragon, and he knows he's going to walk out of that office without a job. The only satisfaction he'll get is to take as many of them with him as he can. Fred strikes like a cobra before Ms. Jacobs can get a breath.

Fred: "I'm glad we're having this opportunity to get together, Priscilla. I haven't had the chance to tell you how much I appreciate the support you've been giving me on the Jenkins scheduling project. I just know that the experience will be invaluable in our planning efforts for the Jones deal. As a matter of fact, I spent most of the weekend running the figures through my PC at home, and I think I can readily adapt the canned software we've got to do the job."

This is a good opening. Note how Fred thanked her for her (nonexistent) help, alluded to future projects, and showed her that he unselfishly worked all weekend to save a few bucks for JB Industries. (Actually, he spent the weekend in Vegas, but it's pull-out-all-the-stops time.) This barrage of guilt leaves Priscilla off balance.

Ms. Jacobs: "Ah, er, yes. That's very interesting, Fred. But I have something else I want to talk about here. We've noticed that you haven't been too happy lately in your work."

Just because he's stuck in a rotten job working for a total cretin? Fred can see that Priscilla is going right for the throat and will not be easily thrown off track. Fred moves in for one more strafing run before dropping the biggie.

Fred: "Unhappy with JB Industries? Oh, no! I love it here. As a matter of fact, I got an offer two months ago from XYZ Widgets, and I told them that I'd never leave JBI. I was personally recruited by J.B. (another total lie, but Ms. Jacobs doesn't know it), and they'll have to carry me out before I leave."

Priscilla is now flushed with emotion. She knows she's going to have to let Fred have it right between the eyes, and she hates herself for not nailing him right away. She's feeling guilty and embarrassed for the whole scene. She raises the ax.

Ms. Jacobs: "Well, ah, Fred, things just aren't working out. I'm afraid that we're . . . ."

Fred can't let her get this sentence out without getting in his last blast. He drops the biggie.

Fred: "You're telling me things aren't working out! Last night we found out that my wife has inoperable brain cancer and has only six months to live. I don't know what we'd do without the medical plan. We've known something was wrong for the last few months, but we hoped it wasn't as serious. At first they thought it was epilepsy. At least then we would've had a chance . . . (sob). . . . Oh, well. I'm really grateful that I have this great job to keep my mind busy. It's strange, but I find that I get a lot of satisfaction from throwing myself into my work even more in these rough times. You can't know how grateful I am for the opportunity and challenge you've given me here."

Priscilla will hate herself for days. Who knows, maybe Fred started her next ulcer. If Ms. Jacobs is the least bit soft, maybe Fred will get a stay of execution for a while. Note how much more effective this fine performance would have been if Fred had gotten a few cancer rumors started ahead of time. That's why it's critical always to watch the signs. If you have any doubt that there could be trouble, start working on your delay tactics. There are other alternatives to employ if you're in a termination interview. Fake a heart attack and fall on the floor, or get up to adjust your chair and go into a back spasm that throws you to the floor. Nobody will fire you while you're rolling around in agony or while you're being wheeled out to the ambulance. If that's a little too much for you (wait until the acting you have to do during the job search), you can always bolt from the interview with the claim, "Omigod, stomach pains, I'm going to throw up!" Then run out, go home, and call in sick.

If you feel the dragon's breath on your career's neck when you get the call to "drop by my office," you could leave a message saying that you suddenly got sick and had to go home. (Since you'll feel sick when you discover you're about to be fired, it's no lie.) You can take a few sick days (might as well use it all up, as well as unused personal days, if you can't take the unused time with you as additional severance pay), and make them sweat it out while you start your job search and maybe some propaganda to delay their action. Don't worry about jumping the gun and thinking it's a termination scene if it really isn't. If you feel it's the end, you're probably right. If you dodge the interview or run out of it and it was a false alarm, it's no great loss; everybody gets sick occasionally. In any case, you owe it to yourself to make it as hard on them as you can. They're putting the hurt on you, and you'll feel better later if you make them suffer a little. People who say revenge doesn't help haven't tried it.

Stick to the basics in the termination interview.

When you realize you're in a termination interview, you'll probably be in a state of shock. If you don't have the composure or the inclination to work the guilt trip on them, you can't trust yourself to rationally make all of the quick decisions about what to do and say. Follow the advice in this section, and remember that the less said at the time the better. You're not going to get anywhere by arguing with them. Working the guilt trip is a desperate last effort to salvage something, but aside from revenge it's a long shot. In real life, deciding to terminate someone is usually a very subjective and emotional decision. Once the decision has been made, there's nothing much you can objectively do or say during the interview to change their minds. Save it for the grievance procedure and any legal action. Once they've made the decision to trash you, it's pointless to try and bargain with them. It really won't matter whether the reasons for your termination are valid or complete, raging, gaping lies. The decision will have been made, and everyone in the decision-making chain will have already considered the deed done. Nobody can or will change their minds. Realize that now so when the moment comes you'll be able to face it with dignity. It will be important for your own self-esteem to know that you stayed calm and mature under fire.

Don't let them talk you into resigning.

Don't let them demonstrate their deep concern by allowing you to resign. If you're a white-collar worker and you resign, you'll most likely forfeit any possible unemployment benefits. The paltry one or two hundred bucks a week may not seem like much at the time, but you'll need it later. Don't worry about the effect of being fired versus resigning. It makes no difference. Most personnel departments are so scared of possible litigation that they wouldn't give a bad reference to Adolf Hitler. Don't let them bargain or coerce you into resigning. You're entitled to all of your earned back pay, vacation pay, and commissions right away. (Commissions don't have to be paid until they'd normally be disbursed.) Don't be afraid to demand them on the spot. (After all, it's past the point where you're worried that they may not like you.) They can't hold your pay until you turn in car keys, the company car, credit cards, and so on. You can't keep those items, but they can't hold your pay until you return them if you don't have them with you. They can't legally offer to "not mention what you did to the police if you resign" in the case where you might have bent the law a bit. That's extortion. If they offer, tell them. If they are concerned about the "way it will look if we fire you," you might be in a position to negotiate a termination. Don't accept what they offer on the spot. If they're concerned about appearances (as when you're a big shot, are well-liked, or have been around a long time), you can probably get a good deal. If you try to negotiate the deal yourself, they'll probably sic their attorney on you, and you'll end up with a crummy four weeks of pay. Forget it. If they want to negotiate, you can probably get six to twelve months, especially if you're well-known and they don't want the publicity. Tell them you want your health benefits extended for a year or until you find a job, whichever comes first. Tell them you want outplacement support. Tell them you want secretarial support, a work phone number, and a message taker during your search efforts. Tell them you want them to pay for your resume printing and preparation and postage costs. Go for it. The main thing is to get aggressive and keep calm. They'll be feeling guilty and keyed up and will probably make concessions in order to ease their discomfort, but they won't offer if you don't ask for it. They won't give you everything, but the more you ask for the more you'll get.

Take everything you want with you when they kick you out.

Don't leave any of your personal files or anything you may need later to back up your claims of superior performance (or projects that may come in useful later on similar jobs). Take all copies of your performance appraisals. If you keep a detailed appointment book, take it along. Take a copy of their phone book. Don't allow yourself to be intimidated by the security or management types who may be escorting you. Take your time and go through your desk and files carefully. You may find yourself faced with a situation in which the organization has cleared out your belongings for you. In this situation, insist that you be allowed to make a careful inventory before you leave the premises. Make sure you have all of your personal files, pictures, and bric-a-brac. It might make you feel better to claim that your fifty-dollar electric pencil sharpener and custom pen and pencil set are gone. Use your imagination, but make sure you get everything you want and must have. If they try to make you clean out your things in front of the whole office at 10:00 A.M., just tell them you're not going to do it. Tell them you won't leave until you can do it in privacy and with dignity. Tell them you'll leave either after work or if they clear the whole area first. I've heard of several cases where management herded an entire floor of two hundred clerks up to the cafeteria in order to allow one person to leave in privacy. Management felt so uneasy about having to drag someone out physically that they went along with the demands. You've got nothing more to lose at that point except your dignity, so don't take any more abuse than you have to.

Insist on knowing what type of reference they'll give.

During the termination interview, ask them what they'll say when a prospective employer calls for references. If they'll give a positive reference, ask if you can have a positive letter of recommendation right away to take with you. If they are lying, maybe you can get a letter out of them anyway because of their embarrassment. If they say you won't get a positive recommendation, ask them exactly what they will say. Point out to them that any allegations that have not been proven in court may be construed as slander or defamation of character. Most organizations know this and give very little information to reference checkers in order to protect themselves. Your employer may not be so enlightened. A new and recent tactic is to have the employee sign a document that specifies whether the employee wishes any data to be given out to reference checkers. The logic is that if an employee was terminated for cause, the employee will specify that no data be given to reference checkers who call or write. Potential employers will know from the employee's request that there's a problem—sort of a "guilty until proven innocent" situation. Don't sign it if you're worried about this implication. Chances are that no one will check references anyway, but if they do the past employer is still going to be very careful about getting in trouble.

Collect everything you need from coworkers as soon as possible.

You've got few, if any, real friends at work. You'll find out just how true that is when you get fired. Your bosom buddies of yesterday will soon not even bother to return your calls. They'll have their own problems, and you'll be just another irrelevant and unimportant imposition on their time. If you need written letters of reference or some leads on another job, make your requests the day you're terminated (or the day you quit, for that matter), and do everything you can to expedite the requests. Volunteer to have something typed for their signature. Do whatever you have to do as soon as possible. Rapid action is even more critical when you're being terminated for something the organization would just as soon not open to general discussion. If this is the case, you can bet your reference that the executives involved will bring pressure to bear on those you might be expected to contact. The organization will come down on your contacts hard and fast with all sorts of pressure. If you wait more than twenty-four hours to collect information in this type of situation, you'll find that your courteous friends of yesterday will suddenly be very quiet on the phone. Every time you call, they'll be on another line or in conference. Given these types of hazards, act fast to collect whatever you need. Put on all the pressure you can as early as you can. When you're making your requests for recommendations, help, or information, whine a little about how busy you're going to be the next day, "what with having to file for food stamps and unemployment and all. Could I please pick it up tonight or tomorrow morning at your house?" This type of maneuver will play on their sympathies before they are faced with pressure from above.

File for unemployment the next working day.

The crummy small fraction of your normal pay may not seem like much now as you go home with severance pay (if you're lucky), vacation pay, and back pay, but it will be important in five months. You're going to need every cent you can get, so don't delay. Get the ball rolling right away. You'll need the extra time to fight for your rights if the organization decides to be rotten and deny your benefits. It will take the unemployment bureaucracy at least two to three months for hearings, meetings, and determinations. By that time, you'll probably still be out of work and will need the money.

Don't do anything rash for two weeks.

No matter what you feel like doing immediately after you're fired, let it wait for two weeks (except for starting your job search materials development and research). If it still feels appropriate, at least you'll be in a position to make a more rational judgment. If you take action any sooner, you're likely to let your emotional responses have too much influence. Wait until you calm down before you move to Australia or shave your head and join a cult.

If you have cause, file a grievance.

Most organizations have a formal grievance procedure. Even if they don't, you may want to file a formal protest with the organization if you feel you've been given the shaft. If you're fired for embezzlement or industrial espionage, you probably won't get anywhere (expect perhaps jail). If you're fired for a nebulous subjective cause (which is generally the case), you may have a slim chance of obtaining redress. Find out what the grievance procedure is and follow it. If there is none, write down the facts and allegations as you see them or as they were told to you and then present your rebuttal. The key here is to see that the right people get the document. The people who fired you aren't even going to read it if they know you only sent it to them. In fact, you don't even care if they read it. You want their boss and everyone right up the line to the executive suite to read it. Simply carbon them on the letter and then mail them all a copy. If the dismissal can be viewed as in any way related to a high-visibility issue such as race, age, or sex discrimination, you might want to send a copy to each member of the board of directors. Your chances are always slim (as organizations just don't admit they're wrong even if it will cost them), but you may get somewhere. What have you got to lose? At the very least, you may stay their hand for a brief moment the next time they consider trashing another innocent victim.

If you've been totally shafted, investigate legal action.

It's expensive, things take years to get to court, and it's a huge bother, especially when you're trying to find a job. On the other hand, you could end up with a large settlement and a lot of satisfaction. You don't have to do anything right away. If you feel that you have a possible case, visit an attorney who's qualified and pay the fifty or hundred bucks to find out what you would have to do and when you would have to do it. See the attorney as quickly as possible after you are fired. It will be important to follow all possible grievance procedures in order to demonstrate that you tried to fix it the company way. If you think you've really been shafted on an age, sex, or race discrimination basis, see the attorney right away, even before you file the grievance procedure. The attorney will have some recommendations. And don't forget all those federal and state regulatory agencies that use our tax dollars. They love to hear about injustices perpetrated upon helpless citizens by organizations who are flouting the rules and regulations.

If you're quitting, avoid giving notice if you have any doubts.

The situation in which you quit for a better job is not a problem in itself. But it's not a situation that's free of potential hazards, even though they might be momentary. It's woven into the fantasy myths of modern business that it's expected and fair for the employee to give the organization at least two weeks notice before quitting. It may be expected and it's more than fair to the organization, but it could mean problems for you. Don't give your organization any notice unless you have extremely consistent and solid evidence concerning their behavior toward short-timers. A lot of organizations routinely throw those who give notice out into the street the very same day they receive the notice. Organizations do this sort of thing because they're suspicious of everyone's motives and they're worried about what the short-timers may say to other employees. They have a point. If management has been so repressive that everyone's unhappy and desperate to leave, it doesn't make any sense to let someone who's about to taste freedom spread a lot of cheer to the slaves who are still in captivity. It makes the place look even worse to those left behind.

If you give notice and they throw you out, they probably won't give you the severance pay to cover the notice period. You'll end up having to eat two weeks of no pay before you start the next job. Who needs to lose that kind of money? It's no time for false morality. Do they ever give anyone two weeks notice prior to being fired? No, they just trash them on the spot and hustle them out the door. So don't give them any more compassion than they deserve. If you observe that people who give notice are generally allowed to remain on the job until their official last day, you're not at serious risk unless there are other problems. There may be situations where you have to give notice for more tangible reasons related to your reputation. If you're highly visible in your field or working in a small, closed industry where everyone knows everyone, you can't afford to be too reckless. But if that's the case, your move up may seem like a promotion to everyone concerned. If not, beware. The bottom line is not to take chances with a few weeks pay out of allegiance to a misguided and ridiculous set of standards that organizations themselves don't use.

Index

A

Accessories in interview, 167–168
Achievements
    questions on, in interview, 181–183
    section on, in resume, 52, 54–58
        optional, 70–71
Action words for resume, 55–57
Administration and recordkeeping, 141–150; *see also* Recordkeeping
Ads, classified; *see* Classified ads, responding to
American Bank Directory, 116
Answering machine, 149, 163
Arguing with interviewer, 160–161

B

Bank Street Writer, 193
Bare bones response to classified ads, 89–91
    sample, 89
BFC; *see* Boldface full capitals
Blind ads, 91, 98–99
Boldface, 192, 196, 197, 198
Boldface full capitals (BFC), 53
Broadcast letter, 11
Business section of newspaper, 86
Business world, basic truths about, 7–10
Business-size stationery, 115

C

Call, guilt, 33

Call monitoring, 163
Callback
    cost to handle, 30
    per hundred items, 29
    quality of, 29–30
    time to handle, 30
Candidates, selection out of, by personnel department, 17–18
Capitals
    boldface full, 53
    first-letter, 53
    full, 53
Career development consultant, 20
Career development outfits, 19
Career planning consultants, 138
Career planning counselors, 138
Career planning firms, 138
Classified ads, responding to, 5, 30–31, 36, 37, 85–102
    blind, 91, 98–99
    cover letter for, 87, 97, 142, 145
        references on, 98
        supplementary qualifications section of, 96
        things to avoid in, 97–98
    geographical considerations of, 101
    guidelines for, 88
    level of effort for, 88–97
        bare bones, 89–91
            sample, 89
        face down through the cactus, 93–96
            sample, 95
        lead 'em by the hand, 91–93
            sample, 92

Classified ads, *cont.*
  log sheets for, 142, 143–145
    sample, 143
  in newspapers, 85–86
  odds of, 101–102
  position wanted, 136
  in professional magazines and
    journals, 87
  qualifications and, 100–101
  salary levels and, 97–98, 99–100
  selection of, 98–101
Clothing in interview, 167
Club, job, 139–140
Commissions, being fired and, 209
Computer, personal, 6, 190–201
  basic equipment requirements,
    190–191
  boldface capabilities of, 192
  databases and, 193
  generating correspondence on,
    192
  mailmerge capabilities of,
    191–192, 193
  memory of, 190
  printer and, 190, 192
  recordkeeping with, 191–192
  resume construction on, 192
  word processing software package
    and, 190, 192; *see also* Word
    processor
Conduct Expected: The Unwritten Rules
  for a Successful Business
  Career, 24, 55, 202
Consultant, 45
Consultants News, 103, 104
Contingency executive recruiting
  firms, 18–19
Contingency headhunters, 103
Copies of resume, 74–75
Copying machines, duplication of
  resume by, 74–75
Cover letter, 11, 77
  in direct solicitations, 142, 147
  in mailings to headhunters,
    109–112, 113, 142, 146
  in responding to classified ads, 87,
    97, 142, 145
  summary of qualifications in, 93
Coworkers, termination and,
  211–212

Creativity, 132–133, 136
Current job on resume, 53

D

Databases, computers and, 193
Deduction of job search expenses,
  federal tax laws and,
  148–149
Degree on resume, 69
Demeanor, general, in interview,
  168–170
Direct solicitation to executives and
  organizations; *see*
  Solicitation, direct, to
  executives and organizations
Directory of Directories, 116
Directory of Executive Recruiters, 103,
  104–105, 106
Disagreeing with interviewer,
  160–161
Duplication of resume, 74–75
  by copying machines, 74–75
  by offset printing, 74
  by photo duplication, 74–75

E

Easy Writer II/Mailer, 193
Editing of resume, 71–72
Education
  questions on, in interview,
    180–181
  on resume, 52, 69–70
  resume showing lack of, 46
Educational experience, summary of
  qualifications based on, 75
Employed, currently, 24–25
  job search situations for, 36–37
  probability of finding out, 30
Employment agencies, 21, 139
Empty spots in interview, 171–172
Evaluation criteria, 29–30
Executive
  direct solicitation to; *see*
  Solicitation, direct, to executives and
    organizations
  health-care, resume of, 80–81
Executive recruiting firms, 18–19

INDEX

Existentialism, 26–27
Expense log, 143, 148–149, 166
Experience on resume, 52, 59
  lack of, 46
  modifiers of, 64, 65
  professional, 59
  substitutions for, 64, 65
Experience section, job; *see* Job experience section

F

Face down through the cactus
  responding to classified ads, 93–96
  sample, 95
Face-to-face interview, 5–6, 151, 162–163, 166–176; *see also* Interview
  accessories and, 167–168
  bad scenes and, 170
  clothing and, 167
  concluding, 172
  conducting, 168–172
  empty spots in, 171–172
  fingernails and, 168
  following up, 172–173
  general demeanor in, 168–170
  general guidelines for, 151–162
  group, 170–171
  hair and, 167
  handshake and, 169
  job offers and, 173–176
  during meal, 169
  purpose of, 167
  preparation for, 167–168
  posture and, 169
  references and, 173
    sample, 174
  schedule change and, 171
  stress, 170
  thank-you letter and, 172–173
    sample, 173
  written offer letter and, 176
Family, questions on, in interview, 178–180
FC; *see* Full capitals
Federal tax laws, deduction of job search expenses and, 148–149

Feedback records
  direct solicitation, 142, 147
  headhunter, 142, 146–147
Fee-for-service executive recruiting firms, 18
Financial magazines and journals, classified ads in, 87
Fingernails, 168
Fired, how to handle being, 6, 45, 202–214
Firmness in interview, 154–155
First-letter capitals (FLC), 53
FLC; *see* First-letter capitals
Full capitals (FC), 53
Functional specialization of headhunters, 106

G

Geographical considerations; *see also* Relocation
  classified ads and, 101
  headhunters and, 105
Giving notice, 213–214
Goals
  questions on, in interview, 181–183
  on resume, 52
Government jobs, classified ads for, 87
Grievances, 212–213
Group interview, 170–171
Group therapy syndrome, 139
Guide to American Directories, 116
Guilt calls, 33
Guilt interviews, 33, 127

H

Hair in interview, 167
Handshake in interview, 169
Header on resume, 52, 59–60, 65–66, 76
Headhunters, 5, 18–19, 45
  cover letter to, 109–112, 113, 142, 146
  fees for, 19
  lists of, 142, 146
  log sheets of, 142, 145–146
  mailings to, 31–33, 36, 37,

INDEX

Headhunters, *cont.*
103–113
Heading in resume, 52
Health-care executive, resume of, 80–81
Health-care magazines, classified ads in, 87
Hit rate, 30–31
Hot buttons, interviewer's, 152
Humor, 132–133, 156–157

I

In before the ad solicitation, 117–119
  sample, 119
In–depth research and proposal, 138
Individual recruiters, 19
Industry specialization of headhunters, 106
Ink, color of, for resume, 73
Intelligence, 132–133, 136
Interview, 151–189; *see also* Face-to-face interview; Phone interview
  acting like winner in, 152–153
  arguing with interviewer in, 160–161
  avoiding humor in, 156–157
  disagreeing with interviewer in, 160–161
  excess information in, 152
  face-to-face; *see* Face-to-face interview
  firmness in, 154–155
  formal and reserved manner in, 154
  general guidelines for, 151–162
  group, 170–171
  guilt, 33, 127
  having answers ready, 178–189
  intimidating interviewer in, 155–156
  jargon and, 158
  negativity in, 153–154
  personal, per hundred launches, 30
  phone; *see* Phone interview
  self-improvement plan and, 159–160
  sharpening skills for, 177–188
  stress, 170
  termination, 206–209
Intimidating interviewer, 155–156

J

Jargon, 59, 158
JES; *see* Job experience section
Job
  current, on resume, 53
  past
    on job experience section, 58–59
    questions on, in interview, 184–185
    on resume, 53
  recent, on job experience section, 58
  resume showing too many, 46
Job assistance outfits, 19
Job clubs, 139–140
Job dates on resume, 53
Job experience section (JES), 52–60
  achievements in, 52, 54–58
  for current position, 53, 76
  heading of, 52
  job dates in, 53
  job title in, 54
  main body of, 54–59
  organization name in, 53–54
  past jobs in, 53, 58–59
  responsibilities in, 52, 54–58
  sample, 53, 58
  word and toning of, 54–55
Job history, resume showing gaps in, 46
Job offers, 173–176
Job openings, creation of, 10–11
Job search, 7–22, 23–40
  miscellaneous strategies of; *see* Miscellaneous job search strategies
  estimates of length of, in weeks, 38–39
  regional guides for, 104
  strategy for, evaluation of, 27–35
Job skills, questions on, in interview, 187–188
Job slots, 7
Job title on job experience section, 54

INDEX

Journals, professional, classified ads in, 87

L

Launching each item, cost and time requirements of, 29
Lead 'em by the hand response to classified ads, 91–93
  sample, 92
Legal action, being fired and, 213
"Let's be friends" solicitation, 27, 123–126
  sample, 125
Letter
  broadcast, 11
  cover; see Cover letter
  thank-you, 143, 149, 172–173
    sample, 173
  written offer, 176
Letter resume, 76–84
  sample, 79
Librarian, reference, 116
Log sheets
  classified ad, 142, 143–145
    sample, 143
  direct solicitation, 142, 147
  headhunter mailing, 142, 145–146
    sample, 146
Los Angeles Times, 86

M

Magazines, professional, classified ads in, 87
Mailings to headhunters, 31–33, 36, 37, 103–113
Mailmerge capability
  of computer, 191–192, 193
  of word processor, 197–201
Master of technology, 136–137
Meal, interview during, 169
Memory in computer, 190
Microspell, 195
Middle-management jobs, summary of qualifications for, 62
Million Dollar Directory, 116
Miscellaneous job search strategies, 34–35, 36, 131–140
  career planning counselors, consultants, and firms, 138
  employment agencies, 139
  in-depth research and proposal, 138
  job clubs, 139–140
  master or mistress of technology, 136–137
  reasons for using, 131–132
  stunts, 137–138
  super tough talk, 133–136
    sample, 135
  "this one's on me," 132–133
    sample, 134
Mistress of technology, 136–137
Monarch stationery, 115

N

National Ad Search, 86, 138
National Business Employment Weekly (NBEW), 15, 85–86, 91, 138
National Job Market, 86, 138
NBEW; see *National Business Employment Weekly*
Negativity in interview, 153–154
Networking, 5, 27, 33–34, 36, 114–130
New York Times, 86
Newspapers, classified ads in, 85–86
Noncontingency executive recruiting firms, 18–19
Noncritical jobs, job experience section for, 58
Notice, giving, 213–214

O

Objective on resume, 52, 66–67
Offer letter, written, 176
Offset printing, duplication of resume by, 74
Organizations, direct solicitation to; see Solicitation, direct, to executives and organizations
Outplacement support, 210
Overseas jobs, classified ads for, 87

P

Page footer, 71
Paper; see also Stationery

INDEX

Paper, *cont.*
  color of, 73
  selection of, for resume, 72–73
  texture of, 73
Past jobs
  questions on, in interview, 184–185
  on resume, 53, 58–59
Personal affairs, questions on, in interview, 178–180
Personal character statement on resume, 61–64
Personal computer; *see* Computer, personal
Personal data on resume, 52, 67–69
Personal flaws, 157–158
Personality, questions on, in interview, 181–183
Personnel departments, 16–18
Personnel end run solicitation, 119–120
  sample, 120
Personnel requisition (rec), 10
Phone charges, 31
Phone interview, 5, 151, 162–166; *see also* Face-to-face interview; Interview
  answering machine and, 163
  conducting, 164–166
  ending, 165–166
  follow–up of, 166
  general guidelines for, 151–162
  keeping records handy, 163
  preparation for, 163–164
  presentation style of, 164
  purpose of, 162–163
  tape recorder and, 164
Phone solicitation telecharts, 142, 148
Phone solicitation tracking sheets, 142, 148
Photo duplication of resume, 74–75
Poors Register of Corporation Directories and Executives, 116
Position wanted ads, 136
Posture in interview, 169
Printer, 190, 192
Printing, offset, duplication of resume by, 74
Procrastination, 26

Production
  for direct solicitation to executives and organizations, 115–116
  of resume, 72–76
Professional employment section of resume, 86
Professional experience on resume, 59
Professional magazines and journals, 87
Proportional spacing, 74
Psychologists, 20
Publications, classification ads in, 86–87

Q

Qualifications
  responding to classified ads and, 100–101
  summary of; *see* Summary of qualifications
Quitting, giving notice and, 213–214

R

Rec; *see* Personnel requisition
Recent jobs on job experience section, 58
Recordkeeping, 141–150
  computer, 191–192
  Inside Track, 142–149
  why job seekers fail to maintain, 141–142
Recruiter
  executive, 18–19
  individual, 19
Recruiting process, typical, 11–16
Reference, 98, 173, 174, 210–211
Reference checkers, 211
Reference courtesy, 98
Reference librarian, 116
Regional job search guide, 104
Relocation, 86–87, 101, 105
Resignation, 209–210
Resources, allocation of, to search strategies, 35–38
Responding to classified ads; *see* Classified ads, responding to

INDEX

Responsibilities section in resume, 52, 54–58
Resume, 4, 5, 41–84
   achievements on, 52, 70–71
   action words for, 55–57
   admitting past firing, 45
   of competition, 42–43
   construction of, computers and, 192
   copies of, 74–75
   duplication of; *see* Duplication of resume
   editing of, 71–72
   education on, 52, 69–70
   employer's attention to, 44–47
   essential, 42
   experience on, 52, 59
   flaws in, 45–46
   gimmicks and flashy approaches to, 47
   goal objective on, 52, 66–67
   header on, 52, 59–60, 65–66, 76
   ink color for, 73
   Inside Track, 47–48, 49–84
     basic format of, 50–51
     page 1, 50, 52, 60–71, 75, 77, 80, 82
     page 2, 51, 52–60, 75–76, 78, 81, 83
   jargon in, 59
   just out of school, 75–76
     sample, 77–78
   letter; *see* Letter resume
   missing data on, 68
   myths about, 41–47
   number of, 75
   paper selection for, 72–73
   personal data on, 52, 67–69
   production of, 72–76
   professional experience on, 59
   purpose of, 44
   showing gaps in job history, 46
   showing less education than job requires, 46
   showing no experience in industry, 46
   showing too many jobs, 46
   summary of qualifications on; *see* Summary of qualifications
   type pitch of, 73–74
   10, 73–74
   12, 74
   type and styles of, 43, 73
   typing of, 71–72
   versions of, 142, 148
   what it must do, 47–48
   word processors generating, 193–195
Retainer executive recruiting firms, 18–19
Retainer headhunters, 103
Right justified entry on resume, 53–54

S

Salary data, 97–98, 99–100, 106–107
School; *see also* Education
   name of, on resume, 70
   resume if just out of, 75–76
   sample, 77–78
Search; *see* Job search
Secretarial support, 28
"See my greatness" solicitation, 120–123
   sample, 122
Self-improvement plan, 159–160
Severance pay, 214
Solicitation, direct, to executives and organizations, 33–34, 36, 114–130
   basic guidelines for, 115–116
   cover letters used in, 142, 147
   lists of, 142, 147
   log sheets for, 142, 147
   production values for, 115–116
   qualifying targets for, 116
   selecting targets, 116
   stationery for, 115–116
   variants of, 116–128
   verifying targets, 116
Solicitation feedback records, 142, 147
SOQ; *see* Summary of qualifications
Spacing, proportional, 74
Spell checker on word processor, 195
Stationery, 115–116; *see also* Paper
Stress interview, 170

Stunts, 137–138
Summary of qualifications (SOQ), 52, 60–65, 67
　based on educational experience, 75
　on cover letter, 93
　for engineering middle manager, 61
　for middle-management jobs, 62
　personal character statement for, 61–64
Super tough talk strategy, 133–136
　sample, 135
Supplementary qualifications section of cover letter responding to classified ads, 96

T

Table manners, 169
Tape recorder, 164, 188
Technical qualifications, 8–9
Technology, master or mistress of, 136–137
Telecharts, 5, 128, 129, 142, 148
10-pitch Type style, 73–74
Termination, delaying, 202
Termination interview, 206–209
Thank-you letter, 143, 149, 172–173
　sample, 173
"This one's on me" strategy, 132–133
　sample, 134
Thomas Register, 116
12-pitch type style, 74
Type pitch of resume, 73–74
　10, 73–74
　12, 74
Type style of resume, 73
Typing of resume, 71–72

U

Unemployed, 25, 36–37, 209, 212

V

Variables, word processors and, 197, 198, 199, 200

W

Wall Street Journal (WSJ), 15, 185–186
"Who do ya know?" solicitation, 126–128
Who's Who in Electronics, 116
Word processors, 72, 190, 192, 193–201
WordStar/Mailmerge, 193, 195
Working conditions, questions on, in interview, 185–187
Written offer letter, 176
WSJ; *see Wall Street Journal*